TAKING DESIGN THINKING
TO SCHOOL

Design thinking is a method of problem-solving that relies on a complex set of skills, processes, and mindsets that help people generate novel solutions to problems. *Taking Design Thinking to School: How the Technology of Design Can Transform Teachers, Learners, and Classrooms* uses an action-oriented approach to reframing K-12 teaching and learning, examining interventions that open up dialogue about when and where learning, growth, and empowerment can be triggered. While design thinking projects make engineering, design, and technology fluency more tangible and personal for a broad range of young learners, their embrace of ambiguity and failure as growth opportunities often clash with institutional values and structures. Through a series of in-depth case studies that honor and explore such tensions, the authors demonstrate that design thinking provides students with the agency and compassion that is necessary for doing creative and collaborative work, both in and out of the classroom. A vital resource for education researchers, practitioners, and policymakers, *Taking Design Thinking to School* brings together some of the most innovative work in design pedagogy.

Shelley Goldman is Professor of Education, Learning Sciences, and Technology Design at Stanford University.

Zaza Kabayadondo is Co-director of the Design Thinking Initiative at Smith College, a pilot program to reimagine liberal arts education.

TAKING DESIGN THINKING TO SCHOOL

How the Technology of Design Can Transform Teachers, Learners, and Classrooms

Edited by Shelley Goldman and Zaza Kabayadondo

Routledge
Taylor & Francis Group

NEW YORK AND LONDON

First published 2017
by Routledge
711 Third Avenue, New York, NY 10017

and by Routledge
2 Park Square, Milton Park, Abingdon, Oxon, OX14 4RN

Routledge is an imprint of the Taylor & Francis Group, an informa business

Library of Congress Cataloging in Publication Data
A catalog record has been requested

ISBN: 978-1-138-10099-2 (hbk)
ISBN: 978-1-138-10100-5 (pbk)
ISBN: 978-1-315-65728-8 (ebk)

Typeset in Bembo Std
by Swales & Willis Ltd, Exeter, Devon, UK

CONTENTS

PART IV
Inspiring Teaching: Design Thinking in the Classroom   **161**

CONTRIBUTORS

Xornam Apedoe is an associate professor in the Department of Learning and Instruction at the University of San Francisco. Her research focuses on improving current educational practices in STEM for diverse students in high-need schools and settings, through the design of authentic learning experiences.

Stephanie Bachas-Daunert is a PhD candidate in Civil and Environmental Engineering at Stanford University. Her interdisciplinary work spans engineering, environmental and public health, microbiology, biogeochemistry, and sustainability. She is passionate about increasing diversity in STEM fields, and began outreach in East Palo Alto through the NSF-funded Stanford REDlab Educating Young STEM Thinkers project in an effort to introduce STEM and design topics to underrepresented groups while mentoring the future generation of scientists and engineers. Stephanie holds a National Institutes of Health Ruth L. Kirschstein Predoctoral Fellowship, and is a National Science Foundation Graduate Research Fellow (NSF GRFP), a Stanford School of Engineering 3D Diversity Fellow, and a Woods Institute for the Environment Rising Environmental Leader Program Fellow.

Phyllis Balcerzak, PhD, is Senior Program Producer at the UMSL College of Education's ED Collabitat, designs, directs, and teaches professional learning experiences for educators in all stages of their professional careers. Balcerzak has contributed to the fields of applied ecological research, science education and teacher preparation. In collaboration with an array of professionals in higher education, informal and formal K-12 education she has built the foundation for programs that cross disciplinary boundaries and respond to the specific and targeted needs of educators, in local and national settings. In concert with the leadership team Balcerzak brings her passion and experience to the ED

Collabitat's infusion of professional creativity into the cultural landscape of our education systems.

Ela Ben-Ur (http://i2iexperience.com/people) has coached and co-experimented with educators and others interested in design thinking since 2012, focusing on her lifelong "extracurricular"—educating of people of all ages. Ela worked 13 incredible years at renowned design firm IDEO. Her design practice and leadership at IDEO spanned diverse geographies, industries, and sectors. She was a co-founder of IDEO's Leadership Studio for developing project leaders, coach for teams, and facilitator for clients. Ela has taught at pioneering Olin College since 2007, and offered workshops through MIT (her alma mater), Sloan, Babson, Dartmouth, and Harvard. Her 2- and 4-year old daughters are her inspiration.

Charles Cox is a registered architect, professional engineer, and instructor of design in the School of Engineering Design, Technology, and Professional Programs in the College of Engineering at the Pennsylvania State University, where he has also taught design studios for the Department of Architecture and the Department of Architectural Engineering. At the time this book chapter was being developed he was performing research during a post-doctoral appointment at the University of Pittsburgh's Learning Research and Design Center.

Meredith Davis is Professor Emerita of Graphic Design at NC State University and has taught for 47 years at the K-12 and college level. She holds degrees in education from Penn State University and in design from Cranbrook Academy of Art. Meredith is author of a two-year study of K-12 design education by the National Endowment for the Arts and served as a member of the development team for the National Assessments of Educational Progress in the Arts and in Technology and Engineering. She is a member of the Cooper Hewitt National Design Museum/Smithsonian education committee and lectures in the museum's teacher education programs. Meredith is also a member of the editorial board of *Design Issues* and *She-Ji*, the journal of design, innovation, and economics, and author of several books and more than 100 articles on design and design education.

Mathias Esmann is a co-founder of Global Minimum and holds an AB in public and international affairs from Princeton University and a joint MSc in international law, economics and management from the University of Copenhagen and Copenhagen Business School. He currently works in the private sector in Copenhagen.

Christelle Estrada, PhD, received her doctorate from Claremont Graduate University (1993) in Education and Religion and is currently the Education Specialist at the Utah State Office of Education. She is also the President of a non-profit, Education Opportunity Now (EON), that supports projects aligned with the vision of Design Thinking and collaborative partnerships with districts, museums and community-based organizations. She is a certified teacher for Stanford's Cultivating Compassion Training and has presented academic papers on the theme of Human-Centered Education at the Parliament of World Religions (2016), the International Global Learning Partners Conference (2013), the Oxford Roundtable (2006) and at the Whitehead International Conferences in Claremont (2016) and at the University of Salzburg (2006).

Jerry Alan Fails is an associate professor in the Computer Science Department at Boise State University in Boise, Idaho. His primary area of research is Human-Computer Interaction, with a focus on technologies that support children's creativity, mobility, and collaboration and promote activity and exploration of the world around them. He has been actively designing technologies with and for children since 2003.

Shelley Goldman is an educational anthropologist studying learning in and out of school. Goldman's work focuses on creating opportunities for rich STEM learning, and for understanding how design thinking and technologies can create access to, and transform, it. A K-8 teacher at heart who helped found three public schools, Goldman is the Director of the Research on Education and Design Lab (REDlab) and a professor at the Stanford Graduate School of Education and by Courtesy, Mechanical Engineering–Design.

Mohanram Gudipati, a molecular biologist by training, is a graduate of the Tata Institute of Fundamental Research in Mumbai, India. After spending approximately 10 years in academic research and industry, during which time his work has been published in multiple peer-reviewed science journals, Mohan rejoined the Riverside School as part of a team working on building a hybrid online teacher training platform to share its processes and practices with educators across the world. Previously, he designed the school's science curriculum.

Mona Leigh Guha, PhD, is affiliated with the University of Maryland's Human-Computer Interaction Lab, where she worked for many years on and eventually led a technology design team of adults and children. Mona Leigh's research focus includes new techniques for design which enable children and adults to better co-design technology, and the impact on children of participating in the design process. Recently, she accepted a position as the Director of the Center for Young Children at the University of Maryland.

Jeffery Hudson has been teaching English in Alton, Illinois since 1996. He holds a Master's degree in teaching writing from Southern Illinois University, Edwardsville. He first became a fellow of the National Writing Project through the Mississippi Valley Writing Project, an experience he marks as one of the most influential in his professional career. In 2008, he jumped at the opportunity to help lead a site, the Piasa Bluffs Writing Project (PBWP). Together with many of the folks that helped found PBWP, he continues to pursue his professional development and action-research interests as a member of the Cultural Landscapes Collabortory (Colab). He currently leads Alton High's Literacy Laboratory, an innovative professional learning community (PLC) supported by the theories of action emerging out of the work of the Colab.

Zanette Johnson, PhD, is a researcher, learning experience designer, and founder of Intrinsic Impact Consulting, based in San Francisco. Her firm helps organizations and teams build adaptive expertise to creatively and effectively solve unexpected problems. Dr. Johnson holds a Bachelor's degree in Neuroscience and Religious Studies, a Master's in Teaching, and a doctoral degree from Stanford University's transdisciplinary "Learning Science and Technology Design" program.

Zaza Kabayadondo works at Smith College as the co-director of the Design Thinking Initiative. She has been using design thinking to tackle "wicked problems" since 2009 when she first started training teachers and students in the San Francisco Bay Area. She is one of the early alumni of the Stanford d.school, and is a founding member of the design thinking research group Research in Education and Design (REDlab). She has a commitment to understanding how learning environments can be shaped to enhance agency, creativity, and community development. Prior to joining Smith College, her energies were focused on introducing design thinking to Zimbabwe, where she facilitates workshops for doctors to develop insightful medical devices and to reimagine their practice. She holds a BA in Media Arts and Sciences from Wellesley College and a PhD from Stanford University's School of Education.

Anna Keune is a graduate research assistant in the Creativity Labs at Indiana University. She studied New Media Art and Design at Aalto University, where she was also the lead designer for the pan-European research project Innovative Technologies for an Engaging Classroom Project. Anna is passionate about participatory making, and has a background in participatory design of digital media tools for learning with educators and youth across Europe and in India. Her personal interests center around maker culture and materials for learning. At Creativity Labs, Anna investigates youth maker portfolios across the US and pursues the design of equitable curricular approaches and spaces for making.

Jennifer Knudsen is a senior mathematics educator for SRI International's Center for Technology in Learning. She is an expert in the design of curriculum and professional development for middle school mathematics. Her research and designs include innovative performatory approaches for learning to teach mathematical practices and technology-enhanced curriculum aimed at mathematical understanding.

David Kwek received his Masters in Curriculum and Teacher Education from the Graduate School of Education at Stanford University and is now a curriculum specialist at the Ministry of Education in Singapore. He is interested in invigorating learning environments with student-centered pedagogies and using real-world problems as a context for students to develop critical and inventive thinking skills.

Deborah Littlejohn is an assistant professor at North Carolina State University's College of Design in the Department of Graphic Design and Industrial Design. As a design researcher, she is guided by questions that address the relations between design and the ability of people to learn, adapt and change. Littlejohn was a fellow at the University of Minnesota Design Institute where she led an investigation of leading type design practice that resulted in the internationally distributed book *Metro Letters: A Typeface for the Twin Cities*. She has been a contributor to journals on design and design education, including *Design Issues*, *Design & Culture*, *Eye* magazine, and AIGA.org. She currently serves as a review editor for the *International Journal of Communication Design* and is a member of the founding editorial board for AIGA's *Dialectic and Dialog*.

Brenna McNally is a PhD student in the College of Information Studies at the University of Maryland. Her research at the Human-Computer Interaction Lab focuses on the design of technologies for children and the considerations around including children in the design process. She received her MS in Human-Computer Interaction from the University of Maryland in 2012 and her BA in Telecommunication-Digital Media, Art, and Technology from Michigan State University in 2008.

Desmond Mitchell is a founding member of GMin's InChallenges and InLabs. Currently he is pursuing a joint Master's degree in business and education at Stanford University and received his BA in Psychology from Harvard University. Previously Demond worked within both the public and private sector within education and technology.

Kylie Peppler is an associate professor of Learning Sciences at Indiana University. An artist by training, she engages in research that focuses on the intersection of arts, media, new technologies, and informal learning. Peppler also leads the Make-to-Learn initiative of the MacArthur Foundation, which leverages DIY culture, digital practices, and educational research to advocate for placing making, creating, and designing at the core of educational practice. Her current work on maker culture is supported by the National Science Foundation, the US Department of Education, the Moore Foundation, and the John D. and Catherine T. MacArthur Foundation. Find out more at kpeppler.com.

Christian Schunn is a senior scientist at the Learning Research and Development Center and a professor of Psychology, Learning Sciences and Policy, and Intelligent Systems at the University of Pittsburgh. He directs a number of research and design projects in science, mathematics, and engineering education. This work includes studying expert engineering and science teams, building innovative technology-supported STEM curricula, and studying factors that influence student and teacher learning and engagement. He is a fellow of AAAS, APA, and APS, as well the Chair of the International Society for Design & Development in Education.

Kiran Bir Sethi is the Founder/Director of the Riverside School in Ahmedabad, India. She is also the founder of "aProCh"—an initiative to make our cities more child friendly, for which she was awarded the Ashoka Fellow in 2008. In 2009, she founded "Design for Change" (DFC) – the world's largest movement of change – of and by children. Design for Change has been declared Lego Foundation's "Reimagine Learning Challenge Champion" in November 2014. In March 2015, she was amongst the Top 10 Educators, nominated for the Global Teacher Prize—instituted by the Varkey GEMS Foundation. Most recently, Kiran was awarded "Asia's Game Changer Award – 2015" by the Asia Society.

Nicole Shechtman is a senior educational researcher at SRI International's Center for Technology in Learning. She leads research and evaluation projects focused on how learning environments can be designed to empower people to succeed in the 21st century. In addition to content knowledge, people need critical social and emotional competencies—including self-management, knowing how to learn, effective communication, teamwork and everyday problem solving. Her work explores how research in education, psychology and other fields can be put into action to improve these capacities, particularly for the most disadvantaged individuals.

Eli Silk is an assistant professor of Professional Practice in the Graduate School of Education at Rutgers. His primary research interest is in understanding processes of learning that integrate concepts and skills across the disciplines of Science, Technology, Engineering, and Mathematics (STEM), with a particular interest on how students can utilize engineering design as a problem solving process. He received his PhD in cognitive studies in education from the University of Pittsburgh in 2011.

Kathy Liu Sun is an assistant professor of education at Santa Clara University. Kathy is a former high school math teacher who earned a Bachelor's degree in Economics and a PhD in Mathematics Education from Stanford University. Her research seeks to understand the barriers that prevent students from succeeding and advancing in STEM-related fields. Her work focuses on understanding how teachers contribute to students' ideas about their own learning potential. She is currently examining math teaching at various grade levels and in a variety of contexts to understand how instruction might influence students' beliefs and academic outcomes.

Verily Tan is a doctoral candidate in Instructional Systems Technology at Indiana University. She has completed a Master's (MSEd) in the Learning Sciences. Verily has extensive experience as a high school teacher and an instructional designer prior to her current study. She enjoys interacting with students and children in K12 settings, in both formal and informal contexts. Verily has presented work on designing with electronic-textiles. Her research interests include designing, making and STEM learning. Her dissertation explores the designerly practice of problem framing by youth in a maker space that strongly focuses on engineering mindsets.

Ann Taylor, PhD, is the Associate Dean for School and Community Parnters, and Professor in the College of Education at the University of Missouri-St. Louis. Her teaching has included mathematics education, teacher leadership and qualitative research methods courses, and she particularly enjoys working with educator-practitioners as they innovate their practice. As a former middle and secondary geography teacher in three urban public institutions in Sheffield, UK, her research has grown naturally from her own study of classroom pedagogy and culture. She is interested in how teachers come to learn, grow and innovate their teaching practices together through developing collaborative cultures and powerful learning spaces.

Tanner Vea is a doctoral candidate in learning sciences and technology design at Stanford University. Formerly an Emmy Award-nominated digital media producer for PBS and PBSKIDS at WNET in New York, Tanner now studies how people learn to act ethically, including in the process of designing new technologies. He also consults with organizations hoping to integrate design thinking into their practices. This work includes leading professional development sessions in design thinking and providing ongoing design coaching. He holds an MA from Teachers College, Columbia University and a BA from Bard College.

Michelle P. Whitacre, PhD, is a senior program producer in the ED Collabitat at the University of Missouri-St. Louis. She has years of experience working as a high school science teacher and instructional coach and in designing professional development programs for educators. She is passionate about drawing on teachers' expertise and creating transformative learning experiences. Based on her research, she believes strongly that professional growth emerges from programs that are targeted towards teachers' individualized needs and contexts. Ultimately, she aims to infuse professional creativity into the cultural landscape of our educational systems.

Susie Wise is motivated by the simple belief that humans are by nature design thinkers. She is the Director of the @K12lab Network at the d.school at Stanford University. She co-founded Urban Montessori Charter School in Oakland, California.

Molly B. Zielezinski is a doctoral candidate at the Stanford Graduate School of Education with dual specialization in Learning Sciences and Technology Design and Curriculum and Teacher Education. As a former teacher, she is deeply committed to identifying and interrogating innovative practices that support the development of critical thinking, collaboration, and creativity in K-12 classrooms. Through this research agenda, Molly has identified the profound potential of design thinking as vehicle for authentic problem solving that promotes creative confidence and scaffolds empathy driven solution finding. She also researches learning associated with the integration digital technologies into K-12 curriculum, mapping these within the myriad of interconnected contextual factors at play in classrooms.

FOREWORD

Bernard Roth

When I first met José he was almost completely shut off. I could hardly get a word out of him. When he did speak, it was mainly an inaudible mumble. He was a fifth grade student in a charter school located in a poor Hispanic neighborhood about 5 miles from Stanford University. Shelley Goldman and Maureen Carroll had invited me to co-teach a class with them in which Stanford students were to devise ways to inspire financially disadvantaged students to become interested in college and STEM subjects. This was the first of nine weekly Thursday afternoons that I spent with the Stanford students at the charter school. Maureen led a kickoff design thinking exercise, and José and I ended up as partners. The design challenge was to redesign the room where your partner's bed is located so that the room better serves their needs.

José and I described to each other what we wanted to use the room for, and then we each drew a sketch of a layout that would accommodate our partner's wants. I inferred that José's most important possession, and perhaps closest friend, was his pet hamster. My design for José's room provided lavishly for his hamster. I made some modifications to my design based on José's feedback and then constructed a small cardboard model that José got to take home. He reciprocated by redesigning my bedroom according to the desires he heard from me. That interaction created a friendship between us, and opened José up so that he became a different person in the classroom.

In my view, that small design thinking exercise did two big things for José. First, he experienced that I truly was listening to him and that I recognized how important the hamster was in his life. My design accepted his priorities and validated him as a person. Second, when I welcomed his redesign of my bedroom he experienced a success that fed into his sense of agency.

Design thinking is the name given to a set of mindsets and procedures that were originally used by designers of physical artifacts. Generally the domain of knowledge in design thinking is process-based rather than content-based. This has allowed design thinking to be used in many other areas of endeavor and to solve problems that are of concern to organizations and individuals in their professional and personal lives. Design thinking has been successfully applied in medicine, law, business, engineering, the physical and social sciences, the arts, and, of course, in education.

At Stanford University's Hasso Plattner Institute of Design (we call it the d.school), design thinking has been the focus of over 40 courses offered to graduate and undergraduate students. In addition, the d.school has a long-standing research and development initiative, with dedicated full-time staff, to promote design thinking to the worldwide K-12 arena. We regularly offer workshops and special sessions for members of school boards, principals, teachers, and students.

This book is based in part on a summer workshop organized by Professor Shelley Goldman, Zaza Kabayadondo, Maureen Carroll, and Adam Royalty. Professor Goldman and her Research in Education Design group (REDlab) have been closely allied to the d.school since the d.school's inception in 2005. The REDlab and the Stanford Graduate School of Education's Learning, Design, and Technology (LDT) program have been the major source of talent that has led the d.school's K-12 initiative.

The d.school at Stanford University has been one of the leaders of the design thinking movement and its application to K-12 education. Our first major K-12 project was for The Nueva School in Hillsborough, California. David Kelley, one of the d.school founders, was a parent of one the students at The Nueva School. He convinced the school to create a design thinking space from a 3,500 square foot space that was originally planned to be a science classroom. The space was named the Innovation Lab, or simply I-Lab. Kim Saxe, a graduate of the Stanford Product Design program, was a teacher at Nueva and she took the lead in implementing the design thinking curriculum that the d.school team led by Susie Wise designed for Nueva. We also designed special furniture for the I-Lab studio. That was our beginning in K-12 education, and our K-12 program has grown to include activities in many other parts of the US and countries throughout the world.

Design thinking is basically a type of learning-by-doing methodology. The roots of the learning-by-doing methodology go back to John Dewey, Maria Montessori, and hosts of other educational innovators. It is obvious that giving students the opportunity to do something real can be inspirational and often more effective than abstract and seemingly meaningless learning. Design thinking has the power to flip students' mindsets. I have seen students move from being powerless learners to confident creators, from passive learners to powerful teachers, from needing mentorship to becoming powerful mentors.

Many surveys of practicing professionals have shown that skills such as making presentations, cooperating with people from different backgrounds, expressing one's ideas, and organizing and meeting deadlines are far more widely used than the specific technical content of their expertise. Design thinking projects enhance these needed interpersonal skills. For students, such projects also have the positive effect of enhancing creative confidence and empowering people like my friend José to live more fully committed lives.

This volume does a great public service since it presents the theory behind design thinking as an educational tool and gives both practical how-to advice on and examples of actual design thinking applications to K-12 education. In reading this book it is best to think of it as a guide rather than a how-to manual to be memorized. The practice of design thinking is being continually modified and enhanced with new concepts, methodology and insights. In fact, it is in the spirit of design thinking to always be prototyping new ways toward the goal of providing the best possible education to our young people. Mindfulness of process and willingness to fail in the pursuit of a better solution are two of the main precepts of design thinking.

This book can only capture what the design thinking adventure has taught us to date. I suggest you use it as a tool to inspire your own use of design thinking. Use the material in this book not only as a tool to educate others—use it to develop your own unique teaching style. Keep in mind that design thinking is a user-centered form of looking at problems, and that you can use its mindsets and processes to design and redesign your own life as well as the lives of your students and colleagues.

PART I

Design Thinking and Its Emergence in K-12 Education

1

TAKING DESIGN THINKING TO SCHOOL

How the Technology of Design Can Transform Teachers, Learners, and Classrooms

Shelley Goldman and Zaza Kabayadondo

Design Thinking in the World and in School

What Is Design Thinking?

Design thinking is a method of problem-solving that relies on a complex of skills, processes, and mindsets that help people generate novel solutions to problems. Design thinking can result in new objects, ideas, narratives, or systems. The excitement over design thinking lies in the proposition that anyone can learn to do it. The democratic promise of design thinking is that once design thinking has been mastered anyone can go about redesigning the systems, infrastructures, and organizations that shape our lives.

Design thinking has been visualized in many ways; most involve a user-centered, empathy-driven approach aimed at creating solutions through gaining insight into people's needs. Design thinking also involves creating conceptual (and sometimes working) prototypes that get improved through feedback and testing with stakeholders. Learning with design thinking often starts with the method. The aim is to move beyond merely going through the steps of the process and to develop mindset change experiences such as empathy development, participation in "team collaborations," commitment to action-oriented problem-solving, a sense of efficacy, and understanding that failure and persistence to try again after failures are necessary and productive aspects of success. As a technology, design thinking is meant to lead to insights that shift design thinkers' perspectives and actions while problem-solving. Design thinking involves empathizing with end-user(s), learning to work collaboratively, and employing hands, minds, and intuitions in ways that drive creative problem-solving. Design thinking has been visualized in many ways: some visualizations emphasize the order of design process by instructing designers to start with *empathy*, then *define* the problem from a fresh perspective, then actively generate ideas (*ideate*). Next, designers must convert the ideas into questions that are embodied in physical artifacts (*prototypes*). Finally, designers answer the questions embedded in those prototypes (which can be products, services, experiences, narratives, or systems) by *testing* the prototypes with other people before finally cycling back to empathy. These five stages of action or modes of thinking—empathize, define, ideate, prototype, test—constitute the design thinking process. Once a learner becomes proficient in design thinking they no longer need to rely on cycling through the steps one after the other—they start to appreciate and fully exploit the fluidity of the design process.

The user-centered, empathy mandate of design thinking refers to many methods of capturing, observing, engaging with, and immersing oneself in the livelihoods of others. The empathy mandate not only puts the "human" in human-centered design; it also asserts that complex problems are not only technical in nature but have an equally complex social and real-world dimension. Design thinking is a technology that brings to life new kinds of inquiry for teachers, learners, and classrooms. In this volume we will explore how taking design thinking to school brings back into focus John Dewey's vision of schooling as a transformative space for creative and collaborative inquiry.

A Short History of Design Thinking With an Eye to the Ideas of John Dewey

The first reference we were able to find to design thinking was as early as 1935 in a discussion about how the incorporation of electrical motors would alter the manufacturing industry (Dennis & Thomas, 1935). As Dennis and Thomas write, "Instances of skillful design thinking in the well-integrated handling of principles, materials, and appearance and style factors are evident in every branch of electrical manufacturing" (1935, p. 25). The authors refer to design thinking as a seamless building of a new component (electrical elements) into an old machine to create an electrically motorized machine with numerous new applications. In this early instance, design thinking is a reference to deftness in "harnessing" engineering principles and aesthetics to build a new age of machinery out of traditional materials.

The phrase gained more currency in the 1940s when industrial manufacturing journals were more prominent. Design thinking began to indicate a state-of-the-art use of engineering to create motors, as seen in an advertisement from a 1944 magazine *Motor Boating*:

> While the sketch above shows no specific controls, it indicates today's design thinking for one type of post-war craft on which BENDIX CONTROLS can function for your added boating pleasure.
>
> *(1944, p. 133)*

The usage hinted at a masterful and complex level of thinking that was simply evident in the finished products and tools. This usage continued throughout the 1950s, as in the periodical *Electronic Design*:

> Undoubtedly a lot of excellent design thinking is being embodied in these devices. Because of the nature of the projects however, these design ideas are part of the working knowledge of a relatively small number of engineers.
>
> *(1955, p. 4)*

Other early uses of design thinking point to the evolution of an idea into a product that can be observed in the methods that designers strategically employ. In 1957 the *American Ceramic Society Bulletin* issued a manifest on how designers could learn good design thinking. They emphasized the need to carry design thinking from the conception of an idea all the way to the production line into "design action" (1957). By 1965 L. Bruce Archer had started to emphasize the cognitive and multidisciplinary aspects of design practice as rationale for developing a methodology and curriculum for design. Archer (1965) called for a methodological approach to training designers who had to find ways to incorporate knowledge from ergonomics, cybernetics, marketing, and management science into design thinking.

From this early history, we can see design thinking invoked as a cognitive process that is evident in the finished product. Design thinking started to influence the study of how people think (cognitive science) and learn (the learning sciences). Unlike the manufacturing and design journals of the mid-twentieth century, the research on design in the 1980s and 1990s sought to shine light on those cognitive processes that were hidden behind designed products. After two decades in which the concept of design thinking was progressively developed in the arts and professional design sectors, more cognitive scientists and learning scientists started to pay attention to what design thinking could mean for general education. Learning scientists were focused on the background thinking and talking and acting that is necessary for designing or building prototypes, what is referred to as "cognitive residue" (Pea, 1993) or "reified ideas in solid medium" (credited to D'Andrade as used in Cole & Engeström, 1993); they suggested that this leftover thinking material was what humans accessed when they used tools. This understanding of the relationship between designed tools and cognitive function built on the work of Lev Vygostky that emphasized the ways tools mediate between a subject and object (see Vygotsky's introduction of the meditational triangle, 1978). Bamberger and Schön (1983) describe the ability of designed things to "hold" meanings as a "reflective conversation with materials." Learning scientists such as Edwin Hutchins later saw the connection between human thinking and the tools designed to ease computation as a "cognitive ecology"—a system of interconnected and interdependent elements that enables humans to perform more sophisticated actions and engage in inquiry.

Building on Dewey's theory of inquiry, Schön set an agenda "to develop the idea of reflective practice, in the spirit of Deweyean inquiry that seeks to integrate thought and action, theory and practice, the academy and the everyday world, but also in the spirit of a constructivist approach to the variety of ways in which we construct the reality of problematic situations" (Schön, 1992, p. 123). We return to Dewey later in this introduction and focus on Schön here because his ideas also inspired research on the relationship between design and learning. The connections between Dewey's and Schön's thinking are often overlooked but Schön clearly set out to emphasize Dewey's influence on his own work. Schön (1992) was interested in designing and discovering as examples of knowing-in-action (knowledge put into action), and he likened the process of designing something to a reflective conversation with its constituent materials and also with oneself. As Schön writes,

> When a designer reflects on the strategies and assumptions that underlie her choices, daring to disrupt them, she may learn critically important things about herself. Mimi, for example, might learn, by reflecting on her work, how she had confined herself unawares to a particularly narrow and untested conception of the task at hand. U-Chin, considering his uses of materials in relation to Rex's, might become aware of possibilities for expanding his vision of the technical universe. These are ways in which designing includes, or stimulates, learning. It is also fruitful, however, to think of learning-in the mode of puzzle or problem-solving as a kind of designing.
>
> *(1992, p. 132)*

In the above excerpt about three designers, Mimi, U-Chin, and Rex, Schön draws parallels between learning and designing. Schön's designers were working through complex, ambiguous, uncertain, or *wicked* problems, a term popularized by Rittel and Webber (1973) to give a new language to the kind of problem-solving design thinkers were engaging in. While Schön credited Herbert Simon for his 1970s support for the need for a science of design, he was, like Dewey, more interested in how designers resolved constraints and how they engaged with wicked problems as a means of developing knowledge-in-action.

Later, Buchanan brought together the connections between design thinking, wicked problems, and Dewey's theory of inquiry in his 1992 article. Buchanan offered a definition of technology that is useful for understanding the role design thinking will play in transforming our shared human culture and in helping our students become responsible agents of that change. As Buchanan writes,

> What Dewey defines as technology is not what is commonly understood in today's philosophy of technology. Instead of meaning knowledge of how to make and use artifacts or the artifacts themselves, technology for Dewey is an art of experimental thinking.
>
> *(p. 13)*

Buchanan went on to demonstrate how design thinking, a process for tackling wicked problems, could be seen as the antithesis of siloed disciplinary thinking. For Buchanan, design thinking is "a common discipline" (p. 21) that has emerged to connect and integrate useful knowledge from the arts and sciences. As Buchanan writes, "Designers, are exploring concrete integrations of knowledge that will combine theory with practice for new productive purposes, and this is the reason why we turn to design thinking" (p. 6).

More recently, David Kelley and Tom Kelley (Kelley & Kelley, 2013) and others at IDEO and Stanford University have been influential in popularizing design thinking as a method to be learned outside of professional design fields for innovating in businesses, university education, and organizations. They take the very democratizing idea that anyone can become a design thinker. We agree, and work closely with the school of design thinking taught at Stanford University.[1] We view this technology—design thinking—as one that provides the agency, the aplomb, the catalysis, and the compassion for others that can transform our schools.

What does design thinking look like in action?

> One Monday morning, three collaborative design teams are presented with a design challenge to transform the meaning of *patient comfort* for seriously ill patients. Forty-eight hours later all three teams show their life-size prototypes to their clients. One client, a cancer survivor, is shown a new concept for a chemotherapy center that accommodates patients, relatives and friends, and includes a smoothie bar and lessons about cooking for the long waits during chemo. Another client, a son who took care of his ailing father, gets to try out a portable shower equipped with wheelchair access, heated floors and towels that could have helped his father stay extra warm. The third client, a hospice caretaker for cancer patients, is presented a hospital room with a high tech wall for video-call messaging, slide shows of family, and a touch-screen patient-readable medical chart and treatment schedule. All three clients are touched by the brilliance of the prototypes, delighted that their concerns as patients and caretakers were listened to so closely, and grateful for how connected the ideas were to their needs. They wanted these ideas to be implemented and thought many others would benefit from them.

These design solutions were not the products of professional medical designers. They were prototypes designed by three teams of ninth-grade students who were brought together for an intensive design challenge over a three-day period.

The students were guided by teacher-coaches using a design thinking process that centered on the students creating designs based on empathy they developed for their clients and their unmet comfort experiences as patients or patient caregivers. For the students, different connections were made with peers and topics of interest—the challenge built confidence. When the teams demonstrated their designs, all that were present recognized the students' contributions—many wept. One principal implored the students to start work with him immediately to "design our school so that students would not want to drop out." Within a week, the newly minted, ninth-grade design thinkers were also asked to train as design thinking coaches for younger students.

What does this example have to do with making education stay relevant to 21st-century demands for productive family members, citizens, and workers who can solve the world's problems? The *patient comfort* challenge shared elements related to design and innovation pedagogies, and those approaches approximate many of the skills that are thought to be essential for next generations of educated adults. The challenge was characterized by deep and critical thinking, active and collaborative learning, relevancy to in-the-world problem-solving, the production of knowledge and products, the use of design practices, and an orientation to creativity and innovation. Teachers and students engaged in hands-on design challenges for real patients that focused on developing empathy, promoting a bias toward action, encouraging ideation, and developing metacognitive awareness (Goldman et al., 2012; Carroll et al., 2012; Carroll et al., 2010). Design thinking involves a focus on acting creatively, thinking critically, communicating widely, collaborating, and exercising meta-cognitive competencies. Design thinking is a reflexive practice and learners often invent something new while reframing and bolstering their own agency in the world. In this volume we use the term *design thinking* as an umbrella term to help us describe these approaches, their variations, and their impacts in both K-12 research and practice. Design thinking pedagogies are complex in their aims, actions, and outcomes. They are about teaching and learning concepts, processes, and dispositions for guiding thought and problem-solving.

Design thinking is especially aimed at generating solutions to undefined and "sticky" problems. Nigel Cross (2005) and others suggest that design pedagogies can be difficult to teach. Cross writes that they are "ill-defined, ill-structured, or 'wicked'" (recall Rittel & Webber, 1973). They are not the same as the "puzzles" that scientists, mathematicians, and other scholars set themselves. They are not problems for which all the necessary information is, or ever can be, available to the problem solver. They are therefore not susceptible to exhaustive analysis, and there can never be a guarantee that "correct" solutions can be found for them. In this context a solution-focused strategy is clearly preferable to a problem-focused one: it will always be possible to go on analyzing "the problem," but the designer's task is to produce "the solution."

Design thinking encompasses active problem-solving by engaging with and changing the world (Dewey, 1916). Design thinking relies on deep collaborations and teamwork, and the opportunities to interact are generally considered an essential environment for learning (Vygotsky, 1986). Like constructionism, design thinking brings an orientation to learning through interaction with materials, objects, and experiences from which the learner reflects and builds knowledge (Papert & Harel, 1991). Design thinking also relies on catalyzing social and epistemic *mindshifts*, which we define as epistemological viewpoints that help learners evolve their orientations to problem-solving (Goldman et al., 2012). These and more learning theory elements are the mirrors through which scholars, researchers, and educators view learners while implementing and studying students engaged with design pedagogies. This volume represents the different ways researchers and educators are thinking about design in K-12.

While educators do not traditionally locate their work in the area of real-world problem-solving, design educators would contend that their students are learning valuable lessons from their interactions with problems in the world, even in the wake of failed solutions. Learning design thinking is complex and transformational, and both the promise and the complexities associated with it can be captivating to educators. With design thinking pedagogies, students might interact with and develop understandings in a domain (such as science, math, or engineering) or develop skills in building empathy with users, collaborating, and prototyping. In the book *Design as a Catalyst for Learning* (1997), Meredith Davis and her colleagues sum up the design process and where it fits in a learning constellation and as a method and a discipline:

> It is a creative counterpart to the scientific method, and it presumes there is more than one right solution to any problem and many paths to each alternative. Designerly modes of inquiry place no hierarchy among various physical and cognitive skills. For designers, doing is a way of knowing. They are as likely to analyze a problem through models, diagrams, walks through an environment, or sketches as they are through statistics or writing. Designers are fluent in several vehicles of thought (images, words, numbers) and methods of communication, storing and recombining experiences for future use.
>
> *(Davis et al., 1997, p. 2)*

The focus of design thinking is human-centered and relies on deeply social engagements with a problem. Design approaches may aim to provide students with experiences such as "radical" collaborations, interdisciplinary thinking and reflection, empathy experiences that lead to deep insights, experience with creating conceptual and real models of ideas, and deep connections to and confidence resulting from problem-solving for real-world situations. Outcomes of design approaches can be broader than traditional subject content learning and include the development of a range of communication competencies and the development of "mindsets" (or dispositions) that enable learners to approach problems in new ways, to experiment in finding solutions, to learn from mistakes, and ultimately to meet the needs of those who would benefit from the solutions.

Since design thinking can be such a complex process, researchers and practitioners involved in providing design-relevant learning experiences are often
guided by a loosely coupled constellation of theoretical rationales. These theoretical rationales include but are not limited to experiential, sociocultural,
constructivist, and constructionist views on learning. These theories may seem
disparate, yet we see them as related and complementary lenses for viewing
and depicting the complexities of learning with design and design thinking
approaches. It is helpful to understand design thinking by using the metaphor
of a kaleidoscope, a mixture of materials and elements that may not shine on
their own, but that dazzle when combined or set in motion in a particular con-
figuration. The point is to connect students to a structure for learning that acts
as a multiplier, mobilizer, and magnifier, by creating reflexive and crystallized
views of the many facets of any concept under design. Like the elements in a
kaleidoscope, students shine when put into action in creative problem-solving.

In many ways, K–12 teachers and classrooms have already been infused with
pre-requisites to design thinking. Design thinking neither negates nor favors
the developmental, sequential approaches that are inscribed in public school
standards documents and curriculum programs. We see design thinking as a
mechanism for bringing these goals into focus. Design thinking has applicability
up and down the K–12 structure and is compatible with many of the ways of
knowing and disciplinary thinking sought after in K–12 education. We feel that
the creative confidence that develops when learners experience design thinking
can and should be in the experience set of all K–12 students.

Although they seem new, design approaches are the most recent waves in
education's hundred-year history with educationally progressive approaches.
The ideas behind these pedagogies have been present for at least a century,
and we see deep connections to the works of educational thinkers such as John
Dewey, Lucy Sprague Mitchell, Lev Vygotsky, and Paulo Freire. Dewey (1916)
suggested that experiencing the world, and its actions, complex issues, and push
and pull are the crux of learning. Mitchell, who was the founder of the Bank
Street College, advocated for taking young children out into the community to
see how people transacted in different local settings. She took her students to the
docks or the market and let them observe and participate, then return to school
and where they constructed models and representations (life-sized physical,
verbal, artistic, and literary) of the world with which they interacted (Sprague
Mitchell, 1934).

Vygotsky (1986) proposed that language and social interaction were hallmarks
of learning and thought, moving the fields concerned with cognition to awareness
about the importance of learning environments that are intensely social and that
include both novices and experts working with each other. Freire took a more con-
frontational approach, arguing for liberation education that was deeply connected
to bettering the world and reorganizing structures in the community and society
(Freire, 1968). Freire spoke of the deep equity issues that plague K–12 schooling,

and to the power of pedagogies that could uplift teachers, students, and communities. The ideas in design approaches to solving problems in light of local needs share a spirit with his writings. Each of these four thought leaders was confident that when you put students together in a compelling, relevant, and real problem-focused learning environment, learning and agency would be omnipresent.

More recently a couple of decades of research and islands of implementation have demonstrated the promise of design approaches (Goldman, 2002; Goldman & Knudsen, 2004; Hmelo et al., 2000). Work has indicated the potential for design in K-12 to contribute to young people's meta-cognitive (Kolodner et al., 2003) and social learning (Cognition and Technology Group at Vanderbilt, 1997) as well as in specific subject areas such as mathematics, science, and computer programming (Kolodner et al., 2003; Goldman et al., 1998; Middleton & Corbett, 1998; Cognition and Instruction Group, 1997; Mastropieri & Scruggs, 1992; Kafai & Resnick, 2000). These efforts suggested that design skills are not merely gimmicks, but can in fact aid students in core subject area learning as well social skills. Research and practice are still in a nascent phase, yet they continue to bring relevant ideas and perspectives to the surface.

Goldman began working on design approaches with a team that developed middle school math curriculum (for students aged 10–14) that integrated mathematics in pursuit of real-world problem-solving (Goldman et al., 1998). That early work helped us view design thinking as conducive to an equity agenda for students. It was impressive how the empathy aspects, brainstorming processes, and the generation of "real-world solutions" enabled students who were otherwise silent in math class to engage and have a voice. The teachers also came to see students in a new light and found promising visions of teaching. Educators and teachers in this volume have similar sentiments as they experiment with and study design approaches.

The Focus of This Volume

The airwaves are alive with urgent calls for innovation in school. This volume brings together a number of fascinating cases where ideological and ontological forces are at play in the production of new attitudes and mindsets towards innovating in schools. We see this volume as an intervention, an event that converses with the realities of and empirical research on implementing design thinking in education. Committing to design thinking education is like standing on a precipice, a moment before something big where we realize that in order to move forward we must take risks and venture into the unknown. The initiatives to integrate design thinking principles in K-12 learning contexts have been decentralized and disparate—they have been initiated by concerned publics, by schools, by teachers, by administrators, and by non-profit organizations acting in parallel as they venture into the unknown. As initiatives they are simultaneously top-down, bottom-up, external, and internal, while also feeding into institutional, everyday and imagined 21st-century contexts. While, on the one hand, design thinking projects make the principles of engineering, design, and technology fluency more tangible and personal for a broader range of young learners, on the other they also embrace ambiguity and failure as opportunities to grow, and in doing so often rub up against institutional values and structures, especially the requirement that new practices are rationalized with data, evaluation, and quick results. The tensions that come up have motivated this volume and its focus on implementation by juxtaposing, in the spirit of Dewey, theory and practice.

We look at students, teachers, principals, administrators, policymakers, international NGOs, and researchers to help us take an ecological perspective on opening up design thinking to schools—and opening up schools to design thinking. How do you study this phenomenon, how do you show learning, how do you describe the kinds of transformations that design thinking allows? It was difficult to bring the practical implications of putting design principles in motion and the theoretical concerns of understanding what design has to offer students into the format of this book without losing the sense of empowerment and multiplicity that motivates the activities we have seen. The volume provides new knowledge on: (1) the theory and practice of reframing teaching and learning contexts as authentic design experiences; (2) attention to equity issues and alternative pathways to introducing design thinking mindsets to young children, girls, English language learners, and minority students; and (3) research-based and classroom integration-focused discussions of design thinking, still under-represented in this emergent field. Our ambition with this book is to affirm the notion of design thinking without borders, and to break through the boundaries between research and practice.

The metaphor of design thinking without borders is broad and evocative in many ways and has the potential to open up dialogue and thinking anew about when and where learning, growth, and empowerment can be triggered. This expansive perspective on design thinking was an outcome of the Research in Education and Design Workshop, a conference from which this volume emerged. The conference was a timely moment to reflect on the theme of equity and inclusive partnerships as our research community set its agenda for the future of research and implementation in the K-12 space. The conference, the first of its kind, was sponsored by a grant from Stanford University's K-12 initiative and was attended by designers and educational practitioners from research institutions in the Bay Area, across the United States, and from abroad.[2] The objectives of the conference were to share work in the field, to facilitate connections between researchers and practitioners, and to generate collaborative research projects. Participants were asked to share freely about successes and mistakes, to embrace curiosity and openness, to experiment with unconventional explanations, and to present their work through the eyes of the partners with whom they collaborate. We worked ideas that would foster connections and effective strategies. How do you introduce an intervention that will stick and have a sustained life beyond the scope of a research project? How might we develop processes of knowledge production that are informed and grounded by attention to what concerns practitioners "in the trenches"? We committed to creating learning interventions and maintaining them as a form of knowledge production that enfranchise the most marginalized of learners.

Many of the chapters in this volume leverage this bias toward action through partnerships with communities, interdisciplinary teams, and young learners voicing their interests. We also networked and invited groups working in the K–12 design space that had not attended the workshops to contribute to this volume. Their accounts contribute to this dialogue by introducing more insights that are useful talking points for researchers and other stakeholders to communicate during those cycles of experimentation. We see opening up to wider spheres of stakeholders as part of the grand scheme for legitimating K–12 design approaches.

Design thinking reflects a way in which a technology can structure experiences that become interventions for changing the human condition. It is an empowering kind of *perceptual* agency (Monson, 1994), a way of paying attention that, for young learners, has profound implications. Learners start to see themselves as effectors of change: they start to be more conscious and deliberate in how they structure their own thinking. It gives them access to knowledge-in-action and works as an entry point for students into fields and disciplines they never would have imagined. Teachers engaged with design thinking see themselves as stewards of the growth of those mindshifts, but must learn to balance their professional roles with ideological commitments. For example, the framing of design thinking as pre-college engineering education and part of STEM and STEAM is helpful and comprehensive, but may limit the possibilities design thinking has to reach out to learners with diverse interests or needs. The chapters in our volume look explicitly at these concerns and questions that are rarely at the center of the STEM/STEAM education discourse. In this sense our book has been a movement toward crafting a new discourse. We imagine each chapter of this volume, whether written by researchers or practitioners, as a chance for the reader to explore novel "spaces" in the rapidly changing landscape of design research and social practice.

The following chapter by Meredith Davis and Deborah Littlejohn supplements our introduction with a historical overview of design's influence on teaching and learning. Davis and Littlejohn critique design's perpetual status as "emergent" in the discourse on school reform. They call for research that establishes a historical record of how design-based teaching and learning has evolved as a culture of practice, and they open up debate on what research methods are appropriate for the study of design in education. They open up an avenue for reimagining and reshaping the patterns of reporting and accounting for learning in the K–12 design space. The introductory section closes with the case of

Utah's statewide efforts to introduce design thinking to K-12 students and teachers. Christelle Estrada and Shelley Goldman's chapter offers a window into the potential of radical and strategic collaborations to spur design-based teaching and learning both bottom-up and top-down across the state.

In addition to the introductory section, the book has three sections addressing various sides of our themes: (2) Young Designers: K-12 Students Take on Design Thinking; (3) Design Thinking as a Catalyst for Reimagining Education; and (4) Inspiring Teaching: Design Thinking in the Classroom.

The second section, Young Designers: K-12 Students Take on Design Thinking, deals with the notion of teaching the attitudes of professional engineers and designers to young learners. How can academic concepts be applied to authentic design tasks for these K-12 learners? How can learning environments best facilitate meaningful and productive planning as a foundational part of design? Furthermore, how does participation in design impact those children? The literature in this field brings together discussions of current research, policy trends, teacher practices, and assessment of learning and creativity in K-12 engineering education (Davis et al., 1997; Purzer et al., 2014; Fosmire & Radcliffe, 2013). The chapters of this section share in common an invitation for the young to embody the forms of leadership and agency that is distinctly different from their usual school experience.

Mona Leigh Guha and her collaborators open this section by showing the social and cognitive experiences of children in partnership with adults as they jointly participate in a Cooperative Inquiry technology design process. They illustrate how the young learners had social and cognitive experiences in the areas of relationships, enjoyment, confidence, communication, collaboration, skills, and content. Next, Desmond Mitchell and Mathias Esmann give an account of experiments with design thinking by African youth engaged in innovation competitions run by the non-profit organization Global Minimum (GMin). GMin's program provides a platform for students to think and act creatively in their communities by prototyping solutions to social problems around them. This chapter both highlights the constraints infrastructure and limited integration with the regular school system pose on design space, and how success is hinged on collaboration with communities and on student ownership in the process of using and implementing design principles. This chapter makes a compelling case for an approach to design that includes communities and students as co-designers.

The next chapter, by Shelley Goldman and the Research in Education and Design Lab (REDlab) team, explores the possibility that design thinking around interdisciplinary STEM topics such as access and conservation of water, energy, shelter, and food can spark interest, learning, and agency in students at far younger ages than previously expected. The REDlab brings design thinking curriculums to middle school students and has begun to assess what is learned about design thinking. The results reported show how empathy and an emergent perception of design as a means for solving people's problems were key outcomes. We close the section with Mohanram Gudipati and Kiran Bir Sethi's chapter on the Riverside School in India. The authors showcase how grade 7 students work as design consultants in a project that goes beyond their school campus and engages the larger community and how design mindsets are integrated in their program. All the authors of this section would agree that students take on design thinking, and the roles of leadership that come with it, in graceful and surprising ways.

The third section of the volume, Design Thinking as a Catalyst for Reimagining Education, presents moments of insight that can be useful talking points between teachers and other stakeholders they must be able to communicate and connect with during design experimentation. The issue of aligning technology and design with teaching goals is not new to the field of K-12 design education. The optimism of technology-*driven* school reform discourse has been critiqued and replaced by technology-*enabled* (Hess & Saxberg, 2013; Todd, 1999) ways of reframing learning opportunities. In many initiatives, learning sciences research has been applied to the question of innovating in schools and specifically targets teachers and school leaders as the designers of these reforms. Innovation in schools is paired with the imperative to reverse-engineer or "backward-design" lessons (Wiggins & McTighe, 1998); and with "instructional journeys" that experiment with how to integrate technologies in the classroom (Swanson & Ferguson, 2014), efforts which better position teachers in their attempts to empower students (Bromley & Apple, 1998). This emphasis on experimentation, reflection, and reiteration could transform how teachers perceive of their role as co-designers jointly engaged in design with students and their communities.

We hope that the different framings of design thinking as a collaborative process of reiteration presented in this section can help teachers-as-designers collaborate with their students and school leadership to include an ecology of partnerships. The section opens with Susie Wise's story about building an urban charter school from ground-up with design thinking as the bedrock. Wise demonstrates how Montessori principles and design thinking converge to create an environment where kindergarteners can learn to notice, care, work together, create, share, and reflect. The section continues with Ralph Córdova and his colleagues' chapter on a theory of action, *ResponsiveDesign*, that emerged from the Piasa Bluffs Writing Project. The initiative enables teachers to come together as a community of practice to steward and build highly customized approaches to teaching and learning.

This section concentrates on the mindsets of embracing ambiguity, learning from failure, and using empathy to carve out educative spaces where young learners believe they belong and develop a sense of ownership over their learning. Zanette Johnson's chapter on teachers in Hawaii further illuminates the power that design thinking has to shape effective designs for context-adaptive learning. Educators apply design process thinking and launch themselves on a trajectory toward adaptive expertise; the resulting context-adaptive educational model has implications for learners, teachers, teacher educators, and policymakers. David Kwek's article describes the importance of failure in coaxing students to experiment. Kwek tells the story of design thinking used to tackle the impulse of perfectionism in Singapore where, to persist in pushing frontiers, students must embrace every failure as a step toward success. Kathy Sun's chapter extends the dialogue to consider how empathy might be integrated into STEM education. Empathy plays a critical role in engineering but also in the types of instructional activities teachers design for students. Sun's findings make a strong case for the importance of professional development in helping teachers integrate empathy into instruction.

The fourth section, Inspiring Teaching: Design Thinking in the Classroom, puts at the center the materials and contexts that spark design thinking. The discourse on school reform is teeming with calls for putting creativity back at the center of education (Speicher, 2009). Creativity in schools is linked to the creative economy and the practices of creative professionals (Araya & Peters, 2010). It is also linked to a technology discourse that values STEM and STEAM education as starting points for young entrepreneurs, engineers, designers, innovators, tinkerers—a future-forward generation trained in lateral thinking. In the discourse, a creative society requires new understandings of learning that reflect the shift from the stability of traditional social structures to the fluidity of the 21st century. There is an imperative for creative confidence (Robinson, 2011), for spaces for free construction and systems thinking (Dillon, 2014), and for harnessing play, games, and imagination as tools, and taking these activities seriously as opportunities for learning (Douglas & Brown, 2011). This fourth section focuses on just how such opportunities for learning might be curated.

Jennifer Knudsen and Nicole Shechtman examine the gains to be made from integrating improvisational theater games in professional development for middle school mathematics teachers in the *Bridging Professional Development* project. By contrasting mathematics and improvisation then highlighting the commonalities between the two, Knudsen and Shechtman explore pedagogical skills that *teach for argumentation*. Verily Tan, Anna Keune, and Kylie Peppler continue this section with a chapter on the learning outcomes of activities framed at the intersection of schooling and interest-driven practice. The authors explore teacher-designers in a workshop who are engaged in the creation of electronic textiles (or e-textiles)—soft, fabric-based electronics projects that dovetail with hands-on crafts, physical construction, and design, as well as material play.

In the following chapter, Molly B. Zielezinski gives insights from her instructional journeys of integrating design thinking in the classroom. Zielezinski's chapter is replete with tips for intrepid teachers eager to rethink their classrooms. Charles Cox and his collaborators invite students to revisit their understanding in a block-stacking task. Their chapter explores how design exposes student sensemaking and provides advice about how foundational engineering ideas might be approached. While the first two chapters of the section focus on making the creativity behind engineering accessible to more diverse learners, the following two chapters emphasize how that sparks sophisticated student problem-solving and leadership. Ela Ben-Ur's chapter closes the section and volume with an example of how the work on developing design thinking mindsets can be made more portable. Readers are invited to hold the compass, like design thinking, as a technology for developing a journey of inquiry personally and professionally.

As you read through this book, you will be reminded again and again of the integration of theory and practice. The sections integrate the perspectives of researchers and practitioners, and bring into view a range of frameworks for understanding design thinking and its impacts on, and possibilities for, K-12 students. The chapters of this volume each provide a new twist of the kaleidoscope and emergent visions of how schooling can be impacted. We hope that these perspectives bring into focus the transformative potential of design thinking in schools.

Notes

1 See dschool.stanford.edu and dloft.stanford.edu for detail on the method and classroom resources.
2 Much thanks to Helen Quinn, who supported our visions for design in K-12 and made it possible to hold the conference and support this book as a productive outcome.

References

American Ceramic Society (1957). American Ceramic Society Bulletin, v. *36–37*. Columbus, OH.
Araya, D., & Peters, M.A. (Eds.). (2010). *Education in the creative economy*. New York, NY: Peter Lang Publishing.
Archer, L.B. (1965). *Systematic methods for designers*. London: The Design Council.
Bamberger, J., & Schön, D.A. (1983). Learning as a reflective conversation with materials: Notes from work in progress. *Art Education, 36*(2), 68–73.
Bromley, H., & Apple, M.W. (Eds.). (1998). *Education, technology, power: Educational computing as a social practice*. Albany, NY: State University of New York Press.
Buchanan, R. (1992). Wicked problems in design thinking. *Design Issues, 8*(2), 5–21.
Cole, M., & Engeström, Y. (1993). A cultural-historical approach to distributed cognition. In G. Salomon (Ed.), *Distributed cognitions: Psychological and educational consideration* (pp. 1–46). New York, NY: Cambridge University Press.
Carroll, M., Britos, L., & Goldman, S. (2012). Design thinking. In S. Garner & C. Evans (Eds.), *Design & designing: A critical introduction* (pp. 20–31). Oxford: Berg Publishers.
Carroll, M., Goldman, S., Britos, L., Koh, J., & Royalty, A. (2010). Destination, imagination and the fires within: Design thinking in a middle school classroom. *International Journal of Art & Design Education, 29*(1), 37–53.
Cognition and Technology Group at Vanderbilt. (1997). *The Jasper Project: Lessons in curriculum, instruction, assessment, and professional development*. Mahwah, NJ: Lawrence Erlbaum Associates.

Cross, N. (2005). *Designerly ways of knowing*. New York, NY: Springer.

Davis, M., Hawley, P., McMullan, B., & Spilka, G. (1997). *Design as a catalyst for learning*. Alexandria, VA: Association for Supervision and Curriculum Development.

Dennis, S.A., & Thomas, L.I. (1935). Design, production, marketing, rebuilding of electrical products including all those that are motor driven. *Electrical Manufacturing, 15*. Grand Rapids, MI: The Gage Publishing Company, Inc.

Dewey, J. (1916). *Democracy and education*. New York, NY: Macmillan.

Dillon, R. (2014). *Engage, empower, energize: Leading tomorrow's schools today*. Lanham, MD: Rowman and Littlefield.

Douglas, T., & Brown, J.S. (2011). *A new culture of learning: Cultivating the imagination for a world of constant change*. Lexington, MA: CreateSpace.

Electronic Design (1955). Editorial: Information Please. *Electronic Design, 3*(1):4.

Fosmire, M., & Radcliffe, D. (2013). *Integrating information into the engineering design process*. Indianapolis, IN: Purdue University Press.

Freire, P. (1968). *Pedagogy of the oppressed*. New York, NY: Bloomsbury Publishing USA.

Goldman, S., Carroll, M.P., Kabayadondo, Z., Cavagnaro, L.B., Royalty, A.W., Roth, B., & Kim, J. (2012). Assessing d.learning: Capturing the journey of becoming a design thinker. In C. Meinel, L. Leifer, & H. Plattner (Eds.), *Directions in design thinking research* (pp. 13–33). Berlin: Springer Berlin Heidelberg.

Goldman, S. (2002). Instructional design: Learning through design. In J. Guthrie (Ed.), *Encyclopedia of Education* (2nd ed., pp. 1163–1169). New York, NY: Macmillan Reference USA.

Goldman, S., Knudsen, J., & Latvala, M. (1998). Engaging middle schoolers in and through real-world mathematics. In L. Leutzinger (Ed.), *Mathematics in the middle* (pp. 129–140). Reston, VA: National Council of Teachers of Mathematics.

Hess, F.M., & Saxberg, B. (2013). *Breakthrough leadership in the digital age: Using learning science to reboot schooling*. Thousand Oaks, CA: Corwin Press.

Hmelo, C., Holton, D., & Kolodner, J. (2000). Designing to learn about complex systems. *The Journal of the Learning Sciences, 9*(3), 247–298.

Kafai, Y., & Resnick, M. (Eds.). (2000). *Constructionism in practice: Designing, thinking, and learning in a digital world*. Mahwah, NJ: Lawrence Erlbaum Associates.

Kelley, T., & Kelley, D. (2013). *Creative confidence: Unleashing the creative potential within us all*. New York, NY: Crown Business.

Kolodner, J.L., Camp, P.J., Crismond, D., Fasse, B., Gray, J., Holbrook, J. Putambeckar, S., & Ryan, M. (2003). Problem-based learning meets case-based reasoning in the middle-school science classroom: Putting learning by design into practice. *The Journal of the Learning Sciences, 12*(4), 495–547.

Mastropieri, M.A., & Scruggs, T.E. (1992). Science for students with disabilities. *Review of Educational Research, 62*(4), 377–411.

Middleton, J.A., & Corbett, R. (1998). Sixth-grade students' conceptions of stability in engineering contexts. In R. Lehrer & D. Chazan (Eds.), *Designing learning environments for developing understanding of geometry and space* (pp. 249–266). Mahwah, NJ: Lawrence Erlbaum.

Monson, I. (1994). Doubleness and jazz improvisation: Irony, parody, and ethnomusicology. *Critical Inquiry, 20*(2), 283–313.

Motor Boating (March, 1944). Everyman's boat . . . tomorrow [Advertisement for Bendix Aviation Corporation (pp. 133)]. Retrieved from https://books.google.com/books?

id=px8KvVtB8L4C&lpg=PA113&dq=%22design%20thinking%22&pg=PA113#v=
onepage&q=%22design%20thinking%22&f=false.

Papert, S.E., & Harel, I.E. (1991). *Constructionism*. Westport, CT: Ablex Publishing
Corporation.

Pea, R. (1993). Practices of distributed intelligence and designs for education. In G. Salomon
(Ed.), *Distributed cognitions: Psychological and educational considerations* (pp. 47–87).
New York, NY: Cambridge University Press.

Purzer, S., Cardella, M., & Strobel, J. (2014). Engineering in pre-college settings:
Synthesizing research, policy, and practices. Indianapolis, IN: Purdue University
Press.

Rittel, H.W.J., & Webber, M.M. (1973). Dilemmas in a general theory of planning.
Policy Sciences, 4(2), 155–169.

Robinson, K. (2011). *Out of our minds: Learning to be creative* (2nd ed.). West Sussex:
Capstone Publishing Ltd.

Schön, D.A. (1992). The theory of inquiry: Dewey's legacy to education. *Curriculum
Inquiry, 22*(2), 119–139.

Sprague Mitchell, L. (1934). *Young geographers: How they explore the world and how they map
the world.* New York, NY: The John Day Company.

Speicher, S. (2009, February 18). IDEO's ten tips for creating a 21st-century class-
room experience. *MetropolisMag*. Retrieved from http://www.metropolismag.com/
February-2009/IDEO-rsquos-Ten-Tips-For-Creating-a-21st-ndashCentury-
Classroom-Experience/.

Swanson, K., & Ferguson, H.J. (2014). *Unleashing student superpowers.* Thousand Oaks,
CA: Corwin Press.

Todd, R. (1999). Design and technology yields a new paradigm for elementary schooling.
Journal of Technology Studies, 25(2), 26–33.

Vygotsky, L.S. (1978). Mind in society: The development of higher psychological processes.
Cambridge, MA: Harvard University Press.

Vygotsky, L. (1986). *Thought and language* (A. Kozulin, Trans.). Cambridge, MA: MIT
Press. (Original work published in 1934).

Wiggins, G., & McTighe, J. (1998). *Understanding by design.* Alexandria, VA: Merrill
Education/Association for Supervision and Curriculum Development College
Textbook Series.

2

THE CULTURE OF PRACTICE

Design-Based Teaching and Learning

Meredith Davis and Deborah Littlejohn

> An area of education requires an educational approach to its development.
> *Anita Clayburn Cross,* Design and General Education, *1980*

Design-based teaching and learning borrow the methods of design practice and the pedagogy of design education in teaching a variety of subjects and thinking skills in K-12 schools. Nationally, designers and design educators work to transform K-12 classrooms as centers of student-guided inquiry and teachers as designers of innovative learning experiences. As an instructional approach, design-based strategies are well suited to developing in children the 21st-century thinking competencies and problem-solving skills demanded of productive adults in an environment of constant change and uncertainty.

While this approach to teaching and learning has attracted significant attention across its long history, it has yet to gain broad adoption by American schools and, with only a few exceptions, by colleges of education in preparing the nation's teachers. Proponents tell compelling stories of student accomplishment, but despite experimentation, there is limited empirical research confirming that design-based strategies produce the kinds of outcomes necessary to drive educational policy and practice at the national level. Further, it is unclear what truly defines the use of design in schools as an organized culture of practice. It is not apparent how proponents of design-based education constitute a learning community that shares and builds consensus regarding research and practice. And, notwithstanding enthusiasm for the approach, there do not appear to be curricular structures and sufficient literature for preparing new teachers that have the endorsement of the profession at large.

The earliest work in design-based education began in the late 1960s and 1970s. In a fifth decade of interest in the contributions of design to education, a number of questions become increasingly urgent. What must occur for design-based teaching and learning approaches to transcend the status of "curricular and pedagogical experimentation"—that is, to be recognized as an established culture of practice? What role does research play in encouraging public confidence in design-based pedagogies and what kinds of research are relevant in arguing for broader adoption? On what theories of action is the practice based and what are the methods and metrics for measuring their efficacy? And what should be the next steps in addressing these issues?

The following discussion traces the history of design-based teaching and learning and suggests criteria for assessing its status as a culture of practice. Further, it expresses concern regarding the shortfall in rigorously researched outcomes that would argue for broader recognition in the pre-service education of teachers and offers a grounded theory approach as appropriate to the current state of the field.

What Is the History of Design-Based Teaching and Learning in K-12 Schools?

Design has a long history in American classrooms. As early as the 1960s and 1970s, designers worked in K-12 schools to help students and their teachers understand the role design plays in the environment. Often focused on the design of products and buildings, these efforts piggybacked on increasing environmental awareness and concern for developing a citizenry capable of making informed decisions about the quality of life in communities (Davis et al., 1997).

In 1970, Richard Saul Wurman and Alan Levy founded the Group for Environmental Education (GEE), authoring a middle school curriculum (*Our Man-Made Environment: Book Seven*) that involved Philadelphia students in activities about the design of urban environments. In 1975, Cranbrook Academy of Art published *Problem Solving in the Man-Made Environment*, a program for seventh-grade social studies students in Michigan that encouraged intelligent choices about products, communication, and environments. Ginny Graves' Center for Understanding the Built Environment, Doreen Nelson's Center for City Building Education, and Sharon Sutton's Urban Network involved elementary school children and their teachers in community planning as a strategy for understanding how the built environment works at a variety of levels, including that of social interaction. Ann Taylor's School Zone Institute focused on the relationship between school design and curriculum, using college-level architecture students in workshops and activities with K-12 students. And the International Technology Education Association (now the International Technology and Engineering

Educators Association) centered its work on the application of design problem-solving to the invention of technology and the design transformation of what was once called "industrial arts" in K-12 schools.

Project-based learning captured the attention of schools nationally as a teaching method in the 1990s. K-12 classroom teachers discovered that the scenario-driven, prototyping strategies of professional design education held relevance for teaching subjects and content other than design. In 1996, the National Endowment for the Arts commissioned a two-year study of design in K-12 schools. Interested in the impact of ten previous years of NEA funding for the use of design in American classrooms, the study identified more than 900 K-12 teacher nominees who used some form of design-based pedagogy or included design content in their curricula. *Design as a Catalyst for Learning* reached a number of conclusions about the positive impact of design approaches to teaching and learning. Yet despite claims of producing more flexible and engaged learners and a more diversified pedagogy that valued problem-solving and making as ways of knowing, the study found that there was little systematic evaluation of these teaching practices or evidence of students' improved content mastery, other than through the anecdotal accounts of the nominated teachers (Davis et al., 1997, p. 113). Further, teachers reported that they acquired their knowledge of design and design methods largely through informal exposure to designers, not through pre-service training, and that they typically worked independently in this approach without the active participation of colleagues or school administrators (Davis et al., 1997, pp. 109–111). These concerns raised questions about how design-based practices could be scaled to the levels of schools and districts as well as how design content might enter the college curricula of teacher preparation programs.

By contrast, the project to evaluate design learning in the United Kingdom was more rigorous and focused on specific aspects of student performance than in the United States. In the 1970s, the British government's Schools Council and the Department of Education and Science argued successfully for Design and Technology as a discrete subject area in schools and sponsored research by the Royal College of Art on *Design in General Education*. The research project described the characteristics of designing as a distinct category of knowledge, analogous to but different from the humanities and sciences. It also introduced writings by Nigel Cross, Ken Baynes, and Brian Lawson on issues of design thinking, which continue to be seminal references among many perspectives on the topic. Cross's *Designerly Ways of Knowing* and Lawson's *How Designers Think* predate the current plethora of books on design thinking, innovation, and creativity written to satisfy the appetite of business for new approaches to management and product/service development (Peters, 2003; Peters, 2005; Brown & *Harvard Business Review*, 2008; Brown, 2009; Martin, 2009; Martin & Christensen, 2013; Nussbaum, 2013; Nixon, 2016).

In 1981, the British Department of Education and Science undertook studies to develop and evaluate assessment strategies for describing student performance in the subject. Ten years later the British School Examination and Assessment Council (SEAC), under the leadership of Goldsmiths College, University of London professor Richard Kimbell, assessed national student achievement in design and technology. The assessment team defined design as "the purposeful pursuit of a task to some form of resolution that results in improvement (for someone) in the made world" (Kimbell et al., 1991, p. 17) and determined that the made world was comprised of "products, systems, and environments in which they function" (Kimbell et al., 1991, p. 18). The team showed less agreement about a definition of the design process, however. They resisted describing a linear or cyclical sequence of task-oriented steps for what they saw as a somewhat confused, interactive process. They worried that to do so would promote "greater concern for 'doing' all the stages of the process, than for combining a growing range of capabilities in a way which reflects individual creativity and confident and effective working methods" (Kimbell et al., 1991, p. 19). Agreeing that the issue was the ability to "convert active capabilities into passive products," assessors ultimately described a relationship between mind and hand in which a sequence of thinking behaviors (hazy impressions > speculation and exploration > clarification and validation > critical appraisal) produce tangible artifacts (discussions, drawings, diagrams, and graphs > models > prototypes or provisional solutions) (Kimbell et al., 1991, p. 20).

The study reached many conclusions, describing student performances systematically under an inventory of the procedural, communication, and conceptual qualities of design, which together produced a holistic score for each student. The test was authentic to design in its performance-based activity and scored independently by multiple reviewers, whose evaluations were in strong agreement about students' achievement (Kimbell et al., p. 145). This national assessment demonstrated that what many view as the "subjective" evaluation of portfolios could produce statistically significant correlations in scores among expert reviewers when they work within a well-defined framework of standards.[1]

The major differences between concurrent efforts in the United States and United Kingdom, therefore, were: (1) the position of design in the curriculum—as a general strategy for teaching and learning versus a discrete subject area in a national curriculum; (2) the level of adoption—by individual teachers versus system-wide curriculum change; and (3) evaluation strategies—anecdotal reporting by individual teachers versus rigorous national assessment of curricular outcomes and evidence of student achievement. Furthermore, educators in the United Kingdom had a more unified theory about what constituted design knowledge, while interests in the United States ranged from design as a distinct discipline of study to its role as a delivery system for other content in the curriculum.

Much of the early work in design-based pedagogy pre-dated the United States' implementation of state and national content standards, which gained momentum under the presidential administrations of George H. W. Bush and Bill Clinton. Congress enacted *Goals 2000* in 1994, an effort to raise academic standards in the nation's schools through common definitions of what "every young American should know and be able to do" with respect to twelve subject areas. Design concepts appeared in the standards of several disciplines—most notably in science, language arts, and civics—but it was all but absent in the visual arts standards, where one might have anticipated greater affinity. Instead, design was included in a list of art media—with clay, wood, stained glass, and others—and presumed to be addressed under rather ambiguous mention of "function" and "structure" (National Visual Arts Standards, 1994). Scrutiny over the politicizing of these national standards and the subsequent expansion of testing tempered enthusiasm for curricular experimentation by raising the stakes for teachers under a more narrow definition of student achievement. In 2001, the *No Child Left Behind Act* further accelerated the influence of standardized testing on pedagogy. While there was no widespread impression that students in design-based classrooms did less well on such tests, there were almost no statistical comparisons of student performance before and after exposure to a design-based pedagogy from which to draw any conclusions that would stand up to the scrutiny of a counting and measuring culture.

During this period, universities, museums, and professional associations expanded their interest in K-12 design education and developed a number of formal and informal learning opportunities for students and teachers. Universities sponsored summer and afterschool design camps, such as those at North Carolina State University, Parsons New School of Design, and the Design Institute at the University of Minnesota. In most cases, students in these camps focus on pre-college preparation for the study of design, hoping to become design professionals when they graduate from four-year universities. Other university programs and cultural institutions, such as the Cooper Hewitt National Design Museum, develop teachers' abilities to deliver design content and to use the pedagogy of design education in teaching other K-12 subject areas. The Cooper Hewitt program is one of the most enduring and its funding sources mandate continuous evaluation. Such evaluation, however, focuses more on the success of its teacher training in delivering design-based instruction, than on the achievement of students against the disciplinary criteria measured by schools. In other words, these programs typically provide valuable opportunities for learning about design and design-based strategies, but they are not structured as research studies to verify their systemic success in achieving particular student learning outcomes.

Efforts by professional associations to promote design education have been spotty, moving in and out of fashion depending on the interests of their changing leadership. Such programs generally make students aware of the design professions and issues of the built environment. The Chicago Architecture Foundation and the American Architecture Foundation, for example, established the Architecture + Design Education Network (A+DEN) in 2005. The network primarily connects teachers to architecture programs throughout the country, and like the Cooper Hewitt program publishes teacher lesson plans.

The National Academy of Engineering developed standards for student performance in engineering design and technology in K-12 schools. The Academy participated in drafting a framework that guided the design of the 2014 National Assessment of Educational Progress in Technology and Engineering Literacy (TEL), a test of eighth-grade students under the supervision of the National Center for Educational Statistics, National Assessment Governing Board, and the Educational Testing Service as the contractor for test development. Commonly described as "The Nation's Report Card," NAEP tests began in 1990 as an attempt to define a nationally representative "yardstick" for assessing, over time, what American students know and are able to do in various subjects. The digitally delivered TEL test included scenario-based challenges related to "design and systems," as well as insights regarding "technology and society" and skills related to "information and communication technology." NAEP reported results of the TEL test in June, 2016. Overall, 43 percent of students tested at the "proficient" level or above, with girls outperforming boys and suburban students doing better than their inner city counterparts. Of greater concern than the less-than-half proficiency of tested students, however, was that students attributed only 13 percent of learning how to make and fix things to schools (The Nation's Report Card, 2016). Because there is no clarity nationally of where the subject is taught in school, if at all, TEL cannot make specific curricular recommendations for how classroom instruction might better develop students' abilities. At the same time, there was broad consensus among educators that the test's real-world problem solving was a breakthrough in standardized testing.

A number of design firms have demonstrated interest in K-12 education in recent years, most notably IDEO, the Palo Alto-based design and innovation consulting firm. In addition to working with education clients, the firm published its popular *Design Thinking Toolkit for Educators* and collaborates closely with the REDlab, the Stanford Graduate School of Education, which conducts research on the value of design thinking for teaching and learning.

Finally, non-profits, such as the MacArthur Foundation through its Digital Media and Learning initiative, have explored the potential of design in education reform. The MacArthur-funded Quest to Learn schools, for example, deliver instruction through design-based challenges and systems thinking using digital technology. MacArthur support of the OECD-authored book *Connected Minds: Technology and Today's Learners*, argues that more rigorous research is required to understand the impact of technology use, and by implication design, on today's students (OECD, 2012, p. 167).

Some proponents of design-based teaching and learning consider its practice as "emerging," but it is difficult to describe fifty years of effort as still emergent. So why has an approach to teaching and learning—one whose outcomes seemingly align with national priorities on 21st-century skills—had such a difficult time in gaining wider recognition?

What Is a Culture of Practice?

Culture is defined by the collective practices, behaviors, beliefs, and values shared by a particular group of people. It is revealed not only by what people exhibit through outward actions and discourse, but also by "unspoken" rules that govern their behavior. A "culture of practice" is comprised of people who share ways of thinking about the work they do and a network of connections that distinguishes them from others. Practice communities are more engaged than special interest groups that merely devote attention to the same subject matter. They build meaningful relationships through which members learn deeply about their work from each other. And because they are typically organized around a domain, they communicate through a common vocabulary and participate in frameworks that have a particular structure (Lave & Wenger, 1991).

Thomas Kuhn, writing in his 1970 *The Structure of Scientific Revolutions*, described a practice culture's work as reflecting an "entire constellation of beliefs, values, and technique" (Kuhn, 1970, p. 181). Individual members bond through a common identity and shared commitment to patterns of thought and practice. Historically situated, publicly transmitted, and collectively upheld, a culture of practice can be understood by examining the values and ideologies the group brings to its activities and discourse: both cognitive and social functions that reflect what people think and do within a field. All cultures of practice are undergirded by a set of related ideas and commonsense beliefs about what is right, what is natural, and what works (Rochon, 1998, p. 9). In other words, they represent "how we do things around here."

A culture of practice is a process: an evolving history passed on to members through their interactions with each other. It nurtures best practices and identifies prominent members who exemplify its character. And it depends on having members with different levels of experience: senior members and other types of mentors to pass along its collective knowledge and new members to sustain it. In this way, practice cultures transmit standards and norms of education and training. Teaching practices used for this transfer of knowledge provide insight into any group and are specific to both time and the nature of the group. Complex relationships exist between group beliefs and pedagogies for inculcating new members in those beliefs; how something is taught is as important as what is taught. Practices of teaching, therefore, reveal what is characteristic about learning in a profession—what educational psychologist Lee S. Shulman called *signature pedagogies* (Shulman, 2005).

As implied, signature pedagogies "define the functions of expertise, the locus of authority, and the privileges of rank and standing" in a profession (Shulman, 2005, p. 54). There are three dimensions that characterize a signature pedagogy: (1) surface structure—the observable actions of teaching such as methods of explaining, demonstrating, showing, and questioning; (2) deep structure—a set of assumptions about how to best impart a body of knowledge and skills; and (3) implicit structure—the beliefs, professional attitudes, values, and dispositions held by academics, as well as their educational programs, who prepare professionals (Shulman, 2005, p. 55). What is emphasized in the curriculum and the method of training, therefore, signals important values and behaviors to individual initiates. In this sense, a culture of practice prescribes proper knowledge, methods, and problems within a larger set of possible perspectives. During their educational training, novices are provided with acceptable theories, professional vocabularies, technical skills, and intellectual procedures that provide a shared sense of identity.

Education and training also regulate a culture of practice through a standard canon of texts that serve to instill a cohesive narrative about what it means to be a member of the group. The survival of a discipline depends upon its ability to produce and hand down its knowledge (Menand, 2010). By governing the process of knowledge building and transmission, senior researchers embody an academic community's intellectual identity. These seasoned veterans, indeed, play an important role in shaping the future identity of the culture by shaping the direction of future research (Atkinson, 1983).

Cultures of practice are influenced by their academic settings. Academic institutions are the dominant places in which young professionals are inculcated into the values and belief systems of their fields and serve as places where tacit knowledge, social skills, and appropriate discourses are transmitted (Larson, 1979). Universities both reflect and reinforce different cultures of practice, and thus establish and maintain expertise and disciplinary knowledge (Gumport & Snydman, 2002). They also play a significant role in determining the type of research the discipline sees as important to the field. As such, they lead change and establish public perceptions of the relevance of the discipline to society.

A culture of practice is demonstrated through shared commitments that have a formal and acknowledged structure. If an activity or behavior is important to the culture, it is supported in a manner that will sustain it over the long term; it will be passed on to all members of the group through curricula and training, reflected in funding priorities, and underpinned by the allocation of human resources and opportunities for practice. Further, it will drive appropriate discourses as practitioners talk about themselves within the context of their field.

Finally, shared values determine how and why things get done in a culture of practice. Practice is structured both by core values that are rewarded and those that are discouraged. They shape the worldview of the discipline and are deployed when there is a crisis that causes the discipline to "choose between incompatible ways of practice" (Kuhn, 1970, pp. 184–185).

Is Design-Based Teaching and Learning a Culture of Practice?

Do practitioners of design-based teaching and learning behave as members of a culture of practice? Do they identify as a distinct group of educators, hold and articulate common beliefs and values about the work they do, actively share knowledge about outcomes of their efforts, build a body of professional literature, establish structures through which new members learn about best practices and develop professional competencies, and influence their academic settings and public perception?

Although it has a substantial history, design-based teaching and learning in K-12 schools is challenged under a straightforward definition of a culture of practice. Figure 2.1 shows the locus of activity in design-based teaching and learning as being largely in outreach efforts under the direction of external curriculum developers and the in-service training of teachers in short workshops. What is missing in this practice are: (1) consensus about the purpose and theories of action about design thinking as applied in education; (2) documentation and interpretation of its history and philosophy in the literature of education; (3) development of systematic methods of evaluation and empirical research that recommend specific practices over others; and (4) inclusion of design-based strategies in the pre-service education of teachers. Although it has been argued that the design-based education culture is nascent, it is difficult to imagine how work in the field can mature if uninformed by these fundamental behaviors that are common to disciplinary cultures of practice.

Among the programs that engage K-12 students (and their teachers) in design, missions range from the pre-professional education of future designers to methodological applications of a step-by-step design process to problem-solving in general; focused discussions of the formal and functional qualities of communication, products, and environments; and the conflation of design with any project-based or scenario-driven learning. With nearly 155 million search engine entries, the term *design thinking* has been used to describe concepts as varied as creativity, spatial thinking, innovation processes, and managerial strategy. It has been contrasted with the scientific method and analytical thinking on one hand, and described as "design science" on the other. Under other definitions, design thinking is all about the "a-ha" moment, the creative leap, or divergent thinking. Even in the year-to-year programming by the same organization, the definition of design thinking often fluctuates among these differing missions and views, or embraces them all, confusing novices about what truly distinguishes the practice. And there is almost no discussion nationally of what these radically different identities mean to the audiences whom proponents seek to persuade.

The relatively slow progress in developing a field about which advocates are so enthusiastic also has something to do with the profile of its members. Classroom support has come largely from individuals outside the educational

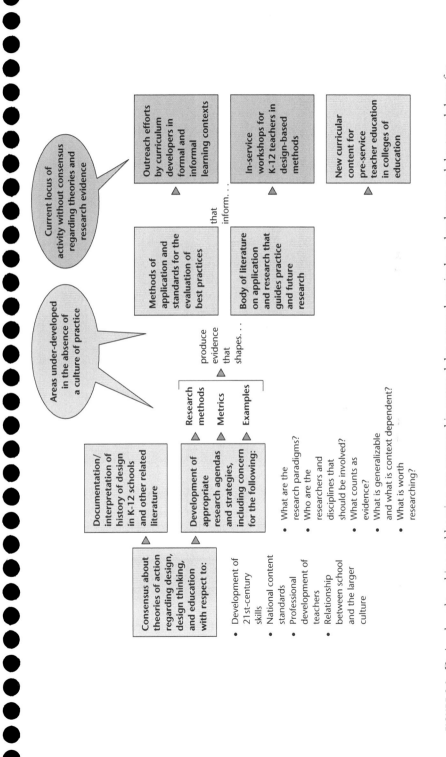

FIGURE 2.1 Design–based teaching and learning concentrated in outreach by external curriculum developers and short workshops for in–service teachers

system or situated in informal learning contexts, such as workshops. As the history shows, much of what was done in the early years depended on the temporary involvement of designers with individual classroom teachers. When designers returned attention to their own businesses, schools often reverted to traditional pedagogies. Rarely did entire schools or districts adopt a design-based approach, so when the inevitable teacher turnover took place, knowledge of design frequently disappeared from the school ethos. In Kuhn's sense, there was little transfer of knowledge from experienced practitioners to new teachers. In other cases, districts designated a few schools as "design magnets," isolating the pedagogical practices in places perceived to favor students with particular talents or interests.

Today, many curricular advocates still work from outside the system, and because they often raise their own salaries through grants or work under year-to-year contracts there are often breaks in the continuity of intellectual support. Conferences frequently feature presentations by energetic, young proponents who have "discovered" design, but who are unlikely to remain in their positions for the time it takes to transform a culture of teaching. Discussion of design-related issues in mainstream professional associations is typically assigned to a special interest group or inspires a splinter organization that lacks the resources to sustain dialogue or to leverage influence in the parent discipline. The uncertainty of the workforce, therefore, means that people are perpetually starting over in developing insights and skills at teaching about and through design.

As the National Endowment for the Arts study found (Davis et al., 1997, p. 95), many of the teachers using design in their classrooms are self-taught or were trained in workshops, usually through a project-based template that engages them in the same design activities they might assign to their students. This strategy falls short, however, in acquainting teachers with relevant literature, showing them how to scale curricular approaches beyond discrete projects, and helping them to conduct credible assessment that addresses measures that are important to administrators and the field at large. Instead, teachers often leave workshops with a shorthand notion about design thinking, but lack the depth of understanding to extend the workshop content in meaningful ways.

In a handful of cases, design-based methods for instruction have been taught in the pre-service education of teachers, but typically this approach is an offshoot of a general college of education with a more dominant pedagogical strategy or is part of an art or technology education curriculum where design is required content. The Design-Based Learning Certificate program at California Polytechnic State University in Pomona and Stanford University's REDlab are two exceptions that offer pre-service teachers the opportunity to explore design as an approach to teaching various subjects in the core curriculum. The REDlab works with pre-service teachers in their very first practicum experiences and they observe and teach in the summer school curriculum in integrated design thinking. Several art education programs and a number of technology education programs have embraced design content as part of their standard curricular requirements. The Art and Design Education program at Rhode Island School of Design, for example, requires significant pre-service instruction in teaching design. This is in contrast to the majority of college-level art education programs in which future teachers study a range of arts media (painting, sculpture, ceramics, textiles, etc.) and art history, but never take coursework related to the design disciplines. The more typical art education curriculum includes study in the arrangement of two- and three-dimensional abstract form—as in a basic design course at the foundation level—but not engagement in the problem-solving strategies of the design professions. For the most part, there has been little exploration of design-based pedagogies in mainstream colleges of education.

There are also a number of K–12 schools that focus instruction around design-based strategies in the service of core content, such as Exploris Middle School in Raleigh, NC, Design Tech High School in San Mateo, CA, and the Henry Ford Institute in Detroit, MI. These are not schools designed to prepare students for careers in design but places where teachers use design-based methods to teach the full range of subjects in the curriculum. It is likely that these schools function as small communities of practice but not that substantive conversations move well beyond their own workforce.

Because there are few well-developed or well-articulated theories of action, advocates for design-based approaches to teaching and learning find it difficult to attract the interest of mainstream teacher preparation programs. According to Chris Argyris and Donald Schön, theories of action involve activities that are designed to achieve specific results and that are monitored for their effectiveness (Argyris & Schön, 1974, p. 4). They take the form of propositions about specific actions that are likely to produce certain kinds of outcomes in particular situations (Argyris & Schön, 1974, p. 6). They are descriptions of "best practices" that have undergone systematic evaluation to ascertain their value.

Under this view, the applied learning of teachers and their students about design-based practices would be understood as the "construction, testing, and restructuring of a certain kind of knowledge" (Argyris & Schön, 1978, p. 1). It is theory-in-use, rather than espoused theory. Argyris and Schön distinguished the two types of theory, saying the former actually governs our actions in situations, while the latter is what we think we follow and communicate to others. What is nascent with respect to design practices, however, is systematic evaluation that determines and supports what is of real value to the overall educational enterprise and the detailed representation of those findings in the mainstream literature and conferences in the field.

The dearth of such evaluation is a symptom of larger concerns. There is almost no discussion of what paradigms should drive research, what should be the backgrounds of researchers who undertake such investigations; what counts as evidence, and what is generalizable and what is context-dependent.

Examples of design learning abound, but the methods used to study them and the metrics that ascertain their worth are either absent or still subject to considerable debate.

What Research Methods Are Appropriate for the Study of Design in Education?

It is not unusual for advocates to argue that favored research strategies in education fail to capture the most important aspects of design approaches to teaching and learning: that such methods devalue learning outcomes that are not easily measured through pencil and paper tests or that ignore the contributions of the social character of the learning environment. Positivist philosophy, which holds that reality can be observed by controlling variables and that the goal of research is objective prediction, may not be the best approach for evaluating all outcomes in the constantly changing learning conditions of K-12 schools. For example, the development team for the National Assessment of Educational Progress in Technology and Engineering Literacy was concerned that the testing agency's desire for scorable elements was often at the expense of a holistic understanding of the student's problem solving. The team searched for ways of assessing reasoning in addition to problem-solutions. They struggled to capture how individual students arrive at particular solutions, value satisfying some problem constraints over others, and regulate their problem-solving behavior across time and in light of new information. Because such behavior is often situational—with successful students adjusting their strategies to problem circumstances—assessing any individual performance or solution only partially represents learning outcomes.

Qualitative methods, on the other hand, are iterative and interpretive—and much more appropriate when a study's focus calls for first-hand observations in real-world settings or an understanding of the meanings people bring to their own unique situations. Research in the qualitative mode also helps make sense of complex contexts and generates guidelines to inform future action. Specifically, educational researchers can use these established methods to gain insight into pedagogic practices and generate new theories about educational phenomena where none exist.

Educational researchers have a variety of qualitative approaches from which to choose, but one method is particularly appropriate in situations where there is no guiding conceptual framework: grounded theory. As a "theory-method" package, grounded theory provides a step-by-step strategy for gathering data as well as a set of analytic tools for building new theory (Clarke, 2006; Glaser & Strauss, 1967). Grounded theory has been used in numerous fields, including education, to generate theories that are typically heuristic, rather than predictive, and about specific settings.

Theorizing, in a grounded theory sense, simply means to reflect and think outside of day-to-day norms in a way that helps the researcher ask new questions. Theory is derived from an "imaginative understanding of the studied phenomenon" (Charmaz, 2006, p. 126) and relies on the researcher's perspective—a perspective that develops from being immersed in the data. The basis of grounded theory, therefore, is to clarify a social practice in which a constructivist approach means "learning how, when, and to what extent the studied experience is embedded in larger and often hidden positions, networks, situations, and relationships" (Charmaz, 2006, p. 130).

In this sense, the grounded theory method is appropriate for revealing the nature of the values-oriented contexts and processes in which design practices must succeed. It is also useful in describing design practices that arise from varied philosophies and for identifying theories of action that underpin application. Grounded theory is consistent with the qualitative concerns of teachers but disciplined in its approach to research in ways that surpass a simple collection of anecdotes.

As an alternative to grounded theory, schools already set benchmarks that can be useful in supporting a design-based approach to teaching and learning: to understanding what and how students learn *through* design, rather than *about* design. A comparison of routinely collected data (if systematically collected and analyzed) can present compelling evidence in favor of design-based practices. For example, sixth-grade teachers Leslie Stoltz and Mark Lantz at Chaparral Middle School in Walnut Valley Unified School District, CA, compared the standardized test scores of students who enrolled in a traditional classroom for their fifth-grade studies with their scores after completion of a design-based classroom for their sixth-grade studies (Nelson, 2009). Scores for four quartiles were compared on the fifth- and sixth-grade Stanford Achievement tests (in Math, Reading, and Language). For all quartiles, students improved their performance from the fifth to sixth grade, although gains by students in the first two quartiles were modest. These were likely students who would excel under any teaching strategy. Improvement by students in the last two quartiles, however, was dramatic in all three subjects. When the 2006–2009 test scores of these students were compared to students in traditional classrooms for the three years from the sixth to eighth grade, students who studied under a design-based approach continued to show improvement in their performance on standardized tests at levels beyond that of their traditional classmates.

It is not clear what specific aspects of design-based teaching practices contributed to this success or whether results are generalizable to other classrooms, but the point this comparison makes is that schools already collect information that can be useful in framing perceptions of design-based learning and that falls within the category of acceptable evidence for policymakers and administrators. Further, although this quantitative evidence is consistent with what the dominant culture values, its collection does nothing to misrepresent the nature of design-based teaching practices. Such low-effort data collection can be useful in making the case that design-based students improve with respect to variety of measures.

Although controversial, the full or partial adoption of the Common Core Curriculum by 46 states and three territories presents another opportunity to relate research on design-based learning strategies to explicit frameworks for student achievement. If student success under a design approach can be measured against these standards, and if teachers can be trained to begin their development of design activities with the achievement of specific standards as a goal, then research studies can investigate the relationship between a design-based pedagogy and the mastery of specific core content.

There are many research possibilities in the study of design methods and their outcomes in student learning, but the message in this discussion is that evidence-based research must be done.

Conclusion

In conclusion, advocates for a design-based approach to teaching and learning have good reason to believe that many students succeed under this approach and that teachers renew their interest in teaching as a creative practice. There are, however, too few serious efforts to articulate and build consensus around theories of action and to engage in the systematic teacher preparation, application, and evaluation of design-based strategies. Many programs still rely on informal accounts of success: anecdotal impressions of student performance that fall outside the normal evidence used by a school system in assessing teaching and learning. Such work is often isolated in small classrooms under exceptional teachers, with no structure for replicating it in others. There is a shortfall of published findings under proven researchers and too little collaboration among institutions to expand available data for confirming and persuading educational policymakers and colleges of education of the effectiveness of design-based approaches.

Teacher education programs need to expand the repertoire of pedagogical instruction. Schools and universities need to partner in methodologically rigorous research and to share findings so that others can build upon it. It is important to develop and publish assessment methods that accurately capture the full range of teacher and student outcomes in design-based approaches. Finally, findings need to be framed in compelling stories and grounded in the evidence that matters to a counting and measuring culture.

For design-based education to establish itself as a culture of practice and influence the wider field of education, these activities are essential. Such deficiencies do nothing to diminish value in the hard work of teachers and designers. But they do explain the perpetual status of the practice as "emergent." For proponents, it is time to change this status.

Note

1 Political turmoil began in 2011 over the content of the Design and Technology curriculum in the UK. Compulsory instruction was reduced to ages 5 through 14, two years less than under the previous administration. Unclear if study in Design and Technology would be dropped from the curriculum, teachers put off specializing in the subject, creating a teacher shortfall. The Department of Education announced that in 2017 content will "emphasize the iterative design processes that all students should understand and be able to demonstrate and which is at the core of contemporary practice" and will not limit students in "the materials they can work with, enabling them to make choices appropriate to their design, rather than creating a design around a particular material" (Gibb, 2015).

References

Argyris, C., & Schön, D. (1978). *Organizational learning: A theory of action perspective.* Reading, MA: Addison-Wesley Publishing.

Atkinson, P.A. (1983). The reproduction of the professional community. In R. Dingwaal & P. Lewis (Eds.). *The Sociology of professions.* London: Macmillan.

Brown, T. (2009). *Change by design: How design thinking transforms organizations and business.* New York, NY: Harper Business.

Brown, T. & *Harvard Business Review.* (2008). *Design thinking (Harvard Business Review).* Cambridge, MA: Harvard Business Press.

Burns, J. (December 16, 2014). Teachers fear for future of design and technology. *BBC News.* Retrieved from http://www.bbc.com/news/education-30484428.

Charmaz, K. (2006). *Constructing grounded theory: A practical guide through qualitative analysis.* Thousand Oaks, CA: Sage.

Creswell, J.W. (2003). *Research design: Qualitative, quantitative and mixed method approaches* (2nd ed.). Thousand Oaks, CA: Sage Publications.

Cross, A. (1980). Design and general education. *Design Studies, 1*(4), 202–206.

Davis, M., Hawley, P., & Spilka, G. (1997). *Design as a catalyst for learning.* Alexandria, VA: Association for Supervision and Curriculum Development.

Gibb, N. (Minister of State for Schools). (2015). "Education Reform: Revised Design and Technology GCSE Content." Written statement HCWS290, November 4, 2015. Retrieved on July 1, 2016 from: https://www.parliament.uk/business/publications/written-questions-answers-statements/written-statement/Commons/2015-11-04/HCWS290/.

Glaser, B.G., & Strauss, A.L. (1967). *The discovery of grounded theory: Strategies for qualitative research.* Chicago, IL: Aldine.

Gumport, P.J., & Snydman, S.K. (2002). The formal organization of knowledge: An analysis of academic structure. *Journal of Higher Education, 73*(3), 375–408.

Kimbell, R., et al. (1991). *The assessment of performance in design and technology.* London: School Examinations and Assessment Council and the General Office of Information.

Kuhn, T.S. (1970). *The structure of scientific revolutions* (2nd ed.). Chicago, IL: University of Chicago Press.

Larson, M.S. (1979). *The rise of professionalism: A sociological analysis.* Berkeley, CA: University of California Press.

Martin, R. (2009). *The design of business: Why design thinking is the next competitive advantage.* Cambridge, MA: Harvard Business Press.

Martin, R., & Christensen, K. (2013). *Rotman on design: The best of design thinking from Rotman Magazine.* Toronto, Ontario: University of Toronto Press.

Menand, L. (2010). *The marketplace of ideas.* New York, NY: Norton.

The Nation's Report Card. (2016). *Technology & engineering literacy: An innovative assessment in an era of rapid technological change.* Retrieved on September 14, 2016 from: http://www.nationsreportcard.gov/tel_2014/.

Nelson, D. (2009) Researched Results. Teaching and Learning through Doreen Nelson's Method of Design-Based Learning. https://www.cpp.edu/~dnelson/results.html

Nixon, N.W. (Ed). (2016). *Strategic design thinking: Innovation in products, services, experiences, and beyond.* New York, NY: Bloomsbury.

Nussbaum, B. (2013). *Creative intelligence: Harnessing the power to create, connect, and inspire.* New York: Harper Business.

OECD. (2012). *Connected minds: Technology and today's learners.* Paris: OECD and Center for Educational Research and Innovation.

Peters, T. (2003). *Re-imagine: Business excellence in a disruptive age.* London: DK Publishing.

Peters, T. (2005). *Design: Innovate, differentiate, communicate.* London: DK Publishing.

Rochon, T. (1998). *Culture Moves.* Princeton, NJ: Princeton University Press.

Sarker, S., Lau, F., & Sahay, S. (2001). Using an adapted grounded theory approach for inductive theory building about virtual team development. *The DATA BASE for Advances in Information Systems, 32*(1), 38–55.

Shulman, L. (2005). Signature pedagogies in the professions. *Daedalus, 134*(3), 52–59.

Suddaby, R. (2006). From the editors: What grounded theory is not. *Academy of Management Journal, 49*(4), 633–642.

3

A PRAXIS MODEL FOR DESIGN THINKING

Catalyzing Life Readiness

Christelle Estrada and Shelley Goldman

Introduction

The philosopher and educator John Dewey is often attributed with saying that "education is not preparation for life; it is life itself." This is a complex statement about how education, every day, at every level, and for every student, should be intricately involved in and a part of real life and societal concerns. Dewey (1893) distinctly rejects the premise that school ought to sequester students from the life forces of society in order to build knowledge that will be integrated when students leave school and enter "real life." We open our chapter with Dewey's quote because it points to a philosophical and practical tension in schooling—its relationship to and staging of life readiness. We experience this tension when we hear students ask, "Why are we doing this?"; when we see curriculum goals broken down into seemingly isolated and unconnected skills; or when we encounter closed school and classroom doors as barriers between the school and its community. We think what students really seem to be asking is, "How is this connected to me and the real world?"

In this chapter, we question when, how, and under what circumstances schools engage in Dewey's vision of school as "life itself" or "life readiness" more generally. We are interested in the pairing of a "life itself" approach with the current imperatives for college, career, and life readiness. One author, Estrada, works at the Utah State Board of Education, striving to bring academic, social, and life learning opportunities to all students in the state with a focus on English learners and refugee and immigrant students; the other, Goldman, works at Stanford University and is committed to understanding how to make school children active, real-world engaged, problem solvers. We see life engagement and life readiness as a version of academic excellence, rather than as a hope and dream that sits apart from the day-to-day workings of schools. Central to the partnership described herein is the potential that design thinking, a real-world approach to problem-solving and innovation, has for the praxis of Dewey's ideas of school as "life itself".

The chapter describes the essential actions we have taken with design thinking as a way to address the imperatives schools face in relation to preparation for college, career, and life readiness. We start by describing life readiness as currently described in order to set the stage for why design thinking can be powerful pedagogy for a "life itself" approach. Next, we examine two essential actions we have taken in order to assist this work in taking hold in K–12 education. The essential actions are at the nexus of design thinking, life readiness, and the real work of teachers and students. They include: (1) well-leveraged and constantly evolving strategic partnerships, and (2) support of forward movement and momentum for teachers, students, and partners. We will discuss each in turn and provide stories for each that exemplify how they come together as a praxis model.

Conceptual Background

Our approach shares much in common with a range of research-based approaches to career and college readiness and emerging K–12 learning practices (Hess et al., 2014; Vella, 2000). Studies have shown that the major reasons students stay in school are not "academic" in the usual sense but rather social and personal (Lieberman, 2013). In a 2014 meta-analysis of research on college and career readiness, Hess and colleagues identified three skill sets necessary for success in post-secondary education: (1) cognitive, (2) intrapersonal, and (3) interpersonal. Typically, the K–12 schooling system focuses on the cognitive with an emphasis on competences such as critical thinking, information literacy, reasoning, and argumentation. In the United States, the forty-six states that have adopted the Common Core State Standards (2010) and the systems of testing that accompany them, teachers have changed their instruction by increasing cognitive rigor so that students provide evidence to justify their reasoning and judgments. This has been the movement with standards in Utah—where the work we describe takes place.

In his research for college success, David T. Conley at the Center for Educational Policy Research at the University of Oregon (2010) suggests that the interpersonal and intrapersonal skills are foundational dispositions, yet often not intentionally taught nor nurtured. As a consequence the more traditional approaches to teaching, such as lecture for information-giving, often dominate what happens in classrooms, especially with the current focus on accountability through high stakes testing as maintained in the 2016 reauthorization of ESEA (Elementary and Secondary Education Act, 1965)—now called ESSA, the Every Student Succeeds Act, which replaced No Child Left Behind in August 2016 (Guinier, 2015).

The intrapersonal domain includes competencies like flexibility, metacognition, self-awareness, and appreciation for diverse perspectives. A focus on the intrapersonal domain entails developing both independence and interdependence in learners, and is essential to the visions for schooling described by both Dewey (1915) and Whitehead (1929). Intrapersonal competencies might be fostered through action with reflection or praxis and the application of learning to the larger social context. Whether in classrooms, after school programs, or more informal settings such as museums, aquariums, planetariums, concerts, or plays, learners are influenced by the very nature of being human in a world that they seek to understand (Varela et al., 1993; Davidson & Begley, 2012).

The experience of learning as personalized and student-centered within any social context is exemplified in the interpersonal domain, which includes communication, collaboration, responsibility, and creative-productive thinking. Interpersonal learning is an essential 21st-century competency and recent research demonstrates the benefit of practices such as working on teams that represent a range of diverse members (Page, 2007). From a very early age, as students learn pro-social skills for the purpose of contributing to and working with others, they are better able to consider other perspectives and see the world from multiple viewpoints (Ballanca & Brandt, 2010). In addition to communication, students acquire the capacity for "creative confidence" or for "experiencing the world that generates new approaches and solutions" (Kelley & Kelley, 2013, p. 7). The capacity for creativity amidst challenge is illustrated in Csikzentmihalyi's (1990) "flow" research when challenge is just beyond the skill level and supports focused attention. Similarly, Zull's (2011) neuroscience research on learning connects action with discovery to bring both joy in learning and an awareness of the world as new experience.

With a history of educational ideas from Dewey and Whitehead to the most current trends in neuroscience, we learn that schools need to be striving for more than cognitive accomplishments, and that they need to attend to intrapersonal and interpersonal skills. These three aspects are necessary to a vision and practice of education that can meet current and future schooling imperatives.

We take seriously the idea that K-12 education meets cognitive and interpersonal imperatives while engaging students in real-world action and problem-solving. Our goal is to break new ground in schools by integrating design thinking as pedagogy for reaching this aim. Synthesizing cognitive, interpersonal, and intrapersonal competencies with design thinking promises to create teaching and learning experiences that are expanded for and responsive to students' needs for life readiness. We purposefully focus on real-world STEM-related problems such as access to water, shelter, food, energy, and health—problems that persist locally and globally, yet are rarely the subject of traditional schooling. These problem spaces are complex enough to incorporate interdisciplinary and applied teaching, and also have the capacity to bring together school subjects in an immersive learning experience that has an innovation mandate. Students learn deep critical thinking; empathetic approaches to problem-solving; and application and action with knowledge in real-world situations.

Design—with its real-world connections, multiple possibilities for solutions, multiple entry points, and attention to content, process skills, and mindsets—has the potential to engage students in ways that are inclusive of their diversity. Design can engender the development of agency, confidence, and identities as change agents in students as they respond to real-world interdisciplinary challenges. Design can teach students to learn from failures and to persevere in solving difficult problems. Design thinking experiences help children learn that they have tools, power, and possibilities to work actively in the world.

Essential Actions

We have worked together for four years in Utah to use design thinking as pedagogy for meeting the life readiness and life itself imperatives. Our work has been guided by "essential actions" that help us work with teachers, administrators, and students to build cognitive, interpersonal, and intrapersonal capacities. The essential actions are strategies for integrating our theoretical and practical considerations and for continually seeking insights into how to retool our approach. We start by providing some background on Utah K-12 education as a context for this work and then describe the two essential actions: (1) create well-leveraged partnerships with people that connect through their overlapping communities of practice; and (2) support forward movement and build momentum. We take each in turn and provide examples that show the ways they have born out in our work.

The Context of Utah Public Education

There are 622,153 students in the Utah public education system: 75 percent White, 16 percent Hispanic, and 8 percent American Indian, Asian, African-American, Pacific Islander, and multiracial (schools.utah.gov). In 2015 the high school graduation rate was 84 percent. Thirty percent of those who dropped out were English Learners; 26 percent were American Indian; 25 percent were African American/Black; 24 percent were Hispanic; and 20 percent were economically disadvantaged. Utah ranks 51st in per pupil spending: $6,555 compared to the national average per pupil spending of $10,667. Since 2014 Utah has developed and used the state developed assessment system for information on achievement gains, federal accountability, and state legislated school grading designations known as Student Assessment of Growth and Excellence (SAGE). Salt Lake City, a federally designated city for refugees, represents 100+ family languages and a significant percentage of low-income families. In the 2015 disaggregated data, the largest proficiency gap on SAGE is for English learners: 9 percent English Language Arts where the state average is 44 percent;

11 percent in Mathematics where the state average is 44 percent; and 8 percent in Science where the state average is 46 percent. As in many states with new end-of-level testing, mandated by federal legislation of ESEA (No Child Left Behind, 2001) and ESSA (Every Student Succeeds Act, 2016), state assessments show large disparities in performance among groups of students who are the least represented in post-secondary education. Many of the efforts to improve Utah's system are centered on 21st-century skills as well as college and life readiness.

Leveraging Partnerships Through Overlapping Communities of Practice

We view design thinking as a method well-situated to build Utah's capacity for "radical collaborations" fueled by a praxis model. Many of the efforts to work on possible solutions in Utah are centered on 21st-century skill learning and college and life readiness. In this context, we came to view design thinking as a method and process best suited and most relevant to the kind of innovation valued in Utah. Design thinking could bring together public school and educators, community-based organizations, non-profits, universities, and private businesses in reflective actions that would allow all to contribute to and benefit from ongoing partnerships.

Our commitment to reflective and collective action is guided by the research of Otto Scharmer, whose "Theory-U" heralds the vision of "leading from the future as it emerges" (Scharmer, 2007). Scharmer bases his research on leaders who are skilful in systems-wide transformative change, and proposes that we deepen our understanding of a new context or challenge in dialog with others in order to uncover the courage to act in the face of the fear of failure or disapproval. He suggests we listen to others with an open mind and open heart, suspend judgment, and broaden our perspective by seriously considering and attending to the viewpoints of others. We move from surface action characterized by reacting to life's challenges and reach the bottom of Scharmer's "U," where we can move, innovate, and take new actions. In the process we uncover the shared perception of a common commitment to collective action. Scharmer's "Theory-U" is compatible with and elucidates the power of the design thinking process and mindsets for strategic and meaningful partnerships: engaging in unusual collaborations, putting purpose into action, designing for a future not yet realized, and moving into a space of open possibilities for other partners. In the sections that follow, we use stories to illustrate how "leading from the future as it emerges" have transformed experiences for our education partners in Utah.

From Insights to Realizing Visions in Action

The first time we planned a Utah teacher workshop we partnered with a local school district's Center for Technical and Career Education and the science specialist for the governor's office of economic development. Together, we planned a two-day design thinking workshop with thirty-eight participants, including teachers who had been facilitators in the previous summer's academy to implement the new Utah Core Standards. We invited middle school teams from four local districts. We added a team from a STEM-focused charter school in Salt Lake City and the Director of Educational Outreach for the Natural History Museum of Utah. We anticipated that during this workshop, we would be sending up test balloons to gauge the interest of educators in the region.

After two days of design thinking introduction and STEM integration, we offered time for school teams to plan how they might offer design thinking activities in their classrooms or schools. A few principals attended these sessions and gave support. Estrada offered supported planning time for teams back at their schools. From this initial workshop there were early adopters who recognized the potential and began to implement design thinking immediately.

The teachers were varied in the kind of design thinking activities they felt they could support, and we thought it best to support a range of implementation strategies. A few teachers adopted specific design thinking processes—the empathy process or the prototyping and testing phases—into classroom activities. At the other end of the range, the charter school forged ahead with an extended challenge for their entire ninth grade. A few teachers walked away believing it all required more chance and change than they were willing to take on. A few teachers had trouble implementing design thinking in their classrooms and either asked for support or for invitations to return for a future workshop.

We relate the story of one sixth grade teacher, Melissa, whose journey with design thinking illustrates how we were able to connect her to partners who could support her teaching. After the first workshop where we introduced a water access and conservation challenge, Melissa decided to begin an after-school enrichment program for fifth- and sixth-grade students. She started with after-school activities because she was not sure she would have administrative support for bringing the program into the classroom where curriculum for the year was decided. Our team supported her efforts, with Estrada helping her conduct an evaluation of the program.

The outcomes of the after-school program were favorable: students were happy, parents were calling the school to say they wanted to learn more about how design thinking was being used, and the principal wanted to hear more. In pre- and post-surveys and filmed interviews, students reported that after their design thinking experiences they were paying more attention during school activities. When asked how design thinking was different from the regular classroom, a fifth-grade student wrote:

> I think that it is different because you have more chances to express your thoughts, ideation, and disagreements. In school, you also don't have as much time to learn things that you might need to know if you want to get

a job or to be a good interviewer. Design thinking has also changed the perspective of many things, especially the way I think of water and how much we take it for granted.

The student is making connections to design thinking, the topic of water, and to the world of work. Other students commented on group work and empathy: "We are in groups who really cooperate better with each other and all listen to each other talk and comment on their ideas." "I really like to deal with problems we get and meet with happiness. And last but not least we work on projects for others not ourselves." One student saw aspects of design thinking that they could imagine aligned with their futures:

> In Design Thinking we learned how to properly interview our client by making them comfortable and asking questions that really make them think or tell stories. We also learned how to use the information from our interview to create a prototype that fits their needs. We were taught to alter our prototypes after getting feedback from the client to make it the best it can possibly be.

The buzz about Melissa's after-school program generated several new clusters of design thinking activities. With the principal's newly found support, Melissa organized workshops for the School Community Council and the Parents' and Teachers' Association. She also brought teachers from the school to our subsequent workshops so they could create in-school design thinking units to support their classroom standards work. Following this participation, the entire sixth grade adopted design thinking units for the next school year.

Melissa facilitated design thinking workshops for after school educators, partnering with Museum of Natural History educators to offer a week-long summer camp with scholarships provided by the principal of a school in a high poverty community. As an early adopter, Melissa continued extending her network of influence to the sixth grade, the school, the district, and schools in the region. She eventually moved to a new position at Brigham Young University in the STEM master's program where she brought the design thinking process into the preparation of science teachers. She has designed an online professional development course for the Utah State Board of Education, and the reach of design thinking has been extended by other organizations like Promise South Salt Lake at their community afterschool learning sites and Women of the World, a non-profit to support refugee women in learning English. She continually attends the workshops we sponsor, talks about her experiences with teachers who attend, and offers help. Her bias toward action is at the heart of acting with design thinking, Theory-U, and taking a praxis approach to change.

Our strategy was to cultivate actions by Melissa and like-minded people. We created opportunities and events where educators such as Melissa could meet, experience design thinking in its many guises, and connect with others who were ready to take a next step in confronting with the status quo. Our strategy also meant making sure that people who heard about Melissa's or others' successes could find their own way to get involved. At city- and state-level, we spread the word to boards, commissions, and committees who were aiming to educate newly capable citizens post-K-12. We connected people from the State Board of Education, local after-school networks in underserved neighborhoods, museums, local businesses, and companies.

Throughout this work, our strategy continued to be to connect partners who share life readiness aims, can build on initial successes, share their goals, combine their resources, and build each others' confidence to act. In trying to build on our many and overlapping connections, we held several workshops to meet people's needs, which included educators from overlapping communities, at the Natural History Museum of Utah. One workshop featured previous and newly recruited partners from across the state as well as twenty-five design thinking experienced students who came to be coaches in the design groups. We catalyzed the energy of such events so we could communicate the power of design thinking and how it could support life itself goals in K-12 settings. During the museum workshop we filmed a group from an underserved community composed of fifth- and sixth-grade students, their principal and a paraprofessional coaching their team. The group interviewed a retired marine colonel to develop an empathy map for brainstorming ideas in response to the colonel's need for transition services for returning veterans. The short documentary film *Design Time* (Cole et al., 2015), co-produced with a Sundance filmmaker, tells the story of the team's journey. *Design Time* premiered at the Stanford d.school and at the University of Utah Eccles Broadcast Center in 2015 and is televised regularly by KUEN, Utah's education network. The networking and connections have had a multiplier effect, extending beyond what had been anticipated.

The connections and clusters of action that have emerged were based on mutual visions for what education could be and the desire and bravery to lead those visions into practice. The partners we connected to each other had different responsibilities and positions and worked in a range of institutions. They each had something to offer and all needed support to take the next step. We conducted some events to ignite passion and know-how, looked for indicators of interest, matched people to other people, and stayed in the conversations as consultants with technical knowledge and experience who encouraged people to wholeheartedly "go for it" when they wanted to take action.

Building on Movement and Momentum

Our initial work was to help teachers experience and understand the potential of design thinking for their students and to support the creative confidence they were developing from their personal design thinking experience. Tom and

David Kelly (2013) write that the principles and strategies of design thinking generate creative confidence—the process of tapping into our creative potential and allowing us to innovate in terms of how we approach and solve problems. The Kelleys write that creative confidence is like a muscle that can be strengthened and nurtured. It is not about being born a creative; it is about learning that you can learn and have efficacy as you take action to create change. This view is also consistent with Carol Dweck's findings on growth and fixed mindsets (Dweck 2006). Dweck found that people who believed that intelligence, talent, or know-how were inborn had the most to lose if they did not immediately succeed. People who believed that they could learn and succeed if they worked at things generally fared better as learners. From the start of our work, we understood that our responsibility was to try to find ways to build on the enthusiasm, commitments, and creative confidence generated in teachers. We saw our introductory workshops as the stepping off place for helping educators and our partners start flexing their new design thinking inspired muscles.

Maintaining the momentum of change making has involved helping teachers recognize that they too are changing as they engage in teaching with design thinking. Our goals were to recognize the energy educators were feeling and find ways to keep momentum for moving their work forward. We engaged in a variety of moves and tactics with various partners in order to keep the synergy high and move people towards action back in their schools and education organizations. Besides connecting people and organizations, we grew our own plans and capabilities for action as interest and implementation by teachers increased. At the very first workshop—when we were still gauging interest and impact—we offered incentives for action that included support for school teams to have planning sessions, resources such as sets of classroom prototyping materials, and connections for teachers and schools to partners who could offer venues for design thinking. To move schools ahead we coached teachers and school staff as they took up planning for design thinking at their schools and brought teachers face-to-face again and again. We realized that these personalized, light touch supports were helpful, but to stimulate more uptake in action we offered new, targeted workshops so educators could return for more training and support. Eventually, we held curriculum design workshops so teachers could build their own creative competence and deeply integrate design thinking with the standards they were addressing.

The story that follows shows the ways partners were brought together to start new efforts and then carry their momentum forward. We tell this story because it was one of the more transformative design thinking challenges we have seen in the state.

We recruited three schools from Salt Lake City School District to be in a challenge: (1) West High School founded in 1890 with a diverse population of 2500; (2) the SLCSE charter school (started design thinking at our first workshop in Utah); and (3) Horizonte Instruction and Training Center, serving nearly 9,000 students each year including high school students, young parents, and refugees, with eighty-two spoken languages.

The design challenge was determined by partners and a participating biotech firm, BARD. We focused heavily on the life itself and life readiness aspects of this challenge. Each school selected a design team of four students from the ninth grade. The suggested criteria for selecting team members was to find students who represented the diversity of the west side of Salt Lake City and who could benefit from work on their self-awareness, metacognition, and career readiness. We all agreed that the problem space would be defined as a patient comfort challenge for those who were ill enough to be recipients of biotech devices.

Stanford facilitators led the two-day workshop for the high schoo! teams and their Utah coaches at the Museum of Natural Curiosity (a partner with a mission to bring design thinking and maker education to students in Utah). The first workshop day was mostly devoted to foundational understanding of experience of patients and their caregivers. Partners from the biotech firm came to be interviewed by the students about a set of medical devices, their uses, and their problems for patients. Museum goers were surveyed by each school team through questions posted on large whiteboards placed on the museum floor in order to elicit responses from museum-goers about their experiences in hospitals. The students also developed interview questions for their "clients": a principal who was receiving chemotherapy; a man who took care of his father through a fatal illness; and a man who cared for his mother during her cancer treatment. These interviews were tough, and full of emotion for the students and interviewers. The interviews involved serious talk about serious caring and interaction with the medical world, and generated strikingly mature conversations with the students. When the conversations finished, students felt strongly that they needed to help their clients and there was a lot of energy focused on learning the process to find innovative solutions for them. The students mined their notes and created empathy maps—a design process tool that helps teams to mine insights from their interviews and observations. Next, students created point of view statements (POVs) about the needs of their informants. All of this complex work was supplemented by team building activities in the museum, instruction in the design thinking process, and improvisation exercises.

On day two of the challenge the students brainstormed ideas and chose one to prototype. The three clients returned for a visit with their respective teams and gave feedback on the design prototypes. The team from the comprehensive high school redesigned and created a life-sized chemotherapy center that had specific emphasis on family space, patient comfort, and ways to help the patient adjust to receiving regular chemotherapy. The team from the personalized alternative school created a portable shower that could be installed in the patient's home. The shower had customized heating panels and towels, wheelchair accessibility, and 360-degree moveable arm supports. The charter school team created a tablet-controlled high tech hospital room environment with a large wall monitor for projecting scenes of a world outside the hospital, video-conferencing with relatives and accessing their health records, schedules, and information. The presentation of each prototype brought an upwelling of emotion and appreciation from each of the clients that affirmed the student's abilities to learn and use design thinking and to experience education with life itself ramifications.

After incorporating client feedback, the teams made adjustments, and presented their work to parents, administrators, and friends at a special final ceremony in Salt Lake City. At the ceremony, one boy, a football player, remarked how he was not that excited to participate in the challenge, but once he met his group's client, he knew he just had to stay involved and really create something that could help her deal with her chemotherapy. This event built on some of the successes our partners had in previous events. Two of the teacher-coaches, two of the patient clients, and the museum partners had done design thinking activities previously. The impact of this challenge has been far-reaching and continues to grow. One client for the challenge and his school-based team developed an approach that integrated design thinking into the school's summer academy. The principal of the comprehensive high school asked his students to engage incoming ninth graders, and as a result thirty more tenth and eleventh graders were trained as design team coaches. Students were recruited from their rival school so they could join forces. Together, they coached middle school students in a youth summit sponsored by the mayor's office, the school district, and the University of Utah in conjunction with Colin Powell's Grad Nation initiative. The Museum of Natural Curiosity has made a commitment to host an annual ninth grade Design Challenge for high schools throughout Utah with support from the Utah State Board of Education and their many partners.

The ninth grade challenge is a story about loosely affiliated, like-minded people coming together to try something new and unique. While some of the educators had prior experience with design thinking, some were new to the process. They joined forces because each believed the outcomes for students would be positive and wanted to see students contributing to design solutions. All were planning for and talking about what they could do next for students, and our job was to help them find a way to make the next action a reality.

Summary and Discussion

This paper has been a tour through the strategies that we have used to bring design thinking into K-12 education practice in the state of Utah. It is a story about how design thinking is a 21st-century pedagogy that has the potential to make education more integrated with its aims to make students "life involved" in the most positive ways.

Loss of momentum can be a serious negative force when people are engaged in taking actions to new, untried, and often untested areas, even when desire is high. Design thinking in K-12 is currently at that level of untried and untested.

While the rationale of education for college, career, and life readiness is compelling, figuring out how to work towards it can be a daunting task, and in an era of standards and accountability it can seem out of reach even when the imperative is clear. We continue to show educators that these aims are doable by exposing them to ways they can make small impacts and connecting them to others who can amplify their actions.

We realize that this may seem to be intensive labor. It is not. We do think that it helps to have people who are willing to connect with those in their professional spheres or networks who are like minded or have similar aims. Some of the connections we make could be the result of a conversation at a meeting of educators or could be built from an activity already organizing people such as content standards meetings or initiatives to have a better workforce. And if it is hard work, then it is a labor of love. This practice of connecting people and institutions who are focused on similar goals and like-minded actions and then building on the momentum in supportive ways can become a way to work on bringing about K-12 change in a variety of settings.

While the history of federal accountability from NCLB (2001) to ESSA (2016) has shaped the experience of educators and students for fifteen years, we see another future that is congruent with Dewey's vision and Scharmer's theory of action. This vision is based on connecting design thinkers in every kind of organization, from schools to museums to community learning centers to universities. The connection, experienced as "radical collaboration" for solving a real issue to benefit others, creates a compelling purpose for collective action—education as life itself.

Acknowledgments

We'd like to thank Madlyn Runburg, Melissa Mendenhall, Nicole O'Brien, and Blake Wigdahl for taking leaps into action and organizing design thinking opportunities. Thanks to Molly Zielezinski, Tanner Vea, and Zaza Kabayadondo for helping to teach design thinking. This work was supported in part by the Utah State Board of Education and the National Science Foundation Grant No. 1029929. Any opinions, findings, conclusions, or recommendations expressed in this working paper do not necessarily reflect the views of the National Science Foundation or the Utah State Board of Education.

References

Bellanca, J.A., & Brandt, R.S. (2010). *21st century skills: Rethinking how students learn.* Bloomington, IN: Solution Tree Press.

Cole, W., Estrada, C. & Goldman, S. (Producers). (2015). *Design time: Learning that is transformative.* Documentary Film. US. Retrieved from https://vimeo.com/122065737

Conley, D.T. (2010). *College and career ready: Helping all students succeed beyond high school.* San Francisco, CA: Jossey-Bass.

Csikszentmihalyi, M. (1990). *Flow: The psychology of optimal experience.* New York, NY: Harper & Row.

Davidson, R.J., & Begley, S. (2012). *The emotional life of your brain: How its unique patterns affect the way we think, feel and live—and how you can change them.* New York, NY: Hudson Street Press.

Dewey, J. (1893). Self-realization as the moral ideal. *The Philosophical Review, 2*(6), 652.

Dewey, J. (1915). *The school and society.* Chicago, IL: University of Chicago Press.

Dweck, C. (2006). *Mindset: The new psychology of success.* New York, NY: Random House.

Guinier, L. (2015). *The tyranny of meritocracy: Democratizing higher education in America.* Boston, MA: Beacon Press.

Hess, K., Gong, B., & Steinitz, R. (March, 2014). *Ready for college and career?* Quincy, MA: The Nellie Mae Education Foundation.

Kelley, D., & Kelley, T. (2013). *Creative confidence: Unleashing the creative potential within us all.* New York, NY: Crown Publishing Group.

Lieberman, M. (2013). *Social: Why our brains are wired to connect.* New York, NY: Crown Publishers.

Page, S. (2007). *The difference: How the power of diversity creates better groups, firms, schools, and societies.* Princeton, NJ: Princeton University Press.

Scharmer, C.O. (2007). *Theory U: Leading from the future as it emerges: The social technology of presencing.* Cambridge, MA: Society for Organizational Learning.

Vella, J. (2000). *Taking learning to task: Creative strategies for teaching adults.* San Francisco, CA: Jossey-Bass.

Whitehead, A.N. (1929). *The aims of education and other essays.* New York, NY: Macmillan.

Zull, J. E. (2011). *From brain to mind: Using neuroscience to guide change in education.* Sterling, VA: Stylus Publishing.

PART II

Young Designers: K-12 Students Take On Design Thinking

4

DESIGN PARTNERS IN SCHOOLS

Encouraging Design Thinking Through Cooperative Inquiry

Mona Leigh Guha, Brenna McNally,
and Jerry Alan Fails

Introduction

For nearly two decades, elementary school-aged children have gathered in a lab
at the University of Maryland every Tuesday and Thursday after school. The
lab is brightly decorated and child-friendly—a place that encourages children
to sit on the floor, design with art supplies, and freely share thoughts in a way
that formal school may not often encourage. The children come together with
undergraduate and graduate students, researchers, staff, and faculty from the university, and together this intergenerational team designs technology for children.
Over the years the team has designed technologies that span content areas and
platforms, such as a multilingual online library of children's books, robots that
emote through stories, and mobile applications designed to support learning
of STEM topics. The team works together as design partners using a design
method called Cooperative Inquiry.

The technologies that have emerged from this process have been ground-
breaking in many ways, producing numerous academic publications and
technologies that are still available to the public today. Likewise, the process by
which these technologies are created, Cooperative Inquiry, has been ground-
breaking for bringing together adults and children to work as equal design
partners in the technology design process. Cooperative Inquiry always encourages and often requires components of design thinking from its members.

Throughout this chapter, we will consider the ways in which Cooperative
Inquiry supports design thinking and the implications and possibilities that
this might have for formal educational settings. We begin with a section
describing Cooperative Inquiry, and then consider the ways in which it incorporates principles of design thinking across its techniques, its process, and the

experiences it affords the children who are a part of the process. Next, we offer two case descriptions of Cooperative Inquiry implementations in formal schools. We conclude by discussing the opportunities we see for Cooperative Inquiry to support bringing design thinking to schools today and in the future.

Cooperative Inquiry and Design Thinking

Readers of this book will be aware that design thinking is a holistic process that promotes collaboration, experimentation, iteration, and the use of physical models to communicate ideas for an authentic or "real world" context. For further reading on how these principles create opportunities for creativity, we encourage readers to refer to other chapters in this volume, as well as Carroll et al. (2010) and Zimmerman, Forlizzi, and Evenson (2007). In this section, we provide a discussion of Cooperative Inquiry to give the reader background knowledge of the method and to better draw connections between this method of design and design thinking.

What Is Cooperative Inquiry?

Cooperative Inquiry is a technology design process in which children and adults work together to create new technology for children (Druin 1999; Guha et al., 2013). This method has been pioneered and refined by Allison Druin and her colleagues at the University of Maryland for nearly two decades. Cooperative Inquiry is founded on the importance of giving children a voice in the design of their technology. (For more information on this method, see Druin, 1999; Druin, 2002; Guha et al., 2013; Fails et al., 2013.)

Cooperative Inquiry grew out of Scandinavian work in Participatory Design, which was originally conceived to give factory workers a voice in the design of the technology that they used (see examples from Floyd et al., 1989; Bjerknes et al., 1987). Participatory Design was built on the user-centered approach, in which the user's needs and not just the technology are considered in the design of new technologies (Sanders, 2008). Participatory Design included the user as a viable and valued member of the design team whose voice was heard and valued throughout the design process. We consider this a type of design partnering, in which all members of a design team are considered equal, regardless of their expertise (Druin, 2002).

Typically, a group of children agree to participate on a Cooperative Inquiry for a year at a time, and each child can choose whether to return in subsequent years. There are generally six to ten children on the team at any one point, ranging in age from six to eleven years old. They are joined by a group of adults that also consistently works with the team for a period of years. While the adults may rotate depending on the project, at any given session there are at least three or four adult design partners present. Together, the adults and children design technology for children. The adults bring expertise in a variety of fields, ranging from computer science to human development to information studies to visual design, and the children bring expertise in being children at that point in time. Philosophically, the belief that all of these expertises are equally important and vital to the team is central to Cooperative Inquiry. Adults on the team look to the children for design input from the developmental level of the children, as well as their intuitive knowledge of being a child in the present day.

Cooperative Inquiry employs an iterative and long-term method of design, in which projects are undertaken over the course of weeks, months, or years. Once the full team has met for design sessions, which happen twice a week for 90 minutes, certain members of the design team may make further work on the technology and then bring it back to the full team for revision, critique, and iteration at a later date. Thus, it is common for the team to be working on multiple projects simultaneously.

Philosophically, the Cooperative Inquiry method operates with a few underlying tenets. The first of these, as mentioned earlier, is that of design partnering. In this method, all partners, adult and child alike, are considered equals on the design team and treat each other as such. Cooperative Inquiry encourages idea elaboration where a team member may have an idea, another iterates on it, and then these ideas are combined with others until no one remembers who had the original idea and how anyone contributed to it. In the end, the idea has emerged from the team working as a collective and collaborative unit. This group design approach and its collaborative attribution are hallmarks of Cooperative Inquiry.

To make design sessions as effective as possible, Cooperative Inquiry includes a large stable of techniques for designing technology throughout an iterative design process (Walsh et al., 2013). These techniques have been adapted or created specifically by researchers and designers using Cooperative Inquiry for projects that involve working with children. There is no set timeline for when each technique must be used, and each technique can be used multiple times during a design cycle; however, there are techniques that are particularly useful at different points in the design process. For example, Bags of Stuff is a low-tech 3D prototyping technique often used for early brainstorming, Sticky Note Critiquing involves using sticky notes to give specific feedback on prototypes, Big Paper is a paper prototyping technique especially suited for early and mid-fidelity prototypes, and Mixing Ideas is a technique created to combine the ideas of the group. For more information on implementing these and other design techniques, see Fails, et al. (2013), Guha et al. (2004), and Walsh et al. (2013).

Cooperative Inquiry as a Space for Design Thinking

Although it was not initially conceived to support design thinking, Cooperative Inquiry incorporates many design thinking principles and thus provides a space for children and adults to practice and implement design thinking. Characteristics shared between Cooperative Inquiry and design thinking include: dealing with open-ended problems, working iteratively and in a hands-on manner, and producing artifacts intended to be largely shared and distributed.

As with design thinking, Cooperative Inquiry promotes attitudes and skills that encourage children and adults to address ambiguous problems with no clear answer, and even no clear way to an answer. Zimmerman et al. (2007) describe these kinds of challenges faced by design researchers as under-constrained problems; Rittel and Webber (1973) referred to them as "wicked" problems that do not have a clear path to an answer. Cooperative Inquiry, in which the team is asked to conceive and create new technology to solve a problem for the future, deals in the realm of open possibilities and wicked and under-constrained problems. One such under-constrained problem that the team recently addressed is: How can we help children solve science inquiry challenges using social media? While there are some general parameters constraining this question, in essence we asked the team to consider ways that science (a broad topic) could be supported by social media (a broad space), and to come up with technology to support this. This lead to ScienceKit (formerly SINQ), a mobile technology designed to support communities of young scientists in their investigations using tools such as video, camera, audio, and connections with others (Yip et al., 2013, 2014). This is an example of how children and adults on a Cooperative Inquiry design team are asked to dream up many creative ideas in response to complex problems, further practicing the skill of solving under-constrained and wicked problems.

Design thinking almost always includes iterative processes or ideation (Carroll et al., 2010; Zimmerman et al., 2007). Cooperative Inquiry is inherently an iterative process. The practice of defining a problem, researching the problem, creating solutions, evaluating solutions, and reflecting on outcomes (Fails et al., 2013) is practiced in Cooperative Inquiry over the course of the design process. Children are heavily involved in many phases of the cycle and thus experience what it means to address a wicked problem from the beginning, through many possible solutions, through evaluating these solutions, and through continuing iteratively. Throughout this iterative process design partners learn that not all ideas in isolation will be ideal, and that the "failure" of an idea can still produce an innovative outcome. Cooperative Inquiry yields positive results by overcoming what could be viewed as an individual failure through use of a collaborative and elaborative process. A good example of this long-term and iterative process was the design of the International Children's Digital Library (http://en.childrenslibrary.org/). Over the course of many years, the children and adults on the team worked to create and iterate this multilingual collection of children's literature online. From the overall look and feel of the website to the ways in which books can be read online, this project took years of iterative designing by the whole team to become the resource that it is today.

Cooperative Inquiry team members engage in hands-on design, as do those engaged in design thinking (Carroll et al., 2010). While this often means using open-ended and low-fidelity art supplies, team members are also asked to explore ideas with the technologies that will be employed or created. Recently, the team helped to design MakerShoe, an interactive e-textile shoe (Kazemitabaar et al., 2015). Throughout the design process, the team worked not only with low-tech art supplies such as cardboard and markers, but also with actual shoes and LittleBits (electronic components) that could be attached to the shoes. This type of hands-on design with low- and high-fidelity materials supports design thinking.

Finally, design thinking is concerned with the production of knowledge and products in a "real" environment. Cooperative Inquiry design teams do work in a real environment; making products that will often be produced and distributed widely. In releasing the products to the world, the children are change agents, engaged in an action-based process (Vande Zande, 2007). Our Cooperative Inquiry design team has had a long-standing partnership with the United States National Park Service. Through this partnership, our team has been involved in the design of the WebRangers site, which is the Park Service's website for children (http://www.nps.gov/webrangers/). Seeing their work produced in the real world is meaningful for children, and working with a group such as the United States Park Service allows the children to have an impact on the broader world; both of which support design thinking principles.

Connecting the Experiences of Cooperative Inquiry to Design Thinking

While the process of Cooperative Inquiry includes many of the characteristics of design thinking, there are further ways in which Cooperative Inquiry and design thinking are related. Cooperative Inquiry has been shown to provide a number of social and cognitive experiences for children when they engage in the process over

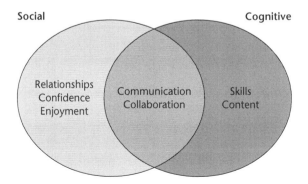

FIGURE 4.1 The social and cognitive experiences of child design partners (Guha, 2010)

the course of a year or longer (Figure 4.1) (Guha, 2010). As depicted in Figure 4.1, children's experiences on a Cooperative Inquiry team can be categorized into two domains: social and cognitive, with some overlap between the two.

While not all of these constructs are linked to design thinking, many are. Below we detail the competencies of design thinking that are supported in the experiences of children on a Cooperative Inquiry design team. For an extended description of these constructs or descriptions of constructs in Figure 4.1 that are not detailed below, please see Guha (2010).

The Cognitive Domain

Iterative problem-solving, prototyping, creativity, and content knowledge are all important aspects of design thinking that educators seek to instill in young learners (Carroll et al., 2010; Scheer et al., 2012; Rauth et al., 2010) and that are reflected in the cognitive experiences of children on a Cooperative Inquiry design team. Empowering and inspiring children to apply design thinking to difficult, real-world problems as done in Cooperative Inquiry includes developing the cognitive *skills* and understanding of *content* that are the basic components of the design process. Through Cooperative Inquiry, children are presented with new design challenges in a variety of content areas, asked to understand what different stakeholders require of the technology they are designing, required to critically evaluate how well a technology accomplishes its goal, and challenged to brainstorm and prototype solutions to the problem using one of the range of techniques. Through the Cooperative Inquiry method, children are able to practice these cognitive components of the processes that underlie design thinking.

The Social Domain

Consistent involvement in Cooperative Inquiry helps children become more outgoing over time, describe their "pride" in their technology creations and design abilities, and increase their comfort with approaching technologies in general. This is precisely the type of creative confidence—and confidence in general—that is an essential part of the learning that design thinking aspires to provide (Kelley & Kelley, 2013; Rauth et al., 2010). This outlook and attitude falls within the social domain of Cooperative Inquiry experiences, which have been shown to provide experiences in the realm of children's *confidence*. In viewing design thinking as not only a set of skills and techniques, but also as an outlook on approaching problems, we acknowledge that children need to develop attitudes toward design processes that enable success. Additionally, a component that is often left out of consideration of design thinking, but which plays a critical role in its success, is *enjoyment*. Children typically find the Cooperative Inquiry process to be enjoyable (Guha, 2010). Enjoyment can encourage further participation, which is beneficial to design thinking and educational scenarios.

The Overlap Between the Social and Cognitive Domains

Working with an intergenerational design team to which children consistently present the ideas they came up with offers the children experience in the areas of *collaboration* and *communication*. Children are challenged to elaborate on the design ideas of their peers and the adult design partners they work with during Cooperative Inquiry design sessions. This can foster skills in multidisciplinary collaboration, which is one of the explicit goals of design thinking (Goldman et al., 2014; Rauth et al., 2010). With regard to design thinking, it is important that children are able to communicate their ideas and why their ideas are important and relevant (Carroll et al., 2010). The Cooperative Inquiry design method affords many opportunities to develop and practice this competency, as children present their design ideas to the team every design session, usually by using the mockup or prototype they have created to illustrate their ideas.

Summary

The design thinking-related experiences that Cooperative Inquiry can encourage over the course of time suggests that it is a promising way to structure the complexities of design thinking with school-aged children. While the Cooperative Inquiry process we have described requires a degree of facilitation that can be difficult to achieve in educational settings, Cooperative Inquiry is a highly adaptable process and has been modified for use in formal schools (Foss et al., 2013, 2014; Guha et al., 2004).

Case Examples of Cooperative Inquiry in Educational Settings

Cooperative Inquiry and the design thinking principles therein are most often implemented in informal educational settings. Nonetheless, there are some instances in which Cooperative Inquiry has been implemented in more formal school settings. Here we present two such cases: one in an early learning center for young children, and one in a middle school for children with learning challenges. We consider the implications of these cases for including Cooperative Inquiry in more formal educational settings.

Case One: A Campus-Based Early Learning Center

Over the course of five years, we implemented Cooperative Inquiry in an on-campus early learning center. During this time, our goal was to determine the feasibility of using Cooperative Inquiry with children aged 4 to 6 years old (Farber et al., 2002). Each year, we worked with a different group of young children to design technology for young children. Although our focus was on considering the use of the Cooperative Inquiry method with young children, this necessarily included the incorporation of many design thinking principles in a formal school environment. The formal school environment in this case was a private early learning center for children in preschool and kindergarten. We worked at the school twice a week for 60 minutes over the course of each academic year in the study.

During this implementation, through Cooperative Inquiry we introduced many principles of design thinking to the young children. We worked on many long-term and iterative projects, all lasting over the course of multiple sessions. Implementing iterative design with such young children required us to add structure to the collaborative process, and one of the ways we did this was creating a technique called Mixing Ideas (Guha et al., 2004). In Mixing Ideas, each team member begins by coming up with his or her own design response to a design challenge. Over the course of many sessions over a period of time (generally on different days), the ideas are combined first in pairs, then in small groups, then in slightly bigger groups, and so on until there is one idea that came from mixing the ideas of the whole group. The Mixing Ideas technique not only provided needed support for these younger children in collaborating, but also facilitated collaboration across multiple sessions in which not all partners are present for each session. This structure may be valuable for other implementations in formal schooling.

We also found that it was possible to work through open-ended problems with this younger population within this school setting. For example, one project began with a prompt to create a new and exciting learning center for the classroom. This center could have been anything that fit into a preschool. With iteration, the group eventually came up with large, collaborative, physical blocks that were technologically enhanced and reconfigurable (Guha et al., 2004). The design team at the early learning center, in conjunction with our older children, also came up with a physically interactive technological game to teach children about environmental health hazards (Fails et al., 2005). These projects, initially presented in an open-ended manner, required children to be creative in their design thinking. The researchers did not assume final answers or products; rather, the team focused on the open-ended, creative design process in order to come up with unique and innovative solutions.

One issue we ran into in this implementation of Cooperative Inquiry in a formal school was that supporting Cooperative Inquiry typically takes a high ratio of adults to children, which may require some creativity to manage in a formal school environment. Working on iterative and open-ended problems common in design thinking often requires significant support from adults, especially for younger children. Due to the large number of children in the class, during each session we typically worked with a small subset of children. Our solution included pulling small groups of children to work outside of the classroom, as the rest of the class remained in the classroom for their typical activities.

With the number of adults that we had on our team, by working with small groups of children, many times we were able to keep to nearly a one-to-one adult-to-child ratio. When working with the children, we generally had them leave their home classroom and work in a common area of the center, such as a great room or conference room. It is also of note that the adults were trained in Cooperative Inquiry methods and were able to moderate and facilitate activities in a manner that has a different dynamic (including power structures) than traditional classrooms.

Case Two: A Middle School for Children With Learning Differences

In another instantiation of Cooperative Inquiry in a formal school setting, we worked with middle-school aged boys in their classrooms at a private school for children with learning differences, including moderate autism, learning disabilities, and ADHD. We took Cooperative Inquiry to two different classrooms of children—one each semester—where we worked within the school day in the children's classroom once a week. The fact that the population was entirely boys was due to the makeup of the classrooms and not manipulated by the researchers. While much of our focus during this time was on implementing Cooperative Inquiry with children with special needs (Foss et al., 2013), as with our experience at the early learning center, we also considered that we were implementing this design process in a formal school setting. Our observations of implementing Cooperative Inquiry in this environment revealed that there were also many instances of design thinking being supported in this formal classroom with these children.

The goal for working with the children in this school was to develop a class technology over the course of each semester. This allowed for a problem that would have a tangible result and thus be understood as a real-world problem, as opposed to making the children feel as though they were simply subjects in a research study (Foss et al., 2013). This required a degree of collaboration and communication among the boys to achieve a single technology project from the entire class working together. Each classroom included 10 boys. The small size was due to the nature of the school. The design prompt also presented an open-ended problem as we asked the team to decide both the content and platform for their technology project. As with the work in the early learning center, implementing Cooperative Inquiry in the middle school allowed us to expose the children to the iterative process often cited in design thinking as we returned week after week to progress the work through the design sessions. Both classes chose to design a computer game, with one class ultimately creating a space exploration game and the second an adventure-based game with multiple settings including a castle (Foss et al., 2014). As a culminating event, the boys were able to visit our university campus and show their game to other researchers in our lab. This offered a chance for the boys to practice communicating their ideas in a real-world setting as well as to feel empowered as they were able to demonstrate what they had created to a group of university professionals who were genuinely interested in what the boys had designed. The university field trip allowed the boys to practice and demonstrate design thinking principles.

While working in the middle school, we worked with the entire classroom of boys for each design session. We again found that this type of exploration in open-ended and iterative design thinking required a high ratio of adults to children (Foss et al., 2013, 2014). Multiple researchers were needed to support each session of Cooperative Inquiry. We also appreciate that in both of the cases that we have described here, though they are very different contexts, they were similar in that they were private schools with flexibility in their curriculum. Each school, though they had different underlying philosophies, found value in Cooperative Inquiry, and thus design thinking, being included in a school day. Because of outside influences such as governmental policies or top-down mandates, some public schools may not have the curricular flexibility to allow this.

Future Directions: How Design Partnering Can Become a Part of Formal Education

Cooperative Inquiry as a method of designing technologies with and for children has been implemented in university design research settings as well as in schools as described in the cases above. Children involved in Cooperative Inquiry design have had beneficial social and cognitive experiences. Because there is such strong crossover between Cooperative Inquiry and the desired outcomes of a curriculum that fosters competencies in design thinking, the incorporation of Cooperative Inquiry into educational activities is a promising area. We have previously published how Cooperative Inquiry can allow children to design the future as it is incorporated into more informal and formal settings (Guha et al., 2011). In this chapter, we have provided illustrative case studies to inspire and suggest guidance for Cooperative Inquiry and design thinking to be implemented in formal school settings.

The requirement for schools to build basic competencies in reading, writing, and arithmetic in order for the children of today to be successful in the workplace of tomorrow is necessary, but is not sufficient. Children will also need to be able to think critically and solve problems ingeniously in order to meet the demands of a more complex workplace. They need to be comfortable with—and adept at—collaborating and communicating with co-workers in the office and around the world. We posit that incorporating design thinking through the Cooperative Inquiry process in formal educational settings will help to meet these ever-expanding needs.

To address the complexities of the workplace, new business models are being employed that espouse several of the principles of design thinking, including focusing on users' experiences, creating models to examine complex problems, using prototypes, and tolerating failure (Kolko, 2015). Cooperative Inquiry addresses each of these. Focusing on users' experiences echoes the design thinking principle of empathy and is a central goal of the user-centered approach employed in Cooperative Inquiry. Using Cooperative Inquiry, children often tackle complex and "wicked" design problems. One of the children's favorite techniques in Cooperative Inquiry is low-tech prototyping (affectionately named "Bags-of-Stuff"). The purpose of this technique is to create a model, or solution, that often addresses an abstract problem. The creation of the model and iteratively prototyping potential solutions echoes the business-oriented design approach. What results is a high tolerance for failure—with children realizing that not all ideas in isolation will be ideal, but that the collaborative and elaborative process of Cooperative Inquiry will yield positive results.

There are several educational best practices that align with employing Cooperative Inquiry in a more formal setting, including active, engaged learning, project-based learning, and chances to fail and iterate to achieve success. Active learning (Prince, 2004) takes place in Cooperative Inquiry, as children are active in physical space as well as co-constructing physical models to represent individual and shared understanding and visions of new ideas. Engaged teaching practices also include allowing the learner to have choice in the types of projects they work on to promote individual investment in working on that project. In Cooperative Inquiry, children work on several projects using the same processes and techniques that allow them to think critically and iteratively improve the design of the project on which they are working. Schools at many levels are engaging in project-based learning (Krajcik & Blumenfeld, 2006), which has theoretical underpinnings including active construction, situated learning, and social interaction. As discussed and illustrated in this chapter, Cooperative Inquiry is built on similar underpinnings whereby co-construction and social interaction are key. The iterative design approach of Cooperative Inquiry allows children to try, fail, get constructive feedback, try again, and succeed, which is seen as an important educational practice (Shechtman et al., 2013).

A defining characteristic of Cooperative Inquiry in relation to other design methods involving children is the long-term commitment and relationship that is cultivated in the team. In the typical instantiation of Cooperative Inquiry, the design team meets two or more times a week for 90 minutes throughout the school year, and adults and children can participate in the team for several years. Most other design methods that include children interact with children once or twice or for the duration of a project that may span a matter of weeks or at most a few months. The extended time and longer-term relationship that is cultivated in Cooperative Inquiry allows for more time to explore and create together. Children are involved with school for several hours a day, multiple days a week, and often forge relationships with peers and adults that last beyond a single year of schooling. Children participating in Cooperative Inquiry have had beneficial experiences in the social areas of relationships, confidence, and enjoyment, in the cognitive areas of skills and content, and overlapping areas of communication and collaboration. With increased frequency and longer durations of time, if Cooperative Inquiry were implemented in a formal school setting, there is potential to magnify the positive experiences in Cooperative Inquiry. For example even if there is a long-term study (i.e., let's grow these beans into plants), oftentimes there is a missed opportunity in taking the time to iteratively approach the problem (i.e., let's design lots of pots and see which is the best for growing these beans into plants, *and then* let's make those pots even better and try it again). Cooperative Inquiry promotes this type of iterative learning approach.

Integrating Cooperative Inquiry into the curriculum can weave several learning best practices into the fabric of the learning environment including: active learning; project-based learning; and chances to fail, to get feedback, and to work toward success. It can also promote beneficial social and cognitive experiences for children. Focusing efforts on incorporating design thinking and Cooperative Inquiry in formal educational settings may empower children to open them further to the important skills including critical thinking and innovative design that they will need as they move on from their formal learning to directly impact society through the things they can think, do, and create.

Acknowledgments

We thank the many children who have participated in the Cooperative Inquiry-based intergenerational design teams we have been on, as well as the parents and teachers who made those collaborations possible.

References

Bjerknes, G., Ehn, P., & Kyung, M. (1987). *Computers and democracy: A Scandanavian challenge.* Aldershot, UK: Avebury.

Carroll, M., Goldman, S., Britos, L., Koh, J., Royalty, A., & Hornstein, M. (2010). Destination, imagination and the fires within: Design thinking in a middle school classroom. *The International Journal of Art & Design Education, 29*(1), 37–53.

Druin, A. (1999). Cooperative inquiry: Developing new technologies for children with children. Proceedings from CHI '99: *The SIGCHI conference on human factors in computing systems.* New York, NY: ACM, 592–599.

Druin, A. (2002). The role of children in the design of new technology. *Behaviour and Information Technology, 21*(1), 1–25.

Fails, J. A., Druin, A., & Guha, M.L. (2013) Methods and techniques for involving children in the design of new technology for children. *Foundations and Trends in Human-Computer Interaction, 6*(2), 85–166.

Fails, J.A., Druin, A., Guha, M. L., Chipman, G., Simms, S., & Churaman, W. (2005). Child's play: A comparison of desktop and physical interactive environments. Proceedings from IDC '05: *Interaction design and children*. New York, NY: ACM, 48–55.

Farber, A., Druin, A., Chipman, G., Julian, D., & Somashekhar, S. (2002). How young can our design partners be? Proceedings from the *2002 Participatory Design Conference*, 127–131.

Floyd, C., Mehl, W. M., Reisin, F. M., Schmidt, G., & Wolf, G. (1989). Out of Scandinavia: Alternative approaches to software design and system development. *Human-Computer Interaction, 4*(4), 253–350.

Foss, E., Guha, M.L., Franklin, L., Clegg, T., Finlater, L., & Yip, J. (2014). Designing technology with students with learning differences: Implementing modified Cooperative Inquiry. Retrieved from: http://hcil2.cs.umd.edu/trs/2014-03/2014-03.pdf.

Foss, E., Guha, M.L., Papadatos, P., Clegg, T., Yip, J., & Walsh, G. (2013). Cooperative Inquiry extended: Creating technology with middle school students with learning differences. *Journal of Special Education Technology, 28*(3), 33–46.

Goldman, S., Kabayadondo, K., Royalty, A., Carroll, M., & Roth, B. (2014). Student teams in search of design thinking. In C. Meinel, L. Leifer, & H. Plattner (Eds.) *Design thinking research: Understanding innovation*. Switzerland: Springer, 11–34.

Guha, M.L., Druin, A., & Fails, J. (2013). Cooperative Inquiry revisited: Reflections of the past and Guidelines for the future of intergenerational co-design. *International Journal of Child-Computer Interaction, 1*(1), 14–23.

Guha, M.L., Druin, A., & Fails J.A. (2011). How children can design the future. In J. Jacko (Ed.) *Human-Computer Interaction*. Heidelberg: Springer, 559–569.

Guha, M.L. (2010). *Understanding the social and cognitive experiences of children involved in technology design processes*. (PhD dissertation). University of Maryland.

Guha, M.L., Druin, A., Chipman, G., Fails, J.A., Simms, S., & Farber A. (2004). Mixing ideas: A new technique for working with young children as design partners. Proceedings from ICD '04: *Interaction design and children: Building a community*. New York, NY: ACM, 35–42.

Kazemitabaar, M., Norooz, L., Guha, M.L., & Froehlich, J. (2015). MakerShoe: Toward a wearable e-textile construction kit to support creativity, playful making, and self-expression. Proceedings from IDC '15: *14th International Conference on Interaction Design and Children*. New York, NY: ACM, 449–452.

Kelley, T., & Kelley, D. (2013). *Creative confidence: Unleashing the creative potential within us all*. New York, NY: Crown Business.

Kolko, J. (September, 2015). Design Thinking comes of age: The approach, once used primarily in product design, is now infusing corporate culture. *Harvard Business Review*, 66–71.

Krajcik, J.S., & Blumenfeld, P.C. (2006). Project-based learning. In R.K. Sawyer (Ed.) *The Cambridge handbook of the learning sciences*. New York, NY: Cambridge University Press, 317–334.

Prince, M. (2004). Does active learning work? A review of the research. *Journal of Engineering Education, 93*(3), 223–232.

Rauth, I., Köppen, E., Jobst, B., & Meinel, C. (2010). Design thinking: An educational model towards creative confidence. Proceedings from ICDC 2010: *1st International Conference on Design Creativity*.

Rittel, H.W.J., & Webber, M.M. (1973). Dilemmas in a general theory of planning. *Policy Sciences 4*(2), 155–166.

Sanders, L. (2008). On modeling: An evolving map of design practice and design research. *Interactions, 15*(6), 13–17.

Scheer, A., Noweski, C., & Meinel, C. (2012). Transforming constructivist learning into action: Design thinking in education. *Design and Technology Education: An International Journal, 17*(3), 8–19.

Shechtman, N., Debarger, A.H., Dornsife, C., Roiser, S., & Yarnall, L. (2013). *Promoting grit, tenacity, and perseverance: Critical factors for success in the 21st century (draft).* U.S. Department of Education, Office of Educational Technology (OET). Retrieved from http://pgbovine.net/OET-Draft-Grit-Report-2-17-13.pdf.

Vande Zande, R. (2007). Design education as community outreach and interdisciplinary study. *Journal for Learning through the Arts, 3*(1), 1–22.

Walsh, G., Foss, E., Yip, J., & Druin, A. (2013). FACIT PD: Framework for analysis and creation of intergenerational techniques for participatory design. Proceedings from CHI '13: *Conference on Human Factors in Computing Systems.* New York, NY: ACM, 2893–2902.

Yip, J.C., Ahn, J., Clegg, T.L., Bonsignore, E., Pauw, D., & Gubbels., M. (2014). "It helped me do my science": A case of designing social media technologies for children in science learning. Proceedings from IDC '14: *13th International Conference of Interaction Design and Children.* New York, NY: ACM: 155–164.

Yip, J., Bonsignore, E., Ahn, J., Clegg, T., & Guha, M.L. (2013). Building ScienceKit through Cooperative Inquiry. Workshop paper in Human-Computer Interaction and the Learning Sciences Workshop. *Computer Supported Collaborative Learning.* Madison, WI.

Zimmerman, J., Forlizzi, J., & Evenson, S. (2007). Research through design as a method for interaction design research in HCI. Proceedings from CHI '07: *Human Factors in Computing Systems.* New York, NY: ACM, 493–502.

5

TAKING DESIGN THINKING TO EAST, WEST, AND SOUTHERN AFRICA

Key Lessons from Global Minimum's Student Innovation Programs

Desmond Mitchell and Mathias Esmann

Design Thinking and Developing GMin's Mission

Educational programs utilizing design thinking principles, as tools for achieving local development goals, provide young people opportunities to tackle development challenges faced by African societies. This has been the central guiding premise for our work over the past four years at Global Minimum (GMin).

Our organization started in Sierra Leone in 2007 with a focus similar to traditional development programs—we started out by distributing mosquito nets. We sought only to be a facilitator that enabled the people of Sierra Leone to shape their own lives, but we quickly discovered that solutions had to come from within the country. We refocused GMin and immersed ourselves in the principles of innovation competitions in the United States such as the MIT IDEAS Global Challenge. The competitions invited participants to identify community needs and to propose new ways of meeting them. Seeing the creativity and passion for change these competitions inspired, we asked ourselves, "Why can't a competition such as the IDEAS Global Challenge showcase the same youthful brilliance within the context of Sierra Leone?"

Design thinking perfectly parallels our refined approach to development. By leading students through the design thinking process (observe needs, ideate, experiment, test ideas, and iterate), we seek to facilitate the acquisition of basic technical literacies that can make hands-on learning a part of the problem-solving process. Design thinking empowers because it allows the individual to define and empathetically approach open-ended challenges frequently created in today's world. We justify creating programs that complement the education systems in the countries where we work because we introduce creative thinking activities with traditional structured problem-solving. Lastly, in addition to the experiential learning, we expose students to mentors and successful innovators who act as additional moral and technical support as students face multiple types of challenges during the problem-solving process.

Our First Innovation Competition in Sierra Leone

In 2012, GMin launched the InChallenge (Innovation Challenge) as a first attempt to prompt young Sierra Leoneans to develop solutions to both local and far-reaching problems. We approached high school students, challenged them to assess their communities, first brainstorm on issues they saw, and identify a specific local problem. We then asked them to use their understanding of their environment to find, through collaborative design, innovative ways of addressing the issues they encountered. Lastly, we asked our student teams to submit proposals to gain mentorship and resources to help their ideas become realities.

After receiving 70 applications and from which we chose eight finalist teams; we conducted our first Innovation camp. We saw finalists' projects come to fruition, and through the week-long camp we saw students gaining confidence in their own ability to be change makers. From a programmatic and experiential standpoint we were able to expose students to new ways of learning and we were able to showcase the promise of holding design thinking challenges in developing economies. We brought together experts and mentors from within the Sierra Leonean community and abroad. The story of one student in particular, Kelvin Doe, was picked up by a film crew who heard of his story through our program and decided to follow him on his journey to MIT as the institution's youngest resident practitioner. Although our first year was a huge success, we faced multiple challenges along the way. We struggled to provide consistent mentorship and to maintain contact with students who lived all across Sierra Leone. We learned that we were overlooking many logistical issues that directly impacted student involvement, but we jumped into our second competition excited to improve.

Our Second Innovation Competition in Sierra Leone

For our 2013 innovation competition round, we reset our competition calendar to better align with the Sierra Leonean calendar. We added additional feedback rounds for students and developed a communications strategy for keeping in better touch with schools. One team endeavored to create a windmill to power their rechargeable batteries; another team proposed to create torchlights from scrap metal; and yet another team wanted to repair local wells to protect the community from an ongoing cholera epidemic. The finalists were once again invited to present their innovations abroad. Representatives from the windmill team, a builder of small helicopters, and a team creating locally sourced dye travelled to the Google campus in California to present at the Science Foo camp, and then again at the Interaction Design for Children Conference at the New School in New York.

The number of applications had risen to more than 100 but the overall quality of the applications had not improved. There were more applicants, but the judges only found five of them qualified for finalist status. We noticed that two of the best applications had something in common. They came from the Prince of Wales school where the student teams had access to SparkFun Inventor's kits. At the school, tinkering and experimenting took place outside of the innovation competitions. This gave us the idea to develop high touch innovation programs which we then later called Innovation Laboratories (InLabs).

The First Innovation Laboratory: Integrating GMin Into the Community and School System

The initial idea behind InLabs was to create an educational program focused around creativity and design so that InChallenge applications would be of higher quality. Through participation in InLabs, students would have a physical space to tinker, experiment, and design so that they could present more refined proposals for prototype funding, implementation, and scaling. Since makerspaces already existed in other parts of the world—FabLab and SparkLab—we were curious to see what ideas would spring from their introduction to Sierra Leone. We drew from the Stanford d.school's Bootcamp and other open source materials to develop a space that was the first of its kind in Sierra Leone.

The precedent for the InLab was the donation of SparkFun inventor's kits to the Prince of Wales school in Freetown in early 2013. The kits allowed the students there to learn Arduino programming and to tinker with breadboards. Mohammed Harding, a student from Prince of Wales, created his own motorized robot and set up the lab's own Facebook page, bringing high publicity to the program. Harding and his peers also made some of the best contributions to GMin's 2013 InChallenge. Their successes inspired us to expose other students to the same kind of learning opportunities.

GMin's first InLab launched in 2014 at the Prince of Wales School with an air of excitement, engagement, and promise. In partnership with a variety of sponsors, we secured 3D printers, laptops, Makey-Makeys and a variety of tools for tinkering with electronics, woodwork, and painting. In addition, we hired a full-time director for the InLab who was in charge of running activities that stimulated the students' ability to formulate local challenges and improved their technical skills. The InLab was open to community members and all students at Prince of Wales as an after-school activity. We also encouraged teachers to use the labs to aid in their teaching.

Expanding Into Kenya and South Africa

After our first two challenges in Sierra Leone, we began to explore more programmatic and logistical questions: Could we create new structures for Kenya to similarly challenge local problems as understood through the eyes of young people? Could we help create structures for students to realize their own potential for impact in South Africa? Could we begin to cultivate a culture of innovative thought across Africa? We decided to branch out to Kenya (Innovate Kenya) and South Africa (Innovate the Cape) where GMin team members lived. We soon learned that building programs there required different approaches.

Innovate Kenya, led by Jacob Lennheden, was established with a heavier focus on mentorship and active engagement in learning. The Kenyan government had established a nationwide inventor's competition and business incubators were beginning to pop up in major cities. The national science-fair competition encouraged students from all over the country to develop innovative ideas and document them, but the competition abruptly ended once finalists were announced. Lennheden and his team found that many teams would stop developing their ideas after the competition because there was little encouragement and help to continue to push these projects along. The two winning teams got a significant amount of exposure, but no additional help was provided past the competition, and the majority of the teams were left with little more than a certificate. To address these problems we redesigned the InChallenge specifically for Kenya with four goals in mind:

1. Establish a platform for creation through a competition.
2. Host innovation workshops at targeted schools.
3. Provide regular mentorship for youth.
4. Support the network of young makers.

The challenge, which was augmented by a week-long innovation camp, provided a learning platform and brought together a community of professionals, teachers, and students who served as mentors and helped develop the teams' ideas while building connections amongst themselves. One team created charcoal briquettes made from waste plant material; another team created paraffin pressure cookers that increased the lifespan of precious fuel; and yet another team designed bamboo coffins to address the prohibitive cost of funerals.

Although we created programs in the hope that teachers shared our goals, we faced resistance in finding times to work with students at the schools. Asking for two hours to hold innovation workshops in many cases proved to be a tall order. Teachers in Kenya, similar to those in so many other countries, are constrained to accomplish their teaching goals within the schedule of the school year. Our programs were often seen as additional curriculum to be added into a packed year. The use of the words "innovation" and "entrepreneurship" were often off-putting to educators outside of the fields of math and science. Many teachers rejected the notion that design thinking principles could be applicable to more than just the sciences. In response, we have been able to facilitate meetings with teachers to discuss the wider definitions of innovation and entrepreneurship, which is a small step in the right direction. The lack of familiarity with the concepts our program is built on remains a major challenge.

Our program in South Africa was initially titled Innovate the Cape (ITC) and was led by GMin member Grant Bridgeman. In South Africa, where the innovation scene was growing rapidly, we noticed a contrast between young people's outward apathetic expressions and their lively, enthusiastic passion for positive change once they were engaged—young people hesitated to excel at innovation competitions because they were afraid of the social repercussions from standing out or "tall poppy syndrome." The GMin team focused a significant amount of their time on curating talks and workshops to help students with presentation skills and with redefining success.

Engineers, philanthropists, business managers, and other community members were the focal points of the workshops. Their talks were built around four main learning objectives:

1. Encourage creativity in assessing local problems.
2. Highlight the importance of communication in developing ideas.
3. Expose young people to a broad range of successful entrepreneurs and intrapreneurs.
4. Introduce students to design thinking frameworks that could be regularly applied to their community surroundings.

Our assessment indicated that the talks were inspiring but needed to be balanced with development of problem-solving skills. We were not seeing much development of the students' own innovative ideas over the course of the program and the notion of innovative change through design thinking is still very foreign to the vast majority of applicants to our competition.

We highlight these three examples to show the cultural and programmatic variance between Sierra Leone, Kenya, and South Africa. What the countries shared in common was an absence of spaces for youth to build ideas, consistent guidance for students, and team-oriented focus on experiential learning. We have determined that having an innovation space, providing consistent high caliber mentorship, and a repository of active learning opportunities for all age groups may be the most effective way of encouraging a "generation of change makers." These insights have helped us to formalize our innovation approach and to develop an emerging theory of change.

Our Emerging Theory of Change: Developing Minds Through a More Robust Structure

We originally gravitated toward design thinking principles out of a frustration with the paternalism and dependency inherent in regular development programs in Africa. Offering design thinking has helped us attract the young self-starters of Kenya, Sierra Leone, and South Africa. We have piqued the interest of local and international media as well as secured a spot at international conferences; but we have also discovered that the competition format undercuts the transformative potential of design thinking principles because it leaves little time to explain the meaning or importance of empathetic human-centered design to those whose creative energy has not yet been kindled. We have redefined our mission statement in light of these findings. Our goal is "to foster a generation of young innovators and leaders who tackle challenges affecting their communities through critical thinking and hands-on learning." We built a theory of change to meet that goal. It draws on other similar frameworks, but also reflects our experience from implementing the InChallenges. Our framework is shown in Figure 5.1, and may be described as follows.

- **Awareness and Exposure:** Challenging young people to assess their communities and see that they have the ability to overlay their lived experiences and their formal education to create change.
- **Tinkering:** Unstructured and playful hands-on learning enables visible progress in building creative skills.
- **Experimenting:** An invitation for students to advance from play encourages them to create a hypothesis about how to meet a community need they have identified.

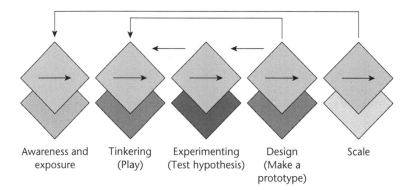

Awareness and   Tinkering   Experimenting   Design   Scale
exposure   (Play)   (Test hypothesis)   (Make a prototype)

FIGURE 5.1 GMin's theory of change framework

- **Design:** Putting a hypothesis in practice. Students create a prototype of their solution, and test it in a real life setting to collect valuable information and to iterate on their design.
- **Scale:** After careful observation and many iterations, students demonstrate to their communities how the challenges they face can be addressed on a broader scale.

We found a good system for awareness and exposure to innovation—the first step in our theory—by reaching hundreds of high schools across three countries, and by highlighting the achievements of our finalists on several media platforms. However, we understood that the journey of learning is much longer and deeper, and our construction of a journey to personal development ran up against formidable foes: interruptions to daily life caused by the Ebola epidemic and the undervaluing of youth potential.

In Sierra Leone, the Ebola epidemic and its concomitant quarantine zones, curfews, and closing of schools wreaked havoc on the academic calendar year. Our students responded admirably: one decided to expand her group's health and sanitation program to share best practices about preventing Ebola transmission; another made an awareness video about the experience of surviving Ebola and reintegrating into society. In response to school closures, our team created the Hack@Home program where students were given challenges over their phones using the Internet communications application WhatsApp. To reinforce collaborative learning through this period, we encouraged students to communicate amongst their WhatsApp groups and to share their solutions via GMin-curated Facebook groups. Students shared ideas on how to combat misconceptions of Ebola and to develop protective gear for caregivers. Hack@Home grew into a high-reach, low-touch pilot program of attempting to teach design thinking from a distance. Eventually, we discontinued Hack@Home because of the logistical challenge related to mobilization.

During the disruption in Sierra Leone, we focused our energies on Kenya. We work closely with the local community leaders and have adapted our curriculum to make challenges and learning even more contextually relevant. We are accounting for infrastructural challenges and relying on the community more for the supply of resources necessary to run a successful InLab. While we understand that our programming is always evolving, we are trying to find new ways to develop teachers and to modify curriculum toward students' needs.

We have dedicated a significant amount of our time to finding new and innovative ways to track the development of students through our programs. The notion that young people have the ability and the right to suggest new ways of meeting a community's needs can be controversial. The need to underscore this may be surprising in societies where tech billionaires emerge before the age of 30, but in many societies, including the ones that fostered the likes of Marc Zuckerberg, age discrimination is a fact. As one student stated,

> At this time and age, and the structure of the education system, there is the fear brought about by the society's indoctrination of the conservative nature in us as youth. "Don't go out into the world. It is a dangerous place. Stick to your books only. It's what will get you through life." I am therefore ecstatic at this opportunity and hope it ends successfully, so that I don't have to listen to the "I told you so" that I foresee.

Students who work with GMin often describe the programs as the first time that they have had a voice in their societies.

Conclusions

We originally set out to utilize design thinking principles to help students approach challenges faced within their communities and we have been successful in taking the first step in creating effective programs. From our experience, we understand that adding simple elements to a pre-existing educational structure can have impactful results. In this exciting time, we observe changes in how our students see the world but hope to better prove how our interventions lead to positive life outcomes. We conclude our chapter with one example of the value we have added to the existing innovation education structure in Kenya.

Tom Osborn and four friends from Alliance High School in Nairobi observed that the fuel used for cooking in homes created smoke that damaged vegetation and made family members sick. The students developed a clean-burning charcoal made from waste plant material. Their product, GreenChar, was entered into Kenya's system of science fair competitions, and although the team passed the local and regional levels, they were not selected for a prize in the national competition. They received no feedback and had not been given the opportunity to make improvements along the way. Within the existing system there seemed nowhere else to go with their enterprise.

When the GreenChar team heard about GMin's Innovate Kenya program, they were at first skeptical. They applied to participate and quickly learned they could be a part of free-flowing idea spaces, mentorship, and workshopping that were all focused on providing structures, and not answers. All the participants gave each other feedback, and seasoned entrepreneurs shared their experience of starting and failing with multiple ventures. The notion that it was fine to fail but preferable to do so quickly and early stuck with the GreenChar team. Taking advantage of the GMin network, the GreenChar team has partnered with more than ten other organizations and has distributed and sold 130 tons of a biofuel called Makaa Poa. In doing so they have, according to their website (http://www.greenchar.co.ke/), "saved over 3,000 trees and impacted over 4,000 households, translating to over 20,000 lives. In addition, we have employed directly a workforce of 15, mainly women and youth and created 10 part time jobs to a sales team."

Young people have the capacity and ability to create substantial and significant change in their communities. By taking a programmatic approach to change, we have seen students grow within their communities, taking on leadership roles and becoming formidable catalysts for change. While there is still a long way to go, we are excited to witness more students becoming their own versions of change in a growing and quickly changing world.

6

CAPTURING MIDDLE SCHOOL STUDENTS' UNDERSTANDINGS OF DESIGN THINKING

Shelley Goldman, Molly B. Zielezinski, Tanner Vea, Stephanie Bachas-Daunert, and Zaza Kabayadondo

Introduction

Study Motivation

Design thinking is a method for solving complex problems that provides those who use it with steps and mindsets for developing innovative solutions that respond to human needs. This powerful method has made successful inroads in the corporate sector and has been gaining prominence in higher education. More recently, it has begun to gain momentum in K-12 education (Carroll et al., 2009). In 2009, the Research in Education and Design lab (REDlab) was founded at Stanford University with the mission of performing research to identify the opportunities and challenges associated with bringing design thinking to K-12 education. In its early work, REDlab held a workshop on design thinking for elementary school teachers where teachers immediately recognized the differences between traditional classroom practices and design thinking pedagogy, and were excited by its transformative potential (Research in Education Design, 2016). Several design thinking challenges for schools ensued: one K-12 teacher created a challenge around the characters of the story *Cinderella*; a middle school teacher gave an Antarctica-inspired design challenge to her students; and one reading teacher discovered that, after several design challenges, some of her reading students improved one year in reading level in only a few months. These early experiments with design thinking propelled the REDlab team to continue exploring the role that design thinking might play in K-12 education.

Through a series of research and design projects, REDlab has worked with educators from every grade level nationwide to introduce them to design thinking. Beyond anecdotal reports of progress from both teachers and students, important questions remained about what students were really learning.

When students engage in design challenges, do they focus on only the surface-level details of design thinking practices or do they deeply understand the mindsets and pro-social purposes of design thinking? We do not see design thinking as an end in itself and we are interested in understanding what makes design thinking meaningful to students, beyond the fun activities and hands-on experiences involved in learning the process. Design thinking has appeal in K-12 education because of its potential to prepare students to tackle the urgent challenges of our ever-changing world. If design thinking is to be considered a viable school-based pedagogy, students should be aware of what they obtain from engaging the process and working with the mindsets, as well as be able to articulate these deeper connections. This paper reports on a study that investigates whether a design thinking-based curriculum on the topics of energy and environmental engineering supported this potential.

Why Design Thinking?

Design thinking is a method of engineering design used to identify new solutions and stimulate innovations around existing products, processes, communication, and structures that can meet the demands of our world. It is derived from a blending of engineering methodologies, social sciences, and the liberal arts (Buchanan, 1992). Design thinking takes on "wicked problems" that may be ill-defined and not conducive to conventional or incremental methods for solving problems (Rittel & Webber, 1973). In design thinking, tried and true solutions might be absent or outdated, and, in some cases, the problem space is constrained by seemingly insufficient resources (Cross, 2006). We research design thinking in K-12 education because we see possibilities for it to help students acquire 21st-century competencies and content knowledge, while also providing possible pathways to science, technology, engineering, and mathematics (STEM) careers. In addition to empathy, the "mindsets" of design thinking that might aid in introducing and engaging diverse K-12 students in STEM include its emphasis on teamwork, multi-modal communication, real-world problem-solving, and the development of can-do attitudes and creative confidence (Kelley & Kelley, 2013).

Learning design thinking comes with a shifting disposition to action and provides an assortment of avenues for engaging students with engineering tools and concepts, while offering them a view of the life-readiness skills that Estrada and Goldman discuss in this volume (see Chapter 3). The approach to design thinking that we implemented is characterized as a human-centered (or user-centered) method for design that relies on developing deep empathy with potential "users" as a pathway to uncovering new insights about an issue or challenge.[1]

Design thinking nurtures mindsets that are consistent with 21st-century competencies such as interdisciplinary collaboration, teamwork, and active prototyping with iteration. Design thinking can help young problem solvers shift from deeply ingrained yet limiting school methods such as completing creative work in isolation, privileging of predetermined correct answers, exposure to pre-selected dominant narratives, and the pursuit of decontextualized skills for solving problems in artificially siloed disciplines. These limiting pedagogical approaches do not align with the kind of thinking and work STEM professionals perform in their practices and can be replaced with more relevant dispositions and skills for tackling real-world problems.

Pathways to Engineering

The engineering fields are still grappling with persistent gender and diversity gaps, and many of the resources put in place to mitigate this disparity have been the purview of post-secondary engineering programs. Eliminating the gap through academics alone may not be enough. Encouraging entrance to these fields necessitates careful attention to the environment in our classrooms and workplaces (Sheppard et al., 2008). Educators increasingly recognize that K-12 education should play a role in preparing diverse students to enter engineering in ways that complement increased academic achievement in math and science classes, and they have been experimenting with offering earlier and more frequent interactions with engineering (NAENA, 2010). The hope is that these early experiences might introduce diverse students to engineering ideas, methods, and pathways.

Research shows that elementary school students possess very limited and stereotypical views toward engineers and engineering work. Capobianco et al. (2011) found that students conceive of engineers as mechanics, laborers, and technicians whose work entails fixing, building, or making and using vehicles, engines, and tools. Our team previously conducted a pre- and post-study of 83 middle school students' conceptions of engineers and design thinkers, and found that on the pre-test the same stereotypical conceptions of engineers prevailed. After a one-month design thinking course, students' perceptions of engineers as inventors, computer scientists, designers, and makers notably increased in comparison to their prior dominant perceptions of engineers as mechanics and laborers. Capobianco et al. (2011) suggest using the demands of national education standards to help widen students' conceptions of engineers. The Next Generation Science Standards (NGSS Lead States, 2013) specifically recommend the development of interdisciplinary curricula to help students engage in engineering and design activities and learn about engineering work, skills, and attributes. With problem-solving, creativity, and engineering design appearing in the latest standards, this work is becoming more feasible. Design thinking—with its combination of empathy, altruism, support for creative confidence, and focus on creating socially initiated change—may open a "third space" (Muller, 2003; Gutiérrez et al., 2003; Gutiérrez, 2008) for engineering, where the unique aspects of design thinking enable diverse visions of, attractions to, and transformative experiences with engineering.

This chapter reports on how students thought about design thinking after they completed a month-long design thinking curriculum integrated with energy and environmental engineering content. The analyses indicate that students demonstrated significant growth in their understanding of design thinking along three dimensions: the steps of the process, the language of design, and the key methods and mindsets. Although an elaborate discussion of the content-specific learning is beyond the scope of this paper, the students showed improved understanding related to energy access and conservation.

Methods

Curriculum Development

The REDlab team developed a month-long, two-hour-per-day curriculum in conjunction with undergraduate and graduate students at Stanford University taking a course entitled Educating Young STEM Thinkers. For six months, the university students engaged middle school students in weekly design thinking-based energy activities in an after-school setting. The curriculum emphasized energy as an entry point for introducing hallmark principles of environmental engineering and sustainability through the lens of design thinking. During development, proposed activities were deemed successful if they garnered interest from middle school students, were hands-on, facilitated inclusive relations among the group, demonstrated a facet of design thinking, or addressed an energy topic at a developmentally appropriate level. Those successful activities were then prototyped further in a one-week spring break camp with middle school students at an additional school site. REDlab team members and course students iteratively revised the most successful activities and included them in the final curriculum used in this study. The final curriculum presented environmental engineering principles through energy-centric material, focusing on different types of energy, drawing from theory (e.g., kinetic and potential energies), practical applications (e.g., solar power, hydroelectricity, geothermal power, etc.), sustainability, and design thinking. The materials included lesson plans for teachers as well as related media for students such as paper handouts, presentation slides, and video segments. Student activity in the unit was divided between learning and applying design thinking and exploring different sources of energy and their relations to the environment.

Curriculum Implementation

Four summer school teachers from one district implemented the curriculum in a summer school science course. In preparation, the teachers attended a four-hour training workshop that covered design thinking and a sample of energy activities from the curriculum, and they met regularly to plan and discuss the course.

They had access to the curriculum developers throughout the summer school session if they needed assistance, and the research team visited the classrooms weekly to address questions that emerged as the curriculum was being implemented.

Study Participants

The four teachers used our curriculum to teach 119 students in grades 6 through 8 who were enrolled in summer school. Enrolled students represented the diversity of the school district, in which approximately 19.2 percent identified as White Not Hispanic, 43.4 percent Hispanic or Latino, 23.8 percent Asian, 7.9 percent Filipino, 2.5 percent African American not Hispanic, and 3.2 percent as Other. Some students were required by the district to attend summer school, and others opted in as a summer enrichment opportunity.

Data and Analysis

Data Sources

A variety of data was collected during the summer school program, but the primary sources for this paper are the pre- and post-tests that were designed by the research team and administered by the summer school teachers. Both tests had the same four multi-step open-ended tasks and were designed to assess students' understandings of engineering content and design thinking. Student data were only included in the sample if the individual completed both the pre- and post-test during the summer school program. As such, the sample we analyzed consists of 101 students.

Developing Codes

Data were de-identified by assigning identifying numbers to individual test-takers. Responses were coded using an open-coding process (as described by Strauss & Corbin, 2008; Emerson et al., 2011). Initial codes were presented to the group by multiple coders; then codes were consolidated and revised with more precise definitions. The end result included more than 60 code families characterizing the form (legibility, types of representation, level of completeness, etc.) and content (accuracy, relevance, vocabulary, evaluative statements, descriptive statements, etc.) of student responses to each of the four assessment questions.

Inter-rater Reliability

Inter-rater reliability was established for all codes that were determined to be relevant to the analysis. The reliability subsample included 20 assessments and two coders coded each variable. According to Banerjee and colleagues (1999), Cohen's *kappa* values of 0.45 to 0.75 represent "fair to good reliability beyond chance," and *kappa* values above 0.75 represent excellent reliability beyond chance. All reported results meet at least the "fair to good" criterion and most would be rated "excellent."

Analysis

After inter-rater reliability was established for the subsample, all of the remaining tests were coded. The coding results were then analyzed using the quantitative method of specifically matched sample *t*-tests to compare the outcomes from pre- to post-test. The present work focuses specifically on two of the test questions that assessed students' understandings of design thinking. Additional qualitative approaches such as narrative and artifact analysis were used to further interpret the data from these two questions.

In the first question, students were shown a graphic representation that labeled the steps of the design thinking process—a diagram they had seen throughout summer school (see Figure 6.1). They were prompted to select two of the five steps and discuss the experiences that they had with the two steps during summer school. Note: on the pre-test, students were prompted to discuss any previous experience they had with these steps. While their prior knowledge of these steps was unlikely situated in design thinking, students were given the

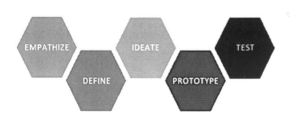

[2] Above is the design thinking process. Pick two steps and write about how you have done during summer school. Tell us a story about what you did and why for each.

Story 1: _____

_____

_____

Story 2: _____

_____

_____

FIGURE 6.1   Design thinking method post-test question

opportunity to show their thoughts about these terms based on their experiences in and out of school.

For this question, codes were applied to capture whether students demonstrated understanding of zero, one, or two design thinking steps. Responses were also coded in terms of which steps students explicitly or implicitly included. The design language used in the responses was tracked (e.g., "design," "designer," "design thinking," "user," etc.). Descriptive statistics for each code were calculated and interpreted to provide preliminary insights. Matched samples t-tests were used to determine whether there was a statistically significant mean difference between scores before and after the curriculum experience.

The second question was constructed to see if students could apply design thinking to a scenario in which they could help a specified user. In this case, the user was the owner of an amusement park, and the item asked students to imagine what they would do to help the owner address the issue of customers waiting in long lines for a roller coaster. The item read: "Imagine a story where you help him by using the design thinking process . . . describe the steps you took to help." The response space had blank lines for written responses and empty boxes for pictures or text.

For this question, codes were applied to capture whether students demonstrated explicit or implicit understanding of the design thinking steps. We also tracked the design language used in the responses. The drawn portions of the responses were coded in terms of seven characteristics describing how the pictures told a story. These included whether the pictures included people, depicted emotion, displayed tools or physical objects, presented a design thinking tool, conveyed humor, or presented personification. Descriptive statistics for each code were calculated and interpreted to provide preliminary insights. Next, matched samples t-tests were used to determine whether there was a statistically significant mean difference between students' scores before and after the curriculum experience. Narrative and artifact analysis methods were also applied to provide a multidimensional perspective of this multimodal task.

Results and Discussion

Students Learned the Steps of the Design Thinking Process

Analysis of the first question aimed to see if students indicated knowledge of the five design thinking steps—empathize, define, ideate, prototype, or test—by sharing a story about an experience using one of these steps. Responses were considered to reflect an understanding if they related a story that included or implied an accurate definition of a design thinking step. Students demonstrated accurate understanding of more steps in the design thinking process on the post-test ($M = 1.15$, $SD = 0.82$) than on the pre-test ($M = 0.19$, $SD = 0.55$). This change reflects a statistically significant mean increase of 0.96 steps,

$t(97) = 9.98$, $p < .001$, d = 1.38. On the pre-test, we observed 19 instances that conveyed an accurate understanding. On the post-test, we observed 162 instances of accurate understanding. In some cases, students conveyed understanding of more than one of the steps within a single answer, and, in other cases, students chose to leave one part of the item (eight students) or both parts of the item (one student) blank. Each of the eight students who only answered one part of the question were successful in demonstrating their understanding of at least one step in the design thinking process. Taking this into account, we are cautioned by the fact that although there was significant improvement from pre- to post-test, not all students were willing or able to tell a story about two different steps. Another limitation of these data is that the format for collection may have led to a ceiling effect. Some students may have understood more than two design thinking steps, but the full extent of their knowledge would not have been solicited within the task. Overall, our analyses illustrate that the students learned at least some of the design thinking steps; had the pre- and post-tests solicited information on all five design steps instead of the two queried, we may have been able to capture even more robust data on curriculum efficacy.

Students Demonstrated an Increased Yet Still Emergent Capacity to Engage With the Language of Design

On the first test question, we see a transformation in the way students use design language from pre- to post-test. On the pre-test, students discussed one of the design thinking steps 38 times, although the use of the word alone did not always indicate a conceptual understanding in the design sense. In fact, students applied the name of a design step to describe non-illustrative experiences 19 times. For example, in Figure 6.2, on the pre-test, Student 6 attempted to describe stories using the design thinking steps "define" and "test." This student used the school definition of "define" (i.e., to give the meaning of a vocabulary word) rather than using "define" in the design thinking sense of the word (i.e., using empathy to identify the root of a problem for a specific user). Student 6 also gave the traditional school-based definition of "test" (an assessment of knowledge in a classroom) and not the design thinking meaning of "test" (evaluating a prototype in the hands of a user). In addition to the 19 non-illustrative uses of the terms, 19 times on the pre-test students demonstrated understanding of design thinking steps based on their previous experiences. These correct responses most frequently described "prototyping" and "testing."

On the post-test, no students misused the term "test," and all students indicated a clear understanding of testing in the context of design thinking. For example, in Figure 6.3, Student 128 writes a story about testing that indicates their understanding of a design thinking "test" in the sense of a user evaluating a prototype by giving feedback.

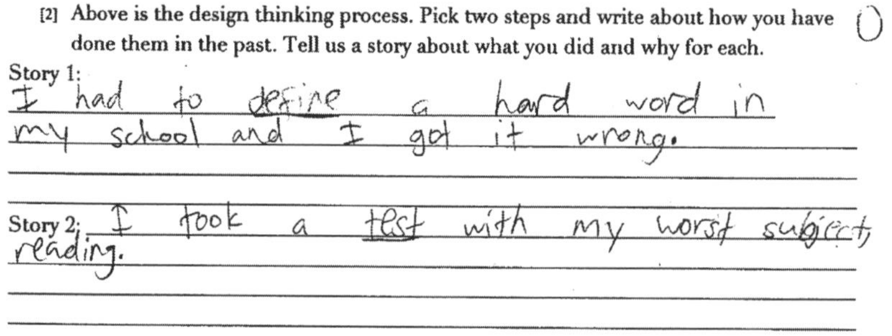

[2] Above is the design thinking process. Pick two steps and write about how you have done them in the past. Tell us a story about what you did and why for each.

Story 1:
I had to define a hard word in my school and I got it wrong.

Story 2: I took a test with my worst subject, reading.

FIGURE 6.2 Student response to pre-test question on design thinking method invoking traditional school-based definitions of "define" and "test"

While this clearly demonstrates a positive shift in how students employ the language of design, room for improvement remains in terms of the consistency with which students are learning these terms. On the post-test, students most frequently discussed the "prototype" step (57 instances). The other steps were discussed in comparatively similar frequencies to each other: "test" (32 instances), "define" (27 instances), "empathize" (26 instances), and "ideate" (20 instances). Our data are not sufficient to determine whether these differences in appropriation of language reflect conceptual understanding, interest, or increased vocabulary, but we can infer that students resonated strongly with prototyping and were significantly less inclined to explore ideation (or brainstorming) on their own terms.

The evidence of emergent uses of design language extends beyond the names of the steps. While neither the first question nor the second question of the tests directly prompted students to use design thinking language, both sets of responses contained evidence of the uptake of this language from pre-test to post-test. On the post-test, students more often included the following design terms in the first question in comparison to the pre-test: "needs statement"

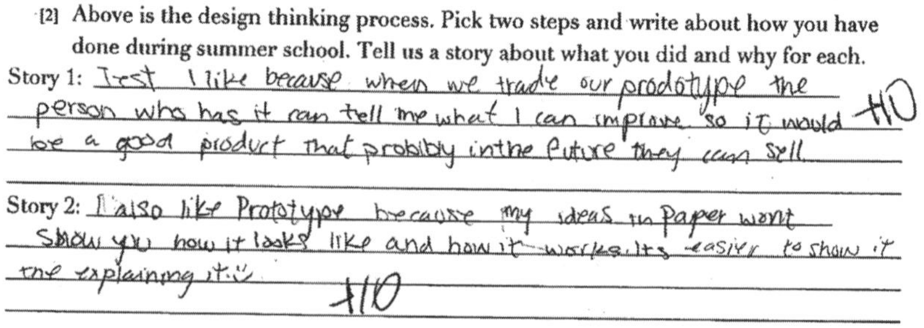

[2] Above is the design thinking process. Pick two steps and write about how you have done during summer school. Tell us a story about what you did and why for each.

Story 1: Test I like because when we trade our prodotype the person who has it can tell me what I can improve so it would be a good product that probibly in the future they can sell.

Story 2: I also like Prototype because my ideas in paper wont show you how it looks like and how it works. Its easier to show it the explaining it.

FIGURE 6.3 Response to post-test question on design thinking method demonstrating an understanding of "testing" in the design thinking sense (pretest-$M = 0.00$, $SD = 0.00$; post-$M = 0.05$, $SD = 0.22$; $t(96) = -2.28$, $p < .05$, $d = 0.33$), "user" (pretest-$M = 0.00$, $SD = 0.00$; post-$M = 0.07$, $SD = 0.26$; $t(96) = -2.73$, $p < .01$, $d = 0.39$), and variations of "design", including "designer" and "design thinking" (pretest-$M = 0.01$, $SD = 0.10$; post-$M = 0.07$, $SD = 0.26$; $t(97) = -2.16$, $p < .05$, $d = 0.32$). In Figure 6.4, Student 73 includes the design vocabulary "user" correctly in their discussion of the design thinking step "empathy." The user, in this sense, is the person for whom the students are designing a solution. This person is responsible for giving the students feedback on the prototype. As shown in the bottom portion of Figure 6.4, Student 102 utilizes both "user" and "needs statement" correctly in discussion of the "define" stage of the design thinking process. This student continued to include their "user" throughout both of their design thinking stories.

In the second question, students' responses were coded "0" if they did not explicitly mention a user as part of their problem-solving, and "1" if a user was explicitly mentioned. Students more frequently mentioned users in their text responses on the post-test ($M = 0.13$, $SD = 0.34$) than on the pre-test ($M = 0.02$, $SD = 0.14$), illustrating a statistically significant mean increase of 0.11 user-mentions ($SD = 0.35$), $t(99) = -3.19$, $p = 0.002$, $d = 0.78$. Some students relied on their own experiences as customers at amusement parks, while others tried to approach the problem from the perspective of a user. This latter group of students explicitly mentioned or illustrated interviews with the roller coaster owner and/or his customers as their starting points and as a way to evaluate the efficacy of their designs.

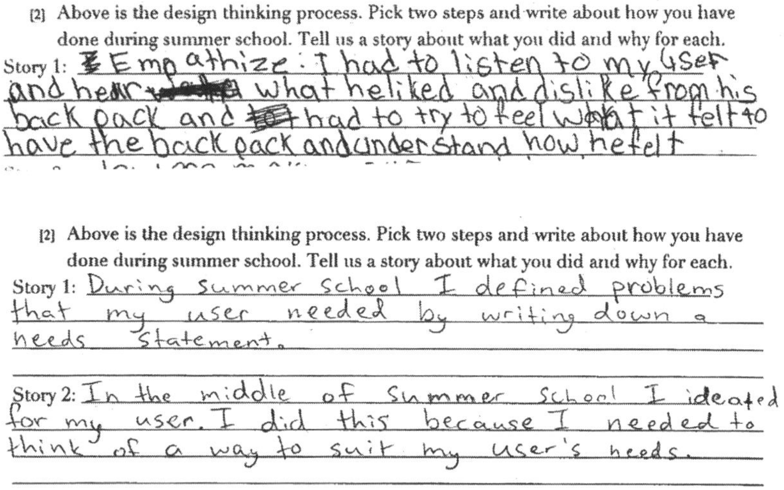

[2] Above is the design thinking process. Pick two steps and write about how you have done during summer school. Tell us a story about what you did and why for each.

Story 1: ~~ℰ~~ Emp athize. I had to listen to my user and hear ~~what~~ what he liked and dislike from his back pack and ~~ℰ~~ had to try to feel what it felt to have the back pack and understand how he felt

[2] Above is the design thinking process. Pick two steps and write about how you have done during summer school. Tell us a story about what you did and why for each.

Story 1: During summer school I defined problems that my user needed by writing down a needs statement.

Story 2: In the middle of summer school I ideated for my user. I did this because I needed to think of a way to suit my user's needs.

FIGURE 6.4   Two student responses on the design method, demonstrating understanding of design language such as "user" and "needs statement"

Naming the "user" is an integral part of the design thinking process. While a significantly higher number of students operationalized design language in this way on the post-test than on the pre-test, the post-test frequency remained relatively low (approximately 13 percent of responses). While there is evidence for an increased capacity of students to spontaneously engage with the language of design, this remains an emergent capability in need of additional scaffolding to positively impact a greater number of learners within the group.

Students Demonstrated an Increased Command of the Purposes and Mindsets of Design Thinking

Students' responses on the second item indicate that students did not merely learn accurate execution of the design process steps—they also illustrated understanding that design thinking can help them change the world in positive ways.

The Purposes of Design Thinking

One purpose of design thinking that students explored was that design work in and out of the classroom can positively impact the experiences of others. This emphasis on improving lives through design was most evident in the pictures students drew in response to the prompt. Students paid close attention to illustrating a change in experience for the user. Some students highlighted their imagined interactions with the roller coaster owner or his customers, while other students showed how users' engagement with the proposed solution led to a more desirable experience at the amusement park. These picture responses could be sorted into two categories: (1) design as a material intervention, and (2) design as a way of relating to people or helping people.

For the first category—design as a material intervention—responses were coded with a "1" if they included representations of tools, structures, or materials. Students more frequently drew new tools, structures, and materials as the means of problem-solving on the post-test ($M = 0.86$, $SD = 0.35$) than on the pre-test ($M = 0.48$, $SD = 0.50$), yielding a statistically significant mean increase of 0.39 ($SD = 0.58$) for drawings of tools, structures, and materials, $t(99) = 6.53$, $p < 0.001$, $d = 0.88$. We consider this category of response important because it highlights how students envision themselves as people who can shape our shared material world. The built environment and the tools we use matter; they help shape our political and economic structures, and influence how we interact with one another. When students depict designers (often, themselves) as people with the power to make a material difference, they illustrate understanding of the potential impact of design, and that they need not be passive recipients of material conditions and environments handed down to them by prior generations.

Figures 6.5 and 6.6 provide vivid examples of the ways that students were thinking about design as a means for impactful material interventions in the

FIGURE 6.5 Designing to solve the user's problem

world. In the panels on the left and the right, Student 102 drew a designer talking with the roller coaster owner. In the left panel, the designer is sympathizing with the roller coaster owner's frustrations, and in the right panel, the designer is presenting a prototype of a new roller coaster that the owner found satisfactory. In the middle panel, the student drew the designer working to create that prototype. The designer is depicted in goggles, suggesting the design thinking process step of experimentation through prototyping. This middle panel shows design as a transformation that has the potential to help someone in need.

In the left panel of Figure 6.6, Student 54 drew a personified sun that took pleasure in burning customers at the amusement park. The sun smiled as its heat set users on fire. The student's design intervention was a structure that thwarted the efforts of this sun by providing shade for people. The sheltered customers celebrated as a fan in the corner cooled them off. These two panels illustrate how the student conceived of design as the introduction of structures to improve people's experience.

For the second category—design as way to improve the lives of others by way of relating to people—responses were coded with a "1" if they included representations of people in their drawings and "0" if they did not. Students more frequently included people in their problem-solving stories on the post-test ($M = 0.75$, $SD = 0.44$) than on the pre-test ($M = 0.34$, $SD = 0.48$), with a

FIGURE 6.6 Building a structure to protect visitors from the sun

Student 56 highlighted the voice of the roller coaster owner (made female here), illustrating how the process is an opportunity to hear others. 	Student 130 drew himself listening closely to the roller coaster owner's frustrations with a smile, a thumbs-up, and a wink that communicated these frustrations had been heard and would be addressed. 	Student 126 depicted the owner of the roller coaster talking with a team of designers. All were engaged in a bouncing back and forth of ideas. 

FIGURE 6.7 Drawings by students depicting talking to users and listening to their needs

Student 96 described empathy as a process used "to help the people being cut in line." Design was presented as an opportunity to foster a sense of fairness. 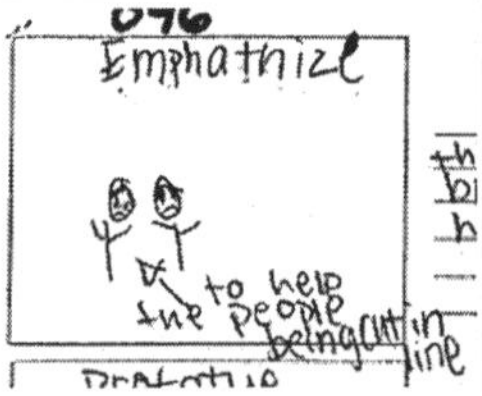	Student 118 focused on the safety of amusement park customers by drawing a seatbelt and chest protection device that ensured a sense of safety for the user. 	Student 130 depicted design as an opportunity to transform the amusement park by emphasizing the importance of having fun. 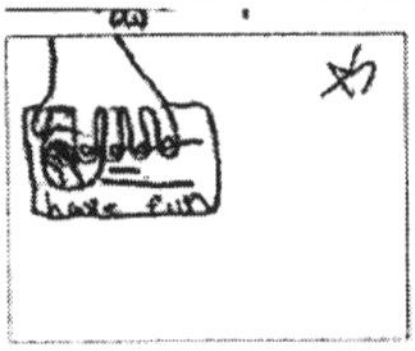

FIGURE 6.8 Students depict design solutions and interventions

statistically significant mean increase of 0.41 for relations to people $(SD = 0.55)$, $t(99) = 7.43$, $p < 0.001$, $d = 0.89$. Consideration of other people may seem like a basic element of all design projects, but, strikingly, only approximately one third of students' stories on the pre-test include people at all.

Such conceptions of design as a means of relating to people (Figure 6.7) and helping people (Figure 6.8) were featured in a myriad of variations in students' drawings. We see three examples depicted where students show interaction with the roller coaster owner. They are listening closely and, as a group, sharing ideas with the owner. These examples relay the students' growing sense of design as a way of relating to and helping others.

When students included other people in their design stories, they indicated an understanding that design is motivated by a desire to connect with others and improve their lives.

Key Mindsets

Key mindsets that develop with design thinking include responding with empathy, engaging teamwork, and building confidence that one can work towards and create solutions. The first key mindset that students explored in the curriculum was the idea that designers use empathy as a driver towards human-centered innovation. This mindset can be characterized by solutions that meet the needs of particular users. Since we were interested in how the human-centered aspects of design thinking would fare with students, we examined the question responses for implicit and explicit mentions of the relevance of empathy to the design process. In their responses to the amusement park test item, students demonstrated a range of storytelling strategies that suggested their increasing sense of centering design on empathy with users. Empathy toward the user was a key feature in students' storytelling that allowed us to distinguish between process knowledge (students understanding activities associated with each step of the design thinking process) and appreciation of the process as *user-centered* (students integrating user participation in their understanding of those steps of the process). We examined both the language and the drawings created by the students.

We defined a basic measure of user-centeredness as the degree to which students represented people in addition to themselves in their responses to the roller coaster test item. Responses were coded with a "1" if people were depicted and "0" if no people were included in the drawings. In the post-test responses, students more frequently drew pictures with people in them—people engaging with and often enjoying or benefitting from the proposed solutions. More students drew people in their design story on the post-test $(M = 0.83, SD = 0.38)$ than on the pre-test $(M = 0.52, SD = 1.17)$, with a statistically significant mean increase of 0.31 drawings of people $(SD = 1.19)$, $t(99) = 14.21$ $p = 0.010$, $d = 0.36$. In the post-test, some students even paid attention to illustrating changes in user attitudes about the amusement park with their drawings (e.g., drawing smiles on the users after the design solution's implementation). These changes suggest that students understood that design thinking is oriented toward human needs, and not the exploration of personally satisfying innovations or the advancement of decontextualized solutions that lack appropriate grounding and evidence.

Investigating written responses to this question more closely gave us further insight into the students' nature of concern for other people. Consider the contrasting responses given by three students below. All three began their responses by situating the human focus of their design activities.

Student 75 wrote, "I am waiting in line for a ride and it [is] taking forever. [T]he line is super long."

Student 80 wrote, "First, I would get to know what he wants, so I am empathizing with him."

Student 93 began, "First I would ask him questions about the problem. [T]hen I would find the overall problem of the problem."

Student 75 clearly expressed a nuanced understanding that the roller coaster challenge requires sensitivity to the customers' experience by imagining what it might be like at the amusement park. However, by using the personal pronoun "I" to describe that experience, the student is positioned and coded as the target of the design. In contrast, Students 80 and 93 integrated the third person pronoun "him" in their stories to refer to the roller coaster owner. Both students introduced an added level of sophistication to their understandings of the user-centeredness of the challenge. Student 80 intended to begin the process by finding out "what he wants," and this indicates an appreciation of going beyond hasty assumptions about the amusement park experience. Student 93's opening remarks suggested an even more careful consideration: that the role of the designer is to extrapolate and infer from their interactions with the user. These three responses convey an appreciation of empathy as (1) the sensitivity to the needs and experience of the user, (2) reaching beyond ready assumptions, and (3) interpreting user stories.

Empathy most often appeared when students approached need-finding (e.g., when students depicted interviewing users before brainstorming solutions) and testing (e.g., when students indicated talking to users to assess a proposed prototype's potential satisfaction of user needs). The stories of students who involved users in multiple design steps were coded as user-centered, as this indicated a pattern of attention to users. Students gave more user-centered responses on the post-test ($M = 0.34$, $SD = 0.26$) than on the pre-test ($M = 0.07$, $SD = 0.48$), reflecting a statistically significant mean increase of 0.27 for user-centered stories ($SD = 0.53$), $t(99) = 5.10$, $p < 0.001$, $d = 0.70$.

The second key mindset evidenced in student work is creative confidence. Students began to see themselves as people who can solve problems for others by creating solutions (Kelley & Kelley, 2013). On the post-test, students often described themselves as the designers directly responsible for helping the roller coaster owner and his customers. In fact, students more frequently referred to themselves as the designer on the post-test ($M = 0.44$, $SD = 0.50$) than on the pre-test ($M = 0.07$, $SD = 0.26$), a statistically significant mean increase of 0.37 for descriptions of the student as the designer ($SD = 0.51$), $t(99) = 7.32$, $p < 0.001$, $d = 0.93$. Students also communicated how the solutions they proposed directly related to an improved user experience. As described above, we witnessed a positive student attitude toward using design to improve the lives and experiences of others. Design thinking allowed students to see a new dimension of engineering, one that contrasted with the prevalent—and misleading—perception of engineering as strictly technical with limited social interest. Students who may not have originally identified with engineering had the opportunity to see it in a new light and as work that can positively transform people's lives.

Conclusion

Our research seeks to understand the role that design thinking could play for K-12 students, and this project interrogated the design learning demonstrated by students after a four-week design thinking course. Our analyses indicated that students demonstrated significant growth in their understanding of design thinking along three dimensions: understanding the steps of the process, the language of design, and the purposes and mindsets of design thinking. This research revealed that students made gains in their understanding of the design thinking process and how it might be applied to address real-world problems. They also represented design thinking as a process for interacting with people and positively affecting their lives. Finally, students demonstrated creative confidence as they described themselves as designers using empathy to solve problems. They placed interaction with users at the core of the design process, capturing the human-centered spirit of design thinking.

Based on these results, we are cautiously optimistic about the potential of design thinking in K-12 education because the curriculum supported students' abilities to confidently solve problems using the design thinking process, language, and mindsets. We are cautious because despite the significant improvement, there remains additional room for improvement both in terms of the level of mastery attained and the number of students reached.

Even with the limitations of a ceiling effect and a pre- and post-test design, we were able to capture a great deal of knowledge regarding students' learning process of design thinking. The results strongly suggest the feasibility of opening up middle school classrooms to design thinking pedagogy. Furthermore, the connections to authentic problems and to people in design thinking reflect the social implications of engineering work done by professionals. By approaching these problems while foregrounding empathy and creativity, students are exposed to a vivid new conceptualization of the engineering profession.

We believe that design thinking is a complex problem-solving method that takes time to cultivate. We see great advantage in introducing design thinking at the middle school level so that students can begin to develop the creative confidence, mindsets, and dispositions that the process engenders well before they approach college and careers. We also recognize that positive results such as the ones we have reported need to be replicated and extended in further studies. We are aware that the promise of engineering-related classroom experiences such as design thinking is part of a larger social and educational ecology, and that many pieces need to converge for there to be real educational change for which design thinking might be a resource. Still, the results here speak to the potential of design thinking curriculum for cultivating interest in students of far younger ages than previously expected, and that through these experiences, students are truly learning the processes and mindsets of problem-solving with the purpose of transforming the lives of those around them.

Acknowledgments

We would like to thank the teachers and students in the summer school program for participating in the design thinking summer school and in our research. We also thank Timothy Huang for helping us to code data. Maureen Carroll and Eng Seng Ng led the curriculum design with our staff and the Stanford students. Nancy Lobell was instrumental in making sure all went well at the school site. Megan Luce read a draft and gave us solid advice and direction. Stephanie Bachas-Daunert acknowledges support by the National Institutes of Health Ruth L. Kirschstein NRSA Diversity Predoctoral Fellowship Grant No. 5 F31 ES023293-03 and the National Science Foundation Graduate Research Fellowship Program (NSF GRFP). This work was supported by the National Science Foundation Grant No. 1029929. Any opinions, findings, conclusions, or recommendations expressed in this working paper do not necessarily reflect the views of the National Science Foundation.

Note

1 This version of design thinking is currently taught at Hasso Plattner Institute of Design (the d.school) at Stanford University. See d.school.stanford.edu.

References

Banerjee, M., Capozzoli, M., McSweeney, L., & Sinha, D. (1999). Beyond kappa: A review of interrater agreement measures. *Canadian Journal of Statistics, 27*(1), 3–23.
Buchanan, R. (1992). Wicked problems in design thinking. *Design Issues, 8*(2), 5–21.
Capobianco, B.M., Diefes-Dux, H.A., Mena, I., & Weller, J. (2011). What is an engineer? Implications of elementary school student conceptions for engineering education. *Journal of Engineering Education, 100*(2), 304–328.

Carroll, M., Goldman, S., Britos, L., Koh, J., & Royalty, A. (2009). Destination, imagination and the fires within: Design thinking in a middle school classroom. *International Journal of Art & Design Education, 21*(1), 37–53.

Cross, N. (2006). *Designerly ways of knowing*. London: Springer-Verlag.

Dewey, J. (1916). *Democracy and education*. New York, NY: Macmillan.

Emerson, R.M., Fretz, R.I., & Shaw, L.L. (2011). *Writing ethnographic fieldnotes* (2nd ed.). Chicago, IL: University of Chicago Press.

Gutiérrez, K.D., Baquedano-López, P., & Tejeda, C. (2003). Rethinking diversity: Hybridity and hybrid language practices in the third space. In S. Goodman, T. Lillis, J. Maybin, & N. Mercer (Eds.), *Language, literacy and education: A reader* (pp. 171–187). Trent: Trentham Books.

Gutiérrez, K.D. (2008). Developing a sociocritical literacy in the third space. *Reading Research Quarterly, 43*(2), 148–164.

Kelley, T., & Kelley, D. (2013). *Creative confidence: Unleashing the creative potential within us all*. New York, NY: Crown Business.

Muller, M.J. (2003). Participatory design: The third space in HCI. In J. Jacko & A. Sears (Eds.), *Handbook of HCI*. Mahwah, NJ: Erlbaum.

National Academy of Engineering of the National Academies (NAENA). (2010). *Grand challenges for engineering*. Retrieved from http://www.engineeringchallenges.org.

NGSS Lead States. (2013). *Next generation science standards: For states, by state*s. Washington, DC: The National Academies Press.

Research in Education Design (2016, February 22). Retrieved from: http://web.stanford.edu/group/redlab/cgi-bin/.

Rittel, H.W., & Webber, M.M. (1973). Dilemmas in a general theory of planning. *Policy Sciences, 4*(2), 155–169.

Sheppard, S.D., Macatangay, K., Colby, A., & Sullivan, W. (2008). *Educating engineers: Designing for the future of the field*. San Francisco, CA: Jossey-Bass.

Strauss, A., & Corbin, J.M. (2008). *Basics of qualitative research: Procedures and techniques for developing grounded theory* (3rd ed.). Thousand Oaks, CA: Sage.

7

ADAPTING THE USER-CENTERED DESIGN FRAMEWORK FOR K-12 EDUCATION

The Riverside School Case Study

Mohanram Gudipati and Kiran Bir Sethi

The founder of a chain of successful ethnic restaurants identified that children were underrepresented among his customers. To target this "missing" market segment directly, he engaged a group of consultants who:

- performed a market survey;
- observed and studied customer behavior;
- created a customized marketing campaign for the targeted demographic;
- developed a new recipe catering to the missing market segment's unique tastes;
- successfully increased sales to the target demographic.

None of this by itself is particularly unusual. What is notable, however, is that the "consultants" in this case were students from grade 7 who worked with the founder to make the restaurants more "child-friendly". The project required the students to step beyond their classroom and engage with the larger community. Having a clear goal in mind established relevance for the students, addressing a common question students ask, "Why do I need to learn this?"

As part of this project, students developed their observation and interpersonal skills; they understood key concepts in sales, marketing, and business studies; they learned data analysis; and learned about human behavior, healthy eating, nutrition, and how to work in teams. Perhaps equally important, they enjoyed learning and were completely engaged in the process. The effects of such engagements translate to exceptional academic performance. Riverside has consistently ranked among the top 10 schools in India in Math and Science in the ASSET test and among the top five international schools across India (Education World India, 2016).

Riverside School (http://www.schoolriverside.com) is a K-12 school with students from ages 3 through 18 and was founded in an attempt to first understand *how students learn* and then transform this insight into appropriate pedagogical and educational practices. We believe that education, at its foundation, must extend beyond "good test results" and needs to help students understand and engage with the world around them with compassion and confidence, and as citizens who add value to society.

Another key pillar of the Riverside approach to education is the recognition that most conventional education approaches do not offer students any choice in their learning, which often leads to disengagement and the development of an "I can't" mentality, where the student often feels powerless. At Riverside, recognizing that our primary user is the student, we consciously focus on instilling the "I CAN" mindset, where every child realizes that they are not helpless and they can make a difference (see the video "Riverside Citizens Leaders", talkingcloud.in, 2016).

Inculcated through a simple four-step design thinking process of Feel-Imagine-Do-Share (FIDS), the "I CAN" (or design thinking) mindset focuses on encouraging children to be more optimistic, collaborative, and human-centered. It gives them creative confidence and prepares them as global citizens to deal with uncertainty, to develop an open mind towards accepting multiple perspectives, and, to come to respect each other as equals by appreciating each one's unique strengths.

The first step of the framework, *Feel*, enables students to observe and understand the issue from the users' perspective, taking into consideration the local environment and context. The second step, *Imagine*, offers students a structured approach to collaboratively developing solutions to the challenges identified in the first step. The third step, *Do*, walks students through planning and executing their solution. Importantly, recognizing that the best solutions are often found through iteration, students are encouraged to reflect and revisit the Imagine and Do steps as needed. Finally, the fourth step, *Share*, encourages students to share the impact of their solution.

Classroom experiences are designed to get children excited about math, science, and literature, *and* to care about ethics, excellence, and engagement. The relevance of the classroom content and its application in the real world context is made visible to students. Through action-based projects, they are empowered to turn their awareness into action, which leads to transformation within them and the world around them. Thus, embedding design thinking in education has resulted in a curriculum that builds critical 21st-century skills and academic achievement in children.

We marry this 'user-centred' approach to education with cutting-edge research on child development. Learning rarely occurs without engagement and we consciously aim to ensure that all school processes and practices build towards this. To distill our experience over the last 15 years: the ingredients for nurturing an engaging learning environment are Relevance, Rigor, and Relationships.

Relevance

It is almost axiomatic to state that when an individual understands the relevance of what they are doing, they will be more engaged in the process: this applies across the board in any institution of human endeavor, be it the work place or a school. At Riverside, establishing relevance is foundational and critical throughout the process of pedagogy, starting from curriculum design to daily classroom practice.

Relevance is a key criterion for identifying the topics and concepts that are included for each grade's yearly plan. For higher grades, this often translates to involving the students in the curriculum design process itself. Some of the questions we ask towards determining relevance are:

- Is this topic appropriate given what we understand about a student's cognitive and emotional development?
- Does this align with/build upon what students have learnt so far and what they will learn in the future? Is this part of a larger narrative, or are we springing this on the students without any context?
- Can we make a persuasive case to students for the need to study this topic beyond the fact that their syllabus requires it?

Moving from planning the curriculum to classroom practice, each new topic or concept is invariably first introduced with a hook or learning experience that aims to establish relevance. In Key Stage 2 (grades 3–7), for instance, one of the key topics is the human body, within which we discuss the circulatory system, respiratory system, skeletal system, and so on. Most students are naturally curious about their body and relevance in this case is understanding more about themselves and the living world that surrounds them. We actively tie this into the importance of topics such as nutrition, exercise, diet, and sleep, and the development of metacognitive skills such as observation, reflection, and critical thinking.

As we go a level deeper, the teachers design multiple activities that first establish the importance of the system. For instance, when the skeletal system is introduced, students are challenged with hands-on activities such as making a tent stay erect without tent poles, packaging/scaffolding eggs from a height so that they do not break upon landing, and so on. This hook or activity establishes the importance of a skeletal system (exoskeleton and endoskeleton). The process also demonstrates to the students how important the skeletal system is for form, shape, and function.

Finally, in terms of daily practice, relevance is again established at the beginning of the day (where the class discusses the agenda for the day) and during the session or at the start of each new topic. To ensure that these critical practices are not lost during the tumult of a busy school day, we have designed a structured board

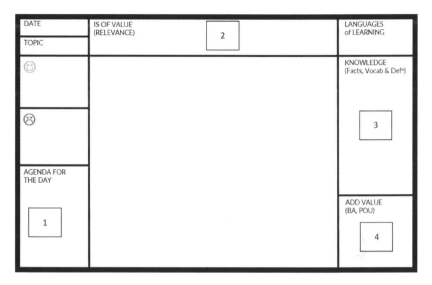

FIGURE 7.1   Structured board protocol for setting agenda and checking progress during a session

protocol aimed at ensuring that these elements are addressed during the session (no. 1 and no. 2 in Figure 7.1). The blackboard in each classroom is designed so that essential elements of effective pedagogical practice—that is, establishing relevance, ensuring rigor and developing and maintaining relationships—are front and center during each and every session.

Rigor

Rigor is critical to ensuring that students retain what they have learned and can call upon appropriate content and concepts as needed, either while learning new concepts or while applying pre-existing concepts to new ideas. The process of rigor, however, varies depending on the student age and topic under discussion.

Note-taking is a key component of rigor, as are student reflections, checkpoints (mid-point assessments while the topic is being taught), and end-of-day consolidation (where students write down the key concepts they have learnt through the day). Another process is bridge-activity (which can be, but is not necessarily, homework), where students are assigned challenges or tasks they need to attempt or complete before the next session on the topic.

Finally, students are also required to demonstrate their understanding of key concepts and content, typically at the end of a unit, through Performance of Understanding (PoU). A PoU for a topic like the skeletal system could be a model or chart with labels, or a skit staged by a group of students (again including all the necessary content and concepts). The key idea here is that students are encouraged to demonstrate their understanding of the concept in multiple ways, with one of the few requirements being that their PoU explicitly includes key content and concepts. Another key requirement of a PoU is for students to demonstrate the application of their understanding of one concept in another area. For instance, in the case of the skeletomuscular system, students could choose to demonstrate their understanding of different joints and associated musculature by mapping them to key ideas in simple machines (or vice versa).

Students also have to demonstrate their understanding through processes such as Making Learning Visible (MLV) or Funderstanding, where they have to present and explain what they have learned to their peers and parents. Such peer and public scrutiny (see the video on "Peer and Public Scrutiny" in TeacherEd, 2014b) ensures that parents are aware of how their child is learning while the student develops critical life skills such as communication and, specifically, speaking in public.

Relationships

Children typically spend more than one-third of their waking hours in schools. Positive relationships between students and their peers or between students and their teachers are essential for engagement and learning. More importantly, strong and positive relationships are essential for the development of emotionally competent students who are compassionate, respectful, confident, and independent. Studies (Klem & Connell, 2004; den Brok et al., 2004) have established the dramatic impact a student's relationship with their peers and teachers has on their academic, personal, and professional outcomes. The school has developed processes that directly address this while allowing us to consciously make space for relationships in the daily timetable. These include processes such as congloms (see video "Congloms I—Timetabling for Relationships" in TeacherEd, 2014a), buddy interactions (see video "Buddy Interaction" in TeacherEd, 2015), and bubble time, all of which are explicitly designed to ensure that students develop positive relationships with their peers and teachers.

Perhaps not as explicitly obvious as the processes mentioned above, programs—such as Artist in Residence (Sethi, 2014), Coffee at Riverside, Citizenship—that aim to build character and to build non-academic (but arguably more critical) life skills, dually require and ensure that students establish strong relationships. The key insight underlying the development and implementation of these processes is an acknowledgement that:

- Every student has a talent and passion that must be identified and allowed to flourish.
- A student's competences go far beyond mere academic performance, and it is the responsibility of the school to help students identify their strengths.

- We must offer each student multiple opportunities to showcase and develop their interests and strengths.
- Positive spotlight and opportunities enable a child to feel more confident, which in turn directly impacts their learning and, perhaps not surprisingly, improves their academic performance.

All the processes developed at Riverside are designed to enable teachers and students to identify and acknowledge a student's contributions to the school culture and classroom activities, leading to the scenario surplus process. Scenario surplus is a conscious, deliberate, timetabled acknowledgement of the idea that one has a responsibility to add a surplus to a place, not draw down from it. Needless to say, while the ideas of relevance, rigor, and relationships have been described individually, every school process integrates these three ideas. This approach extends to the school's interactions with parents. Indeed, our parent community is one of the strongest advocates of the "Riverside Philosophy" since they have seen first-hand the remarkable transformation that such an approach creates in children.

Creating and sustaining a strong learning environment requires intensive planning and organization. Acknowledging that a teacher needs to invest a significant amount of time and thought toward planning sessions and activities that are rooted in relevance, rigor, and relationships, the school sets aside two Saturdays every month to enable planning for the month's sessions. This is in addition to a planning period of roughly three weeks at the beginning and end of each academic year.

Finally, a strong professional development program is part of each teacher's weekly schedule. A user-centered design approach cannot be successfully implemented if the academic and non-academic staff are not aligned with the school's philosophy. Indeed, the professional development programs themselves are developed to keep the teacher (the user) at the center of the design process. Professional development at Riverside is therefore not limited to pedagogy but extends into leadership training and personal development, including stress management, as well as mental and physical health. At an institutional level, this translates to an acknowledgement that the professional development process itself has to be regularly revisited by the school leaders and updated to meet the needs of the school and its staff (academic and non-academic) as the school expands and the profile of the students and society changes. Professional development at the school leverages extensive, ongoing documentation of our processes which enables experienced teachers to reflect and improve current processes while allowing new teachers to quickly come up to speed.

Weekly professional development sessions where key concepts and pedagogical practices are introduced and reinforced serve to update the teachers and allow the school to keep pace with new insights that are either generated internally through our experience or from research and observation of student learning and teacher practice elsewhere. Professional development is embedded in a teacher's day at Riverside. For instance, a key component of PD is peer mentoring, which consists of multiple processes, including:

- Teacher observations: A teacher's practice in a class is observed by another teacher, who observes and provides feedback on what went well and what could be improved.
- Weekly group meetings: Teachers from each Key Stage (KS)—KS1: pre-K to grade 2, KS2: grade 3 to grade 7; KS3: grade 8 to grade 12)—meet on a weekly basis to share observations and insights. This also provides an opportunity to identify areas of collaboration, both inside and outside the classroom.
- Mentoring: New teachers are assigned a mentor teacher who acts as a single point of contact and offers the new teacher professional, emotional, and psychological support.
- Personal projects: Each teacher embarks on a personal project, in which the teacher identifies an issue that is important to their classroom or practice, attempts systematic interventions, and then documents the outcome. This allows teachers to add value back to the school community by becoming valuable resources who can offer insights on key challenges that other teachers may encounter in their practice.

While it can be argued that such an intensive, design-centric approach cannot be replicated or adapted everywhere, our experience with the "Design for Change" (DFC; http://www.dfcworld.com/) movement across 32 countries, involving more than 200,000 students, indicates otherwise. DFC uses the same FIDS framework that has been used by the school to develop our processes. The FIDS framework has been used by children in over 32 countries to lead more than 10,000 stories of change (these stories of change can be found at http://dfcworld.com/stories.aspx). Through the four-step framework of Feel, Imagine, Do, and Share (FIDS), students participating in DFC are taught to implement a user-centered design framework that enables them to identify and solve challenges they identify as most important.

The framework equips children with the tools to be more aware of and informed about the world around them, to believe in and realize the importance of their role in shaping that world, and to take action toward building a more desirable future. The framework redefines failure as prototyping and gives students the confidence to be innovative and to find creative solutions for problems that directly affect them. Teachers get a chance to discover and acknowledge the capabilities of their own children as they listen to their students' voices and ideas.

Teachers share that facilitating DFC projects helps them to discover the strengths of their students, to develop faith in student capabilities, and to get to know what the children think and feel about the world around them. The success of the DFC project is based on teacher participation—and most teachers go back with a stronger sense of belief in their own capacity to make positive change in the world and their roles as teachers. Given the rapid pace at which our world is changing and the constant technological innovation that is transforming how people live, work, and play it seems obvious that students equipped with a "problem-solving" approach—design thinking—will thrive.

The approach developed by the Riverside school can be implemented in any education setting. As part of its outreach, the Riverside Learning Center (RLC) has partnered with many schools who have successfully adopted the school's curriculum. RLC offers multiple professional development programs to schools, school leaders, and educators through intensive on-site training and immersion. Programs can include a school adopting the entire Riverside curriculum, whereby they receive training and extensive documentation including templates, videos, and unit plans. For schools that want to adapt the culture of Riverside, we train teachers and leaders in understanding and implementing our processes. We are now in the process of developing a hybrid blended (online and offline) platform that will allow us to further scale our impact. In Riverside's experience working with schools across the socio-economic and geographic spectrum, the challenge is not access to resources or infrastructure; rather, the challenge is in shifting the perspective of school leaders, teachers, parents, and the larger community.

References

den Brok, P., Brekelmans, M., & Wubbels, T. (2004). Interpersonal teacher behaviour and student outcomes. *School Effectiveness and School Improvement, 15*(3–4), 407–442.

Education World India. (2016). Top School Rankings 2015: Top 5 International Schools. Retrieved from http://www.educationworld.in/rank-school/2015/.

Klem, A.M., & Connell, J.P. (2004). Relationships matter: Linking teacher support to student engagement and achievement. *Journal of School Health, 74*, 262–273.

talkingcloud.in. (2016, January 22). Riverside citizen leaders [Video file]. Retrieved from https://www.youtube.com/watch?v=OgtvRlpUZZU.

Sethi, K. (2014, February 19). *Making of . . . 'I believe I can—Artist in residence 2014* [Video file]. Retrieved from https://www.youtube.com/watch?v=yUh9tK0Sp7w.

TeacherEd. (2014a, September 25). *Conglom: Timetabling for relationships* [Video file]. Retrieved from https://vimeo.com/107136262.

TeacherEd. (2014b, September 25). *Peer and public scrutiny* [Video file]. Retrieved from https://vimeo.com/107136260.

TeacherEd. (2015). *Buddy interaction* [Video file]. Retrieved from https://vimeo.com/139434736.

PART III

Design Thinking as a Catalyst for Reimagining Education

8

BUILD IT IN FROM THE START

A New School's Journey to Embrace Design Thinking

Susie Wise

When a group of intrepid parent-educators first began to think about writing a charter for a new public Montessori school in the city of Oakland, California I was exhilarated. We were all educators in some form or another, but none of us had discovered Montessori until we were parents of preschoolers. As our kids prepared to enter the K-12 system we asked ourselves why Montessori was not an option, and from an equity perspective we thought the model could bring together a wide range of families, some of whom were not being well served with traditional public school offerings. We were drawn to the way the approach allowed for multi-age classrooms, self-paced learning, and support for the growth of the whole child, attending to his or her physical, intellectual, social, and emotional development. We quickly learned that there were many examples of public Montessori, particularly in the Midwest, in addition to several in California, and we sought to follow their lead to create a public Montessori option for families in Oakland.

As I participated in the first few team meetings of those who would quickly form the design team and write the charter, I began to realize that we had an opportunity to do something unique. I started to wonder and then finally braved sharing with the group that I thought perhaps we could powerfully combine Montessori with design thinking. I loved the idea of starting a school from scratch, while also building on the 100-plus year old tradition of Maria Montessori. Because Montessori emphasizes using the tools of our time, it seemed a great set up for combining the old and the new, in a child-centered, asset-based pedagogy.

The school we built is called Urban Montessori Charter School. It opened in 2012 as a K-2 school and will grow to a 600-student, TK (Transitional Kindergarten)-8 school by 2018. It brings together Maria Montessori's pedagogy with design thinking and arts integration processes. The core values of our school are: (1) we embrace our common humanity to build our school community; (2) we notice + care, work together + create, and share + reflect. Underpinning these core values is a strong equity agenda and a belief that all children can become creative innovators and powerful contributors to our city's future.

From the start we were very conscious that we did not want to create an "everything, but the kitchen sink" Frankenstein school model. In crafting the charter we did a rigorous analysis of the essential elements of Montessori curriculum and the process and mindsets of design thinking to ensure that bringing them together was mutually beneficial and would create a rich learning context for children and their families. We found several important connections that bring together Montessori and design thinking. On a global level the child-centered aspect of Montessori combines nicely with design thinking practitioners' goal to help all learners build their creative confidence and know they can change the world. Both Montessori and design thinking practices are grounded in learning to learn independently, each with a guiding process that a child learns to follow and master over time. The emphasis on solving real-world challenges in design thinking and peaceful change making in Montessori also dovetail nicely. Finally Montessori's focus on "grace and courtesy" offers a lovely grounding for young designers as they learn to empathize, synthesize, and prototype in a human-centered way within their school and the broader community.

Design Thinking at Urban Montessori

We did several things to make sure the design thinking piece of our model would grow roots and thrive. The first thing we did was to create our own terms for the design thinking process and we built them into our school's core values (see Figure 8.1). These values engage our children and our community in the creative process. We chose simple and approachable, but powerful words, to represent the process so that it could become a language that we all speak in the classroom, and among teachers and parents. In this way we encourage all parents and caregivers to be a part of the creative process where and whenever it makes sense to them. Below are the words we use with a brief description of what they mean at school.

Notice + Care

The root of notice and care is empathy. Noticing is the first thing children work on. For example, what they notice is or is not working in their classroom, on the play yard, or the way to school. Once they've identified a need, caring means deciding what to focus on, inferring underlying issues, and deciding how they can make a difference. Children learn how to observe, listen, ask questions,

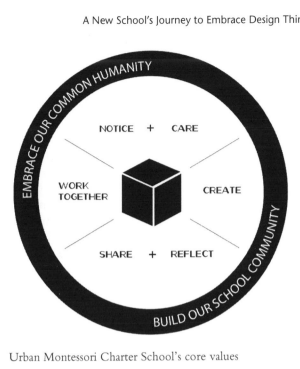

FIGURE 8.1 Urban Montessori Charter School's core values

interview, take notes, make inferences, identify needs, and generate problem and opportunity statements. At school this work can be tied tightly to the curriculum, aimed at building classroom culture, or about the school as a whole.

Work Together + Create

Children work together to learn from each other and the school helps them learn to accept and build upon the ideas of others. We recognize that to come up with a good idea, you need to generate many different solutions so students learn that brainstorming, sketching, and exchanging ideas are all different ways to work together. Children also learn how building prototypes can help them create, modify, and continually develop different solutions to challenges.

Share + Reflect

Throughout the creative process students share their thinking and their work and receive feedback from peers and teachers. They reflect on what they hear, and then use the feedback to further develop their work. Children learn the value of iteration and editing and they learn to communicate what and how they are learning. The most important lesson is to share your ideas and creations early on in order to get feedback.

Design Thinking in the Classroom

In our first three years as a school we have experimented with two primary approaches to exploring design thinking in the classroom. We have had children focus in narrowly on the meaning and experience of each of the key design thinking modes and we have led full-cycle design challenges. In the first approach the teachers divided up the year and took a month to delve deeply into Notice, Care, Work Together, Create, Share, and Reflect. For example, for "notice," which happened at the beginning of the year, the teachers focused the children on using all their senses to look closely at things in their environment. In several classrooms they did a deep exploration of a flower and all of its parts. In other classrooms children investigated different varieties of apples to build a taste chart as a representation of their discoveries. Working in this way, the students were able to try out some of the identified modes in the school's design thinking process flow (see Figure 8.2).

In the second approach, our classroom-based design challenges were the opportunities for students to put the different modes together and experience the creative agency of the full design process. Usually the staff chose the topic, and while the topic was school-wide, there was plenty of room for variation in each classroom. Examples of challenges have included:

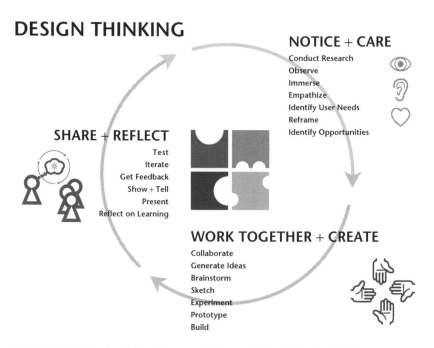

FIGURE 8.2 Modes in Urban Montessori Charter School's design thinking process flow

- How might we create a signature snack for our classroom?
- How might we ready our classroom for a new pet? (Or, how might we improve our current pet's living situation?)
- How might we redesign our classroom's library? (Or, how might we take more responsibility for the books in our room?)

In one case a teacher took the classroom pet topic above and gave it a literary twist to create a challenge: How might we help Stuart Little (the character from the book of the same name by E.B. White) move around our classroom?

These full-cycle design challenges laid the foundation in the school to accomplish more deeply integrated design thinking work across the curriculum. By the end of year three the teachers were ready to create their own curriculum. They have now built design challenges into the upper elementary program in social studies, biology, literature, and the change-maker curriculum. These continue alongside classroom-community focused challenges like: How might we improve our community meetings? Or, how might we redesign the birthday circle?

As the students move from design challenge to design challenge across the curriculum they deepen their understanding of design thinking as a process and begin to embody the competencies we think are important as part of our school community (see Figure 8.3). For example, younger students might work on the garden challenge "How might we help our plants grow?" in which they learn

DESIGN THINKING

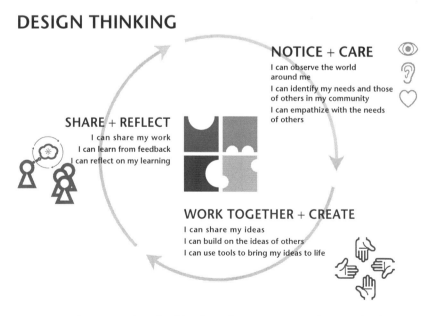

FIGURE 8.3 Competencies valued by the Urban Montessori Charter School community

about what plants need to grow and try out several ways of collecting water or protecting plants from their natural predators. Older children can engage the same challenge, but move to the wider community level to think about mapping resources across the city, investigating food deserts, and potentially starting a business to sell schoolyard produce. In this way the children experience the design process as one that they can return to again and again. They have a process to use at school (and beyond!) when faced with challenges for which there is not an obvious or existing solution.

You may be thinking, "Gosh, these sound like project-based learning projects that I'd expect to see in an elementary classroom or projects that I've heard of in other schools—where's the innovation here?" If you are thinking that, yes, you are right: design challenges are generally examples of project-based learning. What design thinking adds is a consistent scaffold for both teachers and students to use to explore curricular content or community topics. As one teacher put it, design thinking serves as "the final click in the Rubik's Cube of project-based learning." Teachers and students both benefit from the process learning that comes from moving from notice + care, to work together + create, and then to share + reflect. The underlying mindsets—from using empathy to define what you are working on and then prototyping to test if you are on the right track—teach everyone a repeatable process for innovation that is not necessarily found in other approaches to project-based learning. Finally, design thinking

FIGURE 8.4 Parents and caregivers at Urban Montessori are introduced to the design thinking process to help them take action and work across difference

challenges are also differentiated by their emphasis on coming up with solutions that solve real problems in the community. In this way, whether working on the challenge of "making our cafeteria time more peaceful" or "how might we improve our classroom library," children are working to make a positive contribution in their world and becoming change-makers in their community.

Underlying all the work to spiral design thinking throughout the Urban Montessori program is a desire to develop young innovators in Oakland. This is our equity agenda—that all children, not just some children, will know themselves as creative and use their creative confidence to lead in their community. We know we cannot engage all our children if we do not engage their families. We are using design thinking across the parent community because we believe that the grounding in empathy (notice + care) and the bias toward action (work together + create) will give families from diverse situations opportunities to work across difference. We engage families in design thinking challenges just like we do for the children. We have found that parents and caregivers are not usually asked to collaborate in these ways and they find it both intriguing and powerful to come together and learn a new process that helps them take action (see Figure 8.4).

Our effort to use design thinking is linked to our work to hold tenaciously to the equity lens with which the school was founded. Our work, which is always in progress, is to return to the practices of design thinking. When we ground ourselves in notice + care, work together + create, share + reflect, we can continually build a more responsive and inclusive learning community. Visit us in Oakland if you want to see where we are on the journey!

9

RESPONSIVEDESIGN

Scaling Out to Transform Educational Systems, Structures, and Cultures

Ralph A. Córdova, Ann Taylor, Phyllis Balcerzak, Michelle P. Whitacre, and Jeffery Hudson

A Day in the Life: A Glimpse Into Innovative Professional Learning

It's September 2015, 6 am, and the halls of River Bluffs High School (RBHS) are quiet as English teacher, Jeff Hudson, pushes open his classroom door and begins to set tables with agendas, materials, and video equipment for the morning's InnoLab meeting.

The InnoLab meeting is running an "Inquiring into My Practice" (IMP) session that morning. By 6:30 am, Tim Young, the IMP's lead teacher, and a member of the Department of Mathematics, arrives. Jeff will act as Tim's "Thinking Partner." The first component of an IMP is a pre-brief conversation between the lead teacher and the Thinking Partner, in a process of intentional collaborating designed to both make visible and clarify the lead teacher's thinking around the piece of practice to be the focus of inquiry. Colleagues from diverse disciplines arrive, and soon the classroom is filled. In front of their colleagues, Jeff begins by asking Tim what he wants to **explore** both in terms of content and pedagogy, how he **envisions** the sequence of the lesson unfolding, and what he hopes participants take away once the lesson is **enacted**. The lesson Tim envisions will support colleagues in rounds of noticing, wondering, and predicting as we look at already solved Algebra equations.

With the prebrief over, Tim leads his lesson, one rich in language emerging and appropriated from his regular participation in InnoLab sessions. He carefully guides teachers, just as he would his students: many colleagues exhibit insecurity about their mathematical abilities, as they move through rounds of noticing and describing solved Algebra problems.

Later that day, Jeff overhears Amanda teaching her journalism class, across the hall from his office. He recognizes the sequence and even the language of Tim's algebra IMP in Amanda's journalism instruction. By design, what happens in InnoLab does *not* stay in InnoLab. Amanda is guiding her students to read like writers. Students notice bylines, headlines, quotations, and photographs, concise paragraphs with the who, what, when, and so on. She is transforming a lesson about persistence and language in mathematics into a new form, which addresses language use in her journalism students.

When Amanda describes her class to Jeff, "You have to know what just happened," she said. "I've had the hardest time getting my students to write in a more journalistic style. They always want to write these horribly long paragraphs . . . Anyway, I used Tim's IMP to get them looking at pieces of journalism, to notice elements of style and to predict what they might see in other pieces."

This chapter complements our colleague's perspectives in this volume by focusing on work we are doing with students in K-12 settings. We recognized that if design-based approaches are important for our K-12 students, then it matters that our teachers and administrators also have access to the same powerful, creative ways of exploring, envisioning, and enacting in their everyday practices. At River Bluffs High School, the InnoLab emerged as a grassroots, instructional response to the copious data on students' performance that was inundating teachers without any guidance for how to actually improve teaching practices. Twice a month teachers from across the disciplines and grade levels meet in Hudson's room to participate in an Inquiry into My Practice or IMP. The IMP allows teachers regular opportunities to intentionally collaborate, instruct, and critically reflect. The InnoLab at River Bluffs has been making the argument, and collecting data to show that the way to grow in our expertise as educators is through the collective designing and prototyping processes of the InnoLab. The other important facet involves educators crafting prototypes of practice birthed in their classrooms and exporting them across classroom cultural boundaries, with a theoretically sound methodology, allowing it to be revised, translated to a new setting, and thus taken to scale.

The Roots of and Routes to Our Work

The authors of this chapter are founding members of Cultural Landscapes Collaboratory (CoLab) and most are also from the University of Missouri St. Louis, a large public research institution in the Midwest and leaders within the ED Collabitat, our college of education's response to the need for an intentional collaborative space for professional creativity. One author is a K-12 school educator. Other CoLab members are from K-12 schools, the University of California Santa Barbara, the University of Helsinki, and numerous National

Writing Project sites. We are all educators who ground our scholarly work in an Interactional Ethnographic Perspective (Green et al., 2002; Santa Barbara Classroom Discourse Group, 1995). The CoLab is an interdisciplinary nexus where complementary theories from anthropology (Gumperz, 1986; Spradley, 1980), critical discourse analysis (Fairclough, 1992), and literary theory (Bakhtin, 1986) intersect with principles from art and design.

In this chapter we make visible how we are taking to scale our theory of inquiry and innovation, ResponsiveDesign, in both pre-service and in-service settings. In our work in places like River Bluffs High School, we are harnessing the creative potential that links the field of art and design with perspectives from the learning sciences. The challenge we set for ourselves, and the one we report on here, is to understand how that process works, or in other words, methodologizing (Córdova et al., 2012) how to work collectively toward solutions at scale to revolutionize the systems, structures, and cultures of education (Córdova et al., 2015). In this chapter, we offer our approach and learning over the last decade as a contribution from the perspective of a state college of education. The examples we share of our design and innovations work fall into two groups: (1) scaling out an educator preparation model graduating over 300 teacher candidates each year; and (2) seeding half a dozen InnoLabs in local schools, which impact the learning of several hundred teachers and their thousands of students across our bi-state region.

We name our process ResponsiveDesign (see Figure 9.1). ResponsiveDesign places educators at the center of their professional learning by casting them as prototypers of practice. Through iterative and intentional processes of exploring, envisioning, and enacting, ResponsiveDesign becomes a shared theory of inquiry and innovation, and shared language to study, innovate, and improve practice.

On the left side of Figure 9.1 we represent the interacting relationship among several existing theoretical traditions, all of which feature elements of design.

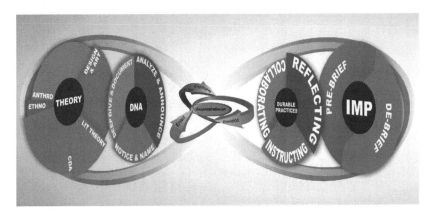

FIGURE 9.1 The ResponsiveDesign process

When we scan across the epistemological and methodological approaches of these traditions—of anthropology, ethnography, art and design, critical discourse analysis, and literary theory—we see a pattern: each tradition uses particular approaches established within their respective fields. We take their salient epistemological and methodological features to construct what we call ResponsiveDesign's DNA: *Deep-Dive & Document, Notice & Name, and Analyze & Announce*. Responsive Design thus becomes a way to translate our theoretical approaches into the sphere of classroom practice by harnessing, reflecting, collaborating, and instructing in the form of the IMP. In this way, the sphere of classroom practice (represented on the right side of Figure 9.1), where the teacher has most control, is informed by theoretical approaches, and the theoretical approaches then are informed by classroom practice, all through the prism of ResponsiveDesign.

Methodological Orientation of Our Work

In order to make visible the levels of resolution involved in scaling out our work, we construct two telling cases, which Mitchell (1984, p. 222) argues is a form of ethnographic inquiry that focuses on particular chains of human activity and events in order to make theoretical inferences. A telling case is a particular kind of case study that makes visible something that may not have been previously known. Our Interactional Ethnographic Perspective illuminates through the telling cases how ResponsiveDesign is shaping professional learning within our educator preparation program and in-service settings, as well as in larger systemic work within educational settings.

In telling case 1, we present an analysis of the ways in which ResponsiveDesign and the three durable practices are being taken to scale in educator preparation within our Studio Schools model. Building on the first case, in telling case 2 we examine the scaling out of our approach in the form of the InnoLabs within the in-service context of a mid-size school district.

Telling Case 1: Scaling Out in Educator Preparation

UMSL offers a new model of teacher education driven by these questions: What is the journey of growth that educators would need to experience in order to complete their studies as innovators confidently able to impact their students' learning? How do we design an intentional curricular journey, rich with theory and research, yet grounded in practical experiences? How can we best ensure that the professionals who emerge fully understand how their own growth, practices, and language are critical to unlocking the potential of their students and who know how to approach their careers in a way that leads them relentlessly forward to become expert educators?

At UMSL this journey moves through three phases, beginning as candidates learn their craft by moving from a stance of *investigating* the broader view of their personal and educational landscape and understanding how to *influence* student learning. In the second phase, candidates learn to *imagine* how to *ignite* learning for all students, using high leverage strategies in inclusive community agency settings and research-based practices in school-based clinics. Finally, candidates *innovate* to impact their students' learning as they collaboratively explore, envision, and enact possibilities for learning in their year-long school practicum.

The structural innovations that support this model include: a new required introductory course; early clinical experience working with youth and adolescents in local urban community agencies rather than passive classroom observations in schools; more integrated special education knowledge and/or focus on English Language Learners; a standards-based developmental assessment system for candidates to document their growth, and for faculty to analyze and report on candidates' growth; and a final year-long practicum in one of 45 partnering "Studio Schools," replacing the age-old semester of student teaching alone in a school.

More specifically, Studio Schools provide a differentiated staffing model where pre-service candidates can be used in flexible ways to meet student needs, as they work in multiple classrooms engaging with several teachers and groups of students during their year-long practicum. In this model, educator candidates are viewed as full staff members in the school and get to experience intentionally designed, realistic, and meaningful interactions to learn in and from practice.

While the model components are important for our educator preparation program, and the structures, systems, and culture within it are critical for the integrity of the program (see Córdova et al., 2015), the story we want to focus on here is how we built out one part of this model over a three-year period, and how that tells us about something previously unknown about the methodology of scaling out a complex system that is an educator preparation program. In our program, ResponsiveDesign undergirds the ways in which educator candidates approach, enter, and practice within their practical experiences in Studio Schools. Additionally, every candidate learns the Inquiry into My Practice (IMP) approach to develop three durable practices. The IMP protocol is a robust and powerful learning tool, tested by practicing teachers and in methods courses for a number of years. As heard in Jeff's story at the start of this chapter, this is the same three-question protocol used by experienced teachers in several InnoLabs in our area. In the IMP, the teacher works closely with a thinking partner who helps guide his or her thinking. During the prebrief, the IMPer describes what he or she wants to explore during the lesson, how he or she envisions the lesson unfolding, and what learners should take away from the lesson. After the lesson is taught, the debrief revisits these same questions in light of the enacted lesson, giving the teacher an opportunity to reflect on his or her instruction. Our intention in using this model was for candidates to learn to build the three durable practices that will sustain them throughout their career. These three durable practices are learning to intentionally collaborate, learning to intentionally instruct in academic practices, and learning to intentionally reflect.

In our first prototype of using this protocol in our educator preparation program, in spring 2013, we introduced the IMP in a foreign language methods course to a subset of Studio School candidates who were also in their Practicum I, and then supported these candidates through both practicums in the field with a clinical educator (student teaching supervisor) who also knew the model. We found that the results were startling in terms of the high-quality conversations and understandings of teaching practice and student learning that emerged (see Córdova et al., 2015). These were documented through video in our web-based partnership with the Teachingchannel.org, which we used as a platform for teacher candidates and faculty to bridge the IMP process learned in the university seminars with candidates' work at their school sites. Before moving on to describe the repeated prototyping around program design, we will look at a snapshot of the rich learnings generated by teacher candidates and faculty interacting when guided by the IMP protocols.

A Snapshot of Practice: The IMP in Action Within Pre-Service Education

We present an analysis of the kind of candidates that our seminar afforded them to become by examining the work of Jake as a representative sample. In doing so, this telling case makes visible the ways in which candidates harnessed the IMP to collaboratively develop and observe each other using Teaching Channel, and collaborate to learn to teach.

As a capstone experience, each teacher candidate prepared an IMP which was enacted and recorded in their practicum and uploaded to Teaching Channel.

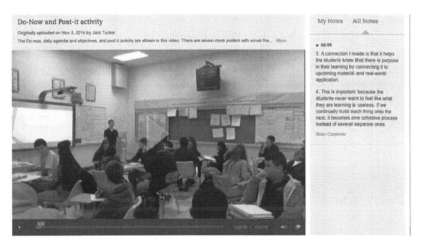

FIGURE 9.2 View of Jake's activity on Teaching Channel

The final assignment involved teacher candidates triangulating 3 data sources from their enacted IMP (described in detail in telling case one): a video record of the lesson, student work, and their lesson plan. Figure 9.2 is a screenshot of Jake's work from Teaching Channel. Jake's video recording of his IMP focused on teaching high school students commands and directions in Spanish.

Jake uses the IMP protocol to explore in his Spanish lesson how he envisions it unfolding, and what he wants the students to walk away with once enacted. Jake's text reads:

What is the IMP's Overall Lesson Context?

The lesson that I taught was for a block period that lasted about 90 minutes, so I'll just upload the PreBrief, DeBrief, and video clips from the main parts. Feel free to watch all of them, but the most interesting parts were the Post-it activity and football field activity. The group map activity is mostly just students working.

Explore: What is the content and pedagogy you set out to explore?

The content that I wanted to explore with my students was giving, receiving, and mapping directions in Spanish. Vocabulary was introduced with visuals and pronunciation practice before students applied the vocab to TL maps in a small group activity. A speaking and listening group activity was also part of the lesson.

Envision: How do you envision the lesson unfolding (beginning, middle, and end)?

1. Beginning—Do-Now question that asks students about the skills they would need when traveling in another country. This led to a discussion and explanation of the daily agenda and objectives. Then I introduced the vocabulary words *para, camina, derecho, izquierda* with a Post-it Note activity that asked students to predict the meaning of words based on visuals, which was followed by modeling of pronunciation and guiding the teacher around the classroom.
2. Middle—Map activity in which small groups followed written directions on a map from the target culture. We first practiced together on a map of the school neighborhood before each group used a map of a Chilean city. Students then wrote their own Spanish directions using the map.
3. End—Football field activity. A blindfolded student is guided along a yarn path with only verbal directions from group members. Students were given directions in the classroom before moving outside to practice for 5 to 10 minutes. Finally, groups took turns "racing" against each other along the yarn paths before we debriefed to review the daily objectives.

Enact: When you enact it, what did you want your students to know? What did you want to learn from this experience?

Students will be able to identify Spanish vocab in written and spoken directions, as well as apply the vocab to a map and giving verbal directions.

This experience helped me learn how students benefit from interacting with the language in multiple ways. While it was a little exhausting after 5 Spanish II classes of about 26 students, all but a few students were engaged in both navigating the map and directing a partner on the football field. I have plenty of room for improvement when redirecting a class during transitions.

In Jake's writing, we see how he took the IMP process as a conceptual base for planning for and enacting instruction. He makes visible the content of the lesson (giving and receiving directions in Spanish) and the group activities as pedagogical meaning-making processes. Further, when Jake articulates how he envisions his IMP will unfold, he engages in a process of making present something that is not yet reality, thus exercising the ability to imagine a future learning experience. Last, when he articulates that he wants his students to identify Spanish vocabulary in spoken and written directions, he identifies the salient practices he wants his students to be able to do.

The IMP process enabled Jake to make his thinking visible across three audiences: himself, his colleagues, and his professors. As such, teacher knowledge of practice—often occurring in isolation and inaccessible to others—becomes a resource for professional learning for Jake and his colleagues. Insights from the learning sciences provide evidence for this as Ericsson states, "self-explanations have been found to change (actually, improve) participants' comprehension, memory, and learning" (2006, p. 228). Because Jake and his colleagues had learned the IMP process as a shared way to live out how to collaborate, instruct, and reflect, the Teaching Channel became a mechanism for extending their emergent practices. The Teaching Channel became a space where candidates took knowledge first formulated (Vygotsky, 1987) and co-constructed in the physical settings of the seminars, allowing them to be later reformulated and appropriated within a digital medium. Here we see collaborating, instructing, and reflecting as Jake transports them to a new setting, manifesting them within his local teaching context.

Barry, a fellow teacher candidate, played the role of the Thinking Partner and responded to Jake's IMP overview in the dialogue box within the Teaching Channel:

A connection I made is that it helps the students know that there is purpose in their learning by connecting it to upcoming material and real-world application.

This is important because the students never want to feel like what they are learning is useless. If we continually build each thing onto the next, it becomes one cohesive process instead of several separate ones.

Upon closer look at Barry's comments to Jake, he makes visible three aspects he witnessed in Jake's post. The first concerns making a rationale explicit to students so that they know there "is a purpose in learning." The second involves Barry articulating two trajectories in how the lesson connects to "upcoming material" and "real-world application." The third is seen by Barry as he names the disjointed nature of school learning for many students, and he identifies how Jake is showing him and others how to construct cohesive learning experiences, "if we continually build each thing onto the next." The principled ways in which Jake and Barry interacted around a shared video record, and their derived insights, were made possible because they participated in the university seminars which afforded them a structured way to learn those very practices.

In addition to receiving feedback from their peers, faculty also viewed and responded to the video record. Here, we see Jake's professor, Ralph, respond:

"Para, para! Derecha! Para!" [Stop, stop! Right! Stop!]

Students give directions . . . you say "Spanish only" (in English).

Question: What sort of message do you implicitly send when you break into English when the goal is to practice the target language?

Ralph's feedback pertains to the need to use the target language more often if Jake is to nurture fluent Spanish speakers. Ralph also asks Jake to consider the implicit messages instructors send to their students about the value of the learning they experience. Teaching Channel became a way for the instructor to observe his students enact lessons they developed in his course, thus making a tighter connection between university and school settings.

Faculty continued their design work on the structures and practices of the Studio School, prototyping to produce a cascade of innovations. We introduced an on-campus seminar for all 60 secondary candidates. Candidates and faculty had previously been siloed into five different teaching seminar courses and now came into one monthly space to collectively learn to understand themselves as professionals. This shift necessitated our next prototype as we introduced the IMP to all 60 secondary candidates in this larger setting, rather than just individual faculty introducing it to select candidates. Thus, Córdova and Taylor shared the practice with 60 candidates through a carefully unfurling sequence of sessions as a way to further deepen their understanding of three durable practices (see Córdova et al., 2015).

By the 2014–2015 academic year, with 220 candidates from all programs, the Seminar had grown into a three-part Grand Seminar. The initial part of the seminar began in a theater-style auditorium with a session led by Córdova and Taylor; the middle section provided ten different breakout sessions for candidates to choose a topic of interest, and then the seminar ended with another collective session in the auditorium. In this third prototype, the IMP was used in every opening session, as a way to introduce a particular teaching insight or idea (noticing, triangulating data, etc.). At this point, we also asked that all of the 25 Clinical Educators use the same IMP protocol with candidates, whom they supervised at their school sites, mirroring the small-scale test we had run with our foreign language secondary candidates.

In spring 2015, we completed a pilot case study to explore the impact of the variability of the clinical educators' understanding of the IMP and the three durable practices on the experience of our candidates. The study drew on analyses from 11 interviews with two clinical educators and nine candidates from two different Studio Schools where each clinical educator used a different level of intensity in their enactment of the IMP. We discovered a direct relationship between candidates' understanding and participation in reflecting, collaborating, and instructing, and their clinical educator's understanding of how IMPing develops these practices. The clinical educator who encouraged their candidates to use the IMP process were preparing candidates whose language indicated a deeper knowledge of collaboration, reflection, and academic practices than those who did not encourage the IMP process. We recognized that this variability between clinical educators was generated and or sustained by the structure we had set up that located a clinical educator's duties only at the school site. This meant that they often did not attend the ten monthly Grand Seminars on campus, where critical components of the program were introduced and refined for all candidates.

Our new knowledge and other data led us to change the system of supervision for the 2015 school year. Instead of 25 adjunct professors, we now have 9 clinical educators working 75 percent time, at higher pay, supervising 330 candidates. Their job structure was changed, requiring three and a half days a week on site supervision, which enabled them to be responsible for 25–35 candidates on four to five school sites, visiting each school building for a full day every other week. This clustering of Studio Schools increased the consistency of instruction of the IMP. We also built in clinical educators' collaboration in the Grand Seminar in three ways. First they would attend the whole group instruction at the beginning, second they would participate as co-creators by leading breakout sessions they had designed and developed, and third, each of them would meet with their full Gallery of candidates for an hour.

We also continued to work intentionally on refining the ways in which candidates, clinical educators, and the Director of Clinical Experience interacted, to intentionally build the culture we were envisioning, in schools and on campus. We now required seminars in school, renamed Collaborative Exchanges, at which the IMPs were used to enact lessons, formally or informally. Our Clinical

Director also prioritized visiting the new team of nine clinical educators to ensure that they were supported in introducing the IMP practice to candidates.

Within this sphere of educator preparation, we see a particular phenomenon of how candidates get better together involving harnessing ResponsiveDesign to develop prototypes of practice. Thus, we see candidates exporting what they learn into their diverse classroom and school settings. This scaling out we are methodologizing in our Studio Schools also applies to the story of how we the teacher-researchers have innovated our way to our current iteration of our educator preparation program.

Telling Case 2: Scaling Out in InnoLabs

We have learned a great deal from scaling out ResponsiveDesign with the context of educator preparation a trajectory-building springboard for future educators. But what happens within the context of practicing educators within in-service settings, particularly struggling schools? The scaled out and mature InnoLab in River Bluffs HS, the story we opened our chapter with, has been in the making for four years now. In this second telling case, we examine the seeding of our InnoLab process within a new setting, a struggling school district with a high percentage of students from homes designated as at or below the poverty level (Northside District, pseudonym). This district, with the loss of its state accreditation in 2013, has been in a constant state of urgency to increase performance of its 3,500 students. In addition to the lost accreditation, the district lost a large student population when the Missouri Supreme Court ruled that students who live within the district could choose to attend a school in an accredited school district instead. Funds were low, morale was lower, and the district began a journey to turn itself around.

In the summer of 2015, with a new school board and under the leadership of its second superintendent in two years, the district initiated a number of changes, structural and procedural, that were intended to improve teaching and learning within the system. Most of these were centered on introducing new instructional programs in literacy and math along with the introduction of professional learning communities in which teachers learned new ways to use student assessment data to make instructional decisions. One of the changes, and the subject of our paper, was the intentional integration of an InnoLab into each of the seven schools in the district, which focused on improving instructional strategies.

The InnoLab, as a structure and process, has a number of constant features that would complement the instructional initiatives underway at Northside School District. First, its solid grounding in empathy creates a space in which teachers can reflect on instruction, without judgment. Indeed, that is the first feature they notice and point to during every initial experience with the InnoLab. Second, it supports a message that they as teachers are the responsible agent in designing the instructional plan for their students. They utilize the district-provided resources but need to help their students make sense of the scripted materials. Implicitly, the process encourages teacher agency by foregrounding the things that teachers do through intentional academic practices that are often left out of the narrative when we talk about our practice to each other. These nuances, seemingly small shifts and moves, are often the difference between a lesson design and student learning.

At Northside, for example, one elementary school had a desire to build a culture of collaboration within each individual grade level, so they implemented grade-level InnoLabs during their Professional Learning Community (PLC) time. The instructional coach used student data to build a series of IMPs constructed around the district-level learning standards for integrating literacy throughout the teachers' content instruction. The coach modeled these lessons to teachers in an InnoLab, in which together they noticed the parts of the lesson in which they learned the desired skills and the parts of her instruction that increased the effectiveness of the lesson.

By IMPing with a thinking partner in front of other empathic teachers, professional creativity is captured and the experience of practicing teachers becomes visible and accessible to other practitioners. In another setting in Northside, seven teachers in the middle school resonated with the process as a way to incorporate more social justice content into their English Language Arts classes. They began to IMP with each other as a way of sharing existing practices and expanding their repertoire of strategies to enter discourse with students around issues of social justice.

In addition to the constant features of each IMP and InnoLab, which are identified by us as the functional unit, there are a number of ways that InnoLabs can be adjusted and modified to fit the needs of individual schools and/or districts. In another school, the principal had a need for teachers in a single grade level to gain competence in applying literacy skills to their science instruction, so they initiated the InnoLab within their fifth grade science teams. In the kindergarten center the principal saw the InnoLab as a way to encourage productive conversation among her faculty about noticing individual students' needs. Each of these variations of the basic InnoLab represents a path of expansion that we view as scaling out, satisfying the criteria of increasing the impact of the prototype as in a "scale-up," while addressing relevant concerns of each site between and within a district and school.

The value of retaining faithfulness to a process while allowing the content to flex can be seen in the continuity of discourse among those who participate in InnoLabs across the country. Teachers as members of a coherent profession begin to reclaim their professional identities as they engage with others in a common language about teaching and student learning. They "notice," they "wonder what would happen if," and they begin to assemble a culture of building on each other's work rather than critiquing what has been implemented to solve isolated problems. When InnoLabs are firmly in place, data on student performance begins to hinge as much on what teachers do in their classrooms as it does on the instructional materials purchased by the district. This change from the culture of isolation to one of collaboration is especially important at Northside, where morale was registering an all-time low and where teachers, especially those with valuable experience, were closing their doors and working alone.

Concluding Discussion: ResponsiveDesign Methodologizes How to "Scale Out"

ResponsiveDesign is a methodology that enables educators to develop prototypes that work at low resolution. ResponsiveDesign is also flexible enough be "scaled out" across a broad assortment of situations with similar goals of improving student learning. Each prototype in its new site is refined and perfected to achieve maximum cultural effectiveness for that setting. When it transfers or re-seeds in a new location it reverts to a low-resolution prototype, poised for more scaling out.

Our approach contradicts the notion of "implementing with fidelity" by beginning with the assumption that the unique qualities of each site add essential pieces to the innovation and cannot be ignored when transferring knowledge and skills to a new site. This changes the notion of fidelity from being faithful to a product we disseminate without change to being faithful to the process that led to the effective impact of a product at the pilot site. We interpret fidelity as faithfulness to a process that is capable of generating highly effective instruction at the new sites. The question is not "are the teachers implementing the lesson in its original form?" but rather, "are teachers implementing the processes shown to generate creative, flexible instruction that is responsive to their students' lived experience?"

The human and design-centric theories that root ResponsiveDesign insist upon a particular shared language and set of practices as evidenced in the IMP and InnoLab that have the power, when scaled out, to transform systems, structures, and cultures.

References

Bakhtin, M.M. (1986). The problem of speech genres. In C. Emerson & M. Holmquist (Eds.), *Speech genres and other late essays* (pp. 60–102). (V.W. McGee, Trans.). Austin, TX: University of Texas Press.

Córdova, R.A. (2008). Writing and painting our lives into being: School, home, and the larger community as transformative spaces for learning. *Language Arts, 86*(1), 18–27.

Córdova, R.A., Kumpulainen, K., & Hudson, J. (2012). Nurturing creativity and professional learning for 21st century education: ResponsiveDesign and the cultural landscapes collaboratory. *Learning Landscapes, 6*(1), 155–178.

Córdova, R.A., Taylor, A., Whitacre, M., Singer, N., Cummings, K., & Koscielski, S. (2015). Three durable practices for approaching video as a reflective tool: From siloed to connected cultures in educator preparation. In E. Ortielb, L.E. Shanahan, & M.B. McVee (Eds.), *Video research in disciplinary literacies* (Online ed., Vol. 6, pp. 167–188). Bingley: Emerald.

Ericsson, A.K. (2006). Protocol analysis and expert thought: Concurrent verbalizations of thinking during experts' performance on representative tasks. In A.K. Ericsson, N. Charness, P.J. Feltovich, & R.R. Hoffman (Eds.), *Cambridge handbook of expertise and expert performance* (pp. 223–242). Cambridge: Cambridge University Press.

Fairclough, N. (1992). Intertextuality in critical discourse analysis. *Linguistics and Education, 4*(3–4), 269–293.

Green, J., Dixon, C., & Zaharlick, A. (2002). Ethnography as a logic of inquiry. In J. Flood, D. Lapp, & J. Squire (Eds.), *Handbook of research on teaching English language arts* (pp. 201–224). Mahwah, NJ: Erlbaum.

Gumperz, J.J., & Cook-Gumperz, J. (1986). Interactional sociolinguistics in the study of schooling. In J. Cook-Gumperz (Ed.), *The social construction of literacy* (pp. 45–68). New York: Cambridge University Press.

Mitchell, C. (1984). Typicality and the case study. In R.F. Ellens (Ed.), *Ethnographic research: A guide to general conduct* (pp. 238–241). New York: Academic.

Santa Barbara Classroom Discourse Group. (1995). Two languages, one community: An examination of educational opportunities. In R. Macias & R. Garcia (Eds.), *Changing schools for changing students: An anthology of research on language minorities, schools and society* (pp. 63–106). Santa Barbara, CA: U.C. Linguistic Minority Research Institute.

Spradley, J.P. (1980). *Participant observation.* New York: Holt, Rinehart, and Winston.

Vygotsky, L. (1987). *Thinking and speech.* (N. Minick, Trans.). In R.W. Rieber & A.S. Carton (Eds.), *The collected works of L. S. Vygotsky: Vol. 1. Problems of general psychology* (pp. 37–285). New York: Plenum Press.

10

TEACHERS AS DESIGNERS OF CONTEXT-ADAPTIVE LEARNING EXPERIENCE

Zanette Johnson

Introduction

Why Does Context Matter?

Rapidly growing cultural and language diversity is altering the future of U.S. schools. The work of teachers is made ever more complex by the flood of new technologies for learning and of new domains of knowledge that teachers must master to serve students well (Goodwin, 2010; Goodwin & Kosnik, 2013). Teacher educators are faced with the challenge of how to prepare today's newly minted teachers for the contexts they will likely encounter over the span of their careers. These diverse contexts are shaped by globalization, political instability, technological innovation, climate shift and migration—and teachers are the primary agents who frame and orchestrate the models of knowledge that children encounter in school.

By 2044, the United States is projected to be a majority-minority nation (Colby & Ortman, 2015). Teacher education cannot ignore the shifts in dynamics this is already bringing about for teachers and students. In places like Hawai'i, where learners' lives are layered thickly with generations of indigenous, settler and immigrant narratives, a majority of the population experiences a hybridized multiculturalism and multilingualism. Hawai'i teachers are called upon to actively and skillfully navigate the multiple worldviews that intersect in local contexts for learning. The respectful pluralism that many Hawai'i teachers have sought to practice forecasts the kinds of solutions that teachers across America will be seeking as the U.S. population under age 18 reaches the "majority-minority" benchmark in 2020.

An American Educational Research Association survey of teacher educators in 2011[1] identified the three most critical areas of teacher preparation:

1. selection of candidates able to work with students of diverse backgrounds and learning preferences;
2. design of teacher preparation to help teachers in a variety of contexts and conditions;
3. how to enable teachers to contextualize and enact teaching practices in a variety of contexts.

All three critical issues converge around context. Whether teacher preparation is examined from a demographic perspective a student advocacy perspective, or a teacher educator perspective, the need for professional preparation and strategies to help teachers become context-adaptive is clear.

What Is Context-Adaptive Teaching?

Context-adaptive[2] teaching considers students' lives, heritage languages, economic circumstances, and cultural repertoires of practice, and the overall ecology from which students grow. Information about the learner is incorporated into practice so that "content" or knowledge to be mastered is not independent of the knower (Freire, 2000; Barab & Duffy, 2000). Teachers who are practicing context-adaptiveness endeavor to learn deeply about learner needs and capacities, observe student responses to learning experiences, and then iteratively adjust instruction in light of the local community needs and globally recognized learning objectives.

Context-adaptive teaching compels teachers to go "beyond subject or instructional strategy to examine learners' needs as nested within multiple socio-cultural-economic-political locations. The teaching methods calls upon teachers to understand and respect the strengths of the students and communities that they work with, and to build upon the existing assets within communities however they can" (Trumbull et al., 2015). Context-adaptive teaching strategies encourage teachers to cultivate the following:

- openness to learning from own setting students;
- reflection upon own practice;
- persisting through initial disequilibrium;
- active interrogation of own weaknesses;
- active challenging of own theories, conceptions, and models;
- analysis of student learning data;
- identification of own growth edges;
- willingness to apprentice themselves to the learning ecology and its members;
- iterative experimentation and 'tinkering';
- attention to discrepancies between expected patterns and realities;
- vigilance in discerning features that are relevant in the learning context;
- seeking of experiences that intervene in the pattern of didactic education;
- embracing of experiences/cycles of failure.

Many paths lead toward similar practices and mindsets; context-adaptiveness is an emerging paradigm for teaching and learning. In fact, all of the following approaches could be considered as aligned with context-adaptive teaching: place-based learning (Gruenewald & Smith, 2014; Gruenewald, 2003; Smith, 2002), culturally sustaining/revitalizing pedagogy (Paris, 2012; McCarty & Lee, 2014), deeper learning (Darling-Hammond et al., 2015), CREDE's five standards for effective pedagogy (Doherty et al., 2003), culture-based education (Kanaʻiaupuni et al., 2010; Castagno & Brayboy, 2008), and so on. Educational researchers know many strategies that encourage context-adaptive teaching, yet they go by myriad names and are rarely seen to have anything in common.

Teachers must have their own active skill set to respond to the changing needs and dynamics that may shift profoundly from learner to learner, class to class, year to year, and school to school. Goodwin describes the challenge for teachers as follows: "no single program, no matter how extensive or comprehensive can possibly prepare each fledgling teacher for every situation that might arise in the classroom" (2010, p. 23). The Hawaiʻi teachers who participated in this study were in a teacher education program created to encourage context-adaptive teaching at unique schools that were:

- based on relationships with people;
- influenced by the physical place and locally valued knowledge;
- transdisciplinary, i.e., not divided by conventional disciplinary categories;
- building cognitive apprenticeship to support learning;
- using concrete experiences as the basis for abstraction;
- practicing problem-solving in context-rich rather than decontextualized scenarios;
- employing multiple assessment streams;
- using iterative methods that respond to changing conditions;
- constructing routines to direct attention and reflection;
- signaling flexible group norms (Johnson, 2013).

Design process was introduced to this group of teachers as an additional strategy—to see what roles it might play among those already practicing context-adaptive methods, and who were able to adopt it freely and fluently in their school contexts.

Why Design Process?

Design process—"design," "designerly ways of knowing," and "design thinking"—offers a tangible, repeatable process that can introduce teachers at any point in their career to a method for becoming context-adaptive that can be learned and shared across the school or professional learning community.

I emphasize design as "process" rather than "thinking" because it is active and, by definition, demands ongoing solution building and actual testing of ideas in the world. To date, design process has been applied primarily to engineering and product development; lately it has also been applied to solving persistent social challenges at scale (Banerjee, 2008). In recent years, design process has been introduced in many schools as a tool for young learners—often as a complement to maker spaces, hands-on STEM curriculum, project-based learning, or other inquiry methods. Design itself is transdisciplinary and while local/transnational lenses shape its practice, it may be applied in any domain or project. At a 2012 Vancouver exhibit of works by the lauded First Nations Kwakwaka'wakw artist Kesu' Doug Cranmer, his words were written in silver above the door: "Design is the key to everything. If you learn how to do design you can do anything."

Typical design process models vary (see Dubberly, 2004), but at their most basic they show problem-solving as a process carried through stages that may be followed in a linear or cyclic fashion or deployed selectively, moving back and forth through many cycles of implementation.

From robotics competitions to solar car races, student use of design process is seen as an exciting plus for schools, but the focus is solidly on *student* use of design. Far less attention has been paid to the ways that teachers use design process to advance their professional practice and enhance student learning, yet it makes sense to involve teachers in the same processes we've come to see as valuable for students (for other examples see the chapters in this volume by Guha et al., Mitchell & Esmann, Goldman et al., and Kwek).

To teach design process, it is essential to have deep experience and flexibility with the design thinking method. Those who facilitate design learning must steadfastly negotiate their own fears as they lead others into the disequilibrium, uncertainty and radical reframing that reliably occur when designing. Schools that focus on delivering design process only to students are missing an opportunity to build a rich foundation of design mindsets and expertise among the teachers who guide them. Design process may also help educators identify the assets of their learning community as affordances, and to work generatively with student needs.

Methods

This study was part of a larger four-year ethnographic study spanning two cohorts of a teacher education program that offered licensure to in-service teachers. Study participants were recruited through the teacher education program; all 32 participants were in the process of fulfilling requirements for a state license. Teacher placements spanned the duration of two full school years, and by the end of the program, teacher candidates had complete independent teaching responsibilities. This structure of preparation gave ample opportunity for observation of teacher candidates in roles that both pre-service and in-service teachers play. Data was gathered through a variety of methods, including individual interviews with teacher candidates and their colleagues, focus groups, analysis of reflective journal writings, video of teacher conversations, examination of artifacts produced by students and teacher candidates, clinical observations of teaching, and "critical event" logs in which teacher candidates documented the

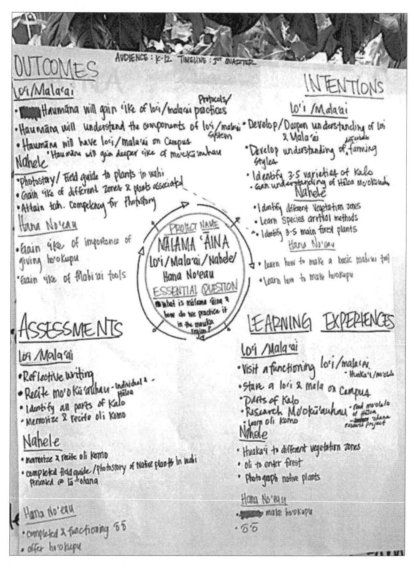

FIGURE 10.1   A sample lesson design produced collaboratively by teachers in the study.

cases and scenarios that presented challenges. Embedded in a larger study, this inquiry lasted just over a year.

Teachers worked in communities with high concentrations of indigenous learners on Kaua'i, O'ahu, and Hawai'i Island. Every school community had its own micro-context (rural, urban, distinctive patterns of Hawaiian language use, heritage traditions like fishing or cattle ranching, etc.), but because they all shared the same root of ancestral Hawaiian traditions there was some convergence in terms of shared values. The schools' stakeholders also shared an intention to positively transform learning experiences in schools. In settings like these, where the organization is not so averse to change, it can be easier for teachers to enact new practices, compared with schools where there is ongoing pressure to reinforce conventional schooling structures.

The study was conducted in two phases, beginning with a course introducing teachers to a human-centered design process (Dubberly, 2004) based on Banathy's divergence and convergence model (1996), and IDEO's sequence (Nussbaum, 2004). Lesson designs before and after the introduction to design process were compared during Phase 1.

The example of a lesson design called *Mālama ʻĀina* (see Figure 10.1) was designed to be flexible enough for students across grades K-12, and was situated in their *mauka* (high-elevation, forested) school region. Many single-page lesson designs like these became part of study data.

Since research took place in indigenous Hawaiian communities we followed an indigenous research methodology, specifically the Empowering Outcomes Model (Smith, 1997), which calls for research to be conducted with indigenous community members, directed by the questions and concerns that are foremost in their minds, and resulting in tangible outcomes that are meaningful for indigenous communities and researchers alike. Phase 2 was a collaborative conversation between a subgroup of the teachers and the researcher, which led to the development of a new way of describing how design process had begun to function within the settings of their work.

Phase 1 Results: Teacher Moves, Visions, and Metacognition

Phase 1 captured the artifacts from teachers' lesson designs and the narratives behind the design. The example of a teacher lesson design shown in Figure 10.1 was produced by a group of teachers who mapped out a quarter-long unit for students on "developing an ethic and practice of caring for the land through diverse relationships." Examples below show the nature of the narratives that were grouped under each category, a primary type of data collected during Phase 1; they also reveal teachers' professional contexts. Teachers' stories brought meaning to the diverse artifacts gathered over the year. The narratives were grouped using open coding, and placed into one of three emergent categories:

1.   Teacher Moves—actions and steps that teachers took in their process of professional decision-making;
2.   Teacher Visions—images and configurations that teachers made and wrote as they described the kinds of education they'd like to enact in their work, and;
3.   Teacher Metacognition—reflections teachers offered about their growth process as professionals.

Example 1: A Teacher Move Using Anticipated Factors as a Basis for Decisions

During a planning session, Lauloa and a partner mapped out a *huakaʻi* (field investigation) for her students; together, they made three different lesson prototypes and tested them by anticipating how students might react. Initially, they did some ideation and came up with the possibility of having students practice "talking story" with *kūpuna* (elders) of the community as a way of getting kids involved in literacy activities in a meaningful way. The two partners (who came from different schools) talked through the ideas and explored the possibility of having Lauloa's students talk to community members about plants in the area—something that could funnel into their end-of-quarter *hōʻike* (knowledge exhibition) and the end-of-year *hula* (dance) performance.

In a later round of prototyping, Lauloa anticipated that her students might not know how to interact appropriately with community partners in order to get information from them about the plants in the area. Lauloa's working hypothesis, based on her knowledge of context, was that the students would run into trouble trying to talk with community members. The two teachers brainstormed how to work through this challenge and first proposed roleplaying the type of interaction students might expect, as a conversation within the class before going out. The teachers continued to ideate and came up with a strategy for having each student storyboard the steps they would use in a culturally appropriate "talk story" method. This way, the students could have a lasting reference point, look at the differences in one another's storyboards, and also remind one another without speaking of the expectations.

Lauloa was pleased with this lesson design and elected to carry it forward. Students would gain information about plants in the area, they would practice and share their expertise about how to interact with knowledgeable elders and community members, they would have the chance to articulate through visual means (maybe even in fun comic book style animation, thanks to an app), and they could better calibrate their guesses and experiences of what made for effective communication with elders and community members.

Example 2: A Teacher Vision of Expanded Purposes for School Activity

Makuahine developed a hands-on project for her students that went far beyond her original idea of "a lesson on invasive species" that would generate positive outcomes for the community as well as help them learn about native plant ecology. She used design process to transform a simple lesson into an expanded approach that was aligned with her vision of meaningful learning.

In her vision, students would leave their classroom and go to the forested edge of campus where they would learn a procedure for doing line transects. With this method, the students could conduct species assessments in areas they traveled to—at different altitudes and at varying heights off the ground, creating a picture of the "health" of certain areas in terms of the balance of native and invasive species.

Makuahine anticipated that, using these methods, the invasive *waiwī* (strawberry guava) growing ubiquitously in yards, reserves, and forests would clearly stand out as a focus for the group's attention—reflected in the data from students' own investigation. Students could research its historical spread through "*kūkākūkā* (listen and talk story) with local ranchers, county workers, and Department of Land and Natural Resources staff. Making sense of that information would be deepened by comparing county maps over the last twenty years. As Makuahine wrote, "each group works with maps in that *'ahupua'a* (land division) and come together later to share findings of *waiwī*'s growth."

Together the students would *huaka'i* (travel to explore a new location) to observe firsthand the effects of *waiwī* on the forests, asking questions like these:

- What native flora and fauna have decreased since *waiwī's* arrival?
- What did we learn from looking at historical and current maps?
- What did we learn from our own observations and transects?
- Do we believe the current maps are accurate, or is the spread of *waiwī* not fully documented?
- How can we apply this data we've gathered in our community?

In Makuahine's vision, students might propose strategies for invasive plant removal, test them on a small scale during a whole-school *mālama 'āina* day, and perhaps go on to coordinate a community work day, during which they would share their data and proposed solutions with the community—teaching the methods they'd found effective for limiting the spread of *waiwī*.

Example 3: A Teacher Vision of a New Structure for Knowledge

Kaleionaona taught mathematics and Hawaiian cultural arts at a small, rural, student-centered school. Although she was mostly assigned math classes like

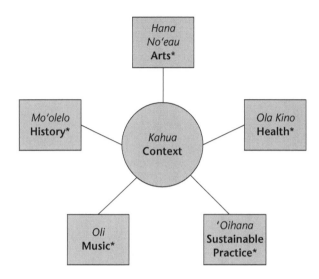

FIGURE 10.2 Kaleionaona's *Kahua* context diagram

Note: *Content standards and skills are associated with *specified activities* within each subgroup.

Geometry during the school day, her desire to focus on more comprehensive place-based curriculum and teach in a more integrated, transdisciplinary way was evident from her earliest proposed lesson plan. Even though the content of her daily teaching was circumscribed by disciplinary boundaries, Kaleionaona nurtured this vision of how she wanted to teach over the year, using every opportunity after school and on *huaka'i* (excursions) to develop content. When she found the opportunity to ideate and articulate her vision for teaching, the design for learning that emerged from her work was transformative not only for herself but also for her peers at the school.

Kaleionaona felt strongly that the structure of the school's "curriculum should reflect the *place* that is our central guide," and created a new vision for curriculum that could support a deep coherence with this important cultural value of place as the context for meaning. She eventually proposed it for adoption school wide, in the form of a manifesto arguing formally for "context" to serve as the *kahua* (foundation or platform) of all curricula (see Figure 10.2).

The goal of Kaleionaona's *kahua* manifesto was to spread the idea that, rather than having Hawai'i State Content and Performance standards as the starting point for lesson planning, the teaching staff should begin with context/place as the *kahua* (foundation) for all lessons and make the connections to content through the indigenous lens of identification through place.

Kaleionaona's place-based manifesto is an expression of a transformation that took place in her teaching—one that had been brewing since the beginning of the program, and which reflected her desire to break out of the limitations imposed by the public school system. Making "adjustments" within the existing school model had stopped making sense, and a new model was needed to reflect her current understanding of required solutions. This spillover from Kaleionaona's process positively affected not only the students she worked with, and spurred new debate among her colleagues—it ultimately influenced the structure of the school itself. Her story reveals precisely the kind of generative innovation that can come from teachers who are actively engaging context-adaptive practices like design process.

Example 4: Teacher Metacognition About the Results of Reframing Their Questions

Leimana and Kūpono were two teachers from the same rural, bilingual school who collaborated during a design exercise. As they envisioned a lesson, they anticipated the kinds of knowledge students would come up with during the pre-assessment test they drafted, and sought to adapt-in-advance based on their best guess—refining the lesson design a little more to fit the "essential question" that students were inquiring about. Essential questions focus curricular units on genuine, complex issues in the world and are meant to stimulate student curiosity and sustained inquiry due to their open-ended structure (see Wiggins & McTighe, 2011). Both Leimana and Kūpono expressed frustration that the essential questions driving their units were so broad, and laden with so much content, that students had difficulty in clearly answering the essential question after completion even though they had gained sophisticated understanding of the subject.

Using design process, Leimana and Kūpono began to tackle another genuine issue in teaching: how to assess and encourage capacities that take a lifetime to develop. As Kūpono put it, they often "got frustrated that some goals/objectives surpass the time frames available in school, like 'demonstrating internalized *kuleana* [sense of responsibility to self, to others],' because that evidence may come years from now." They saw design process as giving them the ability to resolve the short-term technical issue of problematic essential questions, and refocus on the less visible, long-brewing issue of assessment timelines that seemed impossible to measure.

Phase 2 Results: A Teacher Proposal for Different Design Language

Ten weeks into Phase 1, Kekahi and Hoapili worked through a cycle of design process together as part of a curriculum planning exercise. Debriefing the activity, they wrote a critique of design process and shared it with the group: "We liked having a process-sequence, but we felt like we had to fit the format which was so technical; [it] needs to include things beyond the basic." This reaction that the language and diagrams for design process were simultaneously "too technical" and too "basic" struck a chord with the larger group of teachers. They responded in an extended discussion, stating they would benefit from having: simpler language, representation of the hands-on learning phase, guidance on the role and timing of feedback integration, and cues for when to "let go and ho'opuka"—break through to the next level.

From that conversation onward, the model of design process initially presented was under active revision by the group of teachers. Early on, the debate centered on the way that indigenous Hawaiian culture placed high value on iterativity through concepts like maka'ala (vigilant attention) and makawalu (seeing from multiple perspectives)—and how underlying cultural processes for "designing" were a very deep part of Hawaiian tradition (for additional detail, see Johnson, 2013). After multiple rounds of conversation, the visual language they agreed to represented their experience of design process.

One teacher, Hoapili, was energized by this visual representation and helped to facilitate its development into two parallel cycles: the external cycle of enacting teaching that is visible to students and other participants in the learning ecology, and the internal cycle, that constitutes a teachers' process of making sense of all the key contextual factors that matter for learners (see Figure 10.3). The visual reflected the teachers' understanding that "after experiencing a lesson that does not work, a teacher's insight grows." This became a topic of conversation for months. As Hoapili describes it:

> When the lesson is working . . . the students will grow in their sophistication. When the lesson does not work, then the teacher's insight grows and hopefully they will be able to improve student ability using a different learning opportunity.

Day after day, teachers complete the external cycle of teaching followed by the internal cycle of anticipation and ideation. The parallel cycles are based on *and* newly inform their current mental model of the learning ecology and context for learning.

These teachers captured their understanding of how design thinking process intersected with their mental model for context-adaptive teaching in Figure 10.3. In their understanding, the internal cycle is where the pedagogical content knowledge of the teacher plays a very critical role—and the teacher's command of information about the learning context is also vital, particularly for those teachers who are actively seeking to practice in context-adaptive ways. During the "Ideation" stage teachers prioritize and consider the outcomes of possible options. Teachers take time to think through the scenario of how their plans in the current state would actually play out among students—given what they know about current factors in the learning context. This step is specifically based on awareness of the contextual factors in the learning ecology that teachers had identified as influences on learner growth. The "Anticipation" phase is based on informed guessing

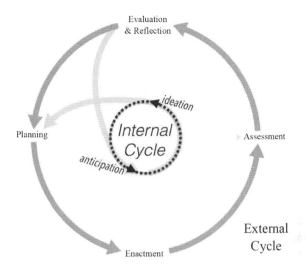

FIGURE 10.3 Internal/external cycle for teachers using design process

or "anticipation" of how students will respond to the various lesson designs generated, based on how they've responded in the past, and it leads to ideation or brainstorming about the next external cycle of enacted teaching.

The grey arrows represent the external, visible cycle of teaching in which a lesson is planned, taught, assessed, and evaluated by the teacher in view of students and peers. The external cycle comprises "Evaluation and Reflection," "Planning," "Enactment," and "Assessment." The "Evaluation and Reflection" stage includes a look both backward (to Assessment) and forward (to Planning) at the connection between recent realizations and future directions. During reflection teachers ask, "What must be strengthened in order to have students grasp the *waiwai* (true wealth or enduring value) of these lessons?" Teachers consider how students are reaching learning goals. Making into the "Assessment" stage, teachers review assessments to determine what kinds of changes need to be made to keep everyone on track. These proposed changes, based on the last teaching cycle, provide fodder for planning in the "Planning" stage. The "Enactment" stage includes the time when teachers are present with students and embodied, contextualized learning takes place for both parties. Teachers make stepwise adjustments from student-to-student and class-to-class in order to ensure that learning experiences are well-fitted.

Following a cycle of enactment, the teacher then makes sense of those experiences through an internal, non-visible cycle, as represented by the dotted black arrows. This inner cycle starts with prospective guesses about "what might have worked better," or "what I'd do differently next time," yet that same lesson won't be taught again. Teachers' use of design process is fundamentally different than that of engineers or product designers because they aren't simply teaching and refining the same lesson over and over again, as with material engineering. The diagram these teachers created to represent their experience of design process looks profoundly different from the simple six-stage circle that they were introduced to because of their focus on context-adaptiveness. When context-adaptive teachers teach the same topic to different students in the morning, and again in the afternoon, it is never the same lesson. Teachers make thousands of decisions in a day and Lampert (2003) reminds us that, while the setting of the classroom may look the same, the parameters of the professional "problems" teachers solve are constantly changing. Context-adaptive teachers use assessments to learn about contextual factors that are relevant for their students, like links with a heritage language, attitudes toward written language, preferences for collaborative work over individual work, and so on. These contextual factors inform different parts of the learning ecology that help teachers to filter information and organize it.

Findings: Teachers Use Design Process to Develop Adaptive Expertise

For teachers, the learning context where their designs are enacted varies in essential ways every day. A prototype that was successful one day would likely fail miserably the next if the same students were engaged in only slightly modified learning activities the very next day. This study's results suggest that, rather than refining an external lesson prototype, the teachers' mental model may be the 'thing' refined during cycles of design process.

When teachers develop lesson plans they are designing a prototype for a lesson and testing it in the learning context with one or more groups of students/users. The parameters for which they design it are not all visible, and some must therefore be held within the teachers' internalized representation of the learning context, as part of the mental model.

Mental models are considered to be a "cognitive structure" that helps people model and think through how things work in the world using analogical thinking (Collins & Gentner, 1987). Researchers recognize that mental models are:

> context-dependent and may change according to the situation in which they are used . . . [they have to] adapt to continually changing circumstances and to evolve over time through learning. Conceptualizing cognitive representations as dynamic, inaccurate models of complex systems acknowledges the limitations in peoples' ability to conceive such complex systems.
>
> *(Jones et al., 2011: pp. 46–47)*

When one teacher, Hiipoi, commented that she had been able to anticipate her students' questions on the material, she was using her mental model of the learning ecology (including all the contextual factors she was aware of, like personality, role in group, prior patterns of questioning, etc.) to reason and predict what they might wonder about. Similar to the way that developing professional vision helps teachers to see and grasp over time what has always been before their eyes, "the nature and richness of models one can construct, and one's ability to reason develops with learning domain-specific content and techniques" (Nersessian, 2002, p. 140). Background knowledge of contextual features (gained through assessment strategies, for example) has a direct impact on the construction of the mental model, just as a person's goals, motives, expectations, and biases do.

Given the data from participants, we can assert that as teachers are designing lessons iteratively within a specific context they are engaging in "cognitive mapping" of their learning ecology as they test, identify, organize, and recall information about the local contextual features that matter in the particular learning environment where they work. Analogical thinking across domains helps people to "create new mental models that they can then run to generate predictions about what should happen in various situations in the world" (Collins & Gentner, 1987, p. 243), and it is plausible that such mental models are being refined through teachers' use of design process.

Teachers' refinement of mental models is an indicator that they are engaging in the kind of generativity that characterizes adaptive expertise. Adaptive expertise may be a key outcome of teachers' use of design process and other context-adaptive practices that support ongoing learning through practice. Adaptive expertise is a learning sciences framework for describing a particular way of thinking and solving; development of adaptive expertise results in solution outcomes that exhibit a balance between efficiency and innovation (Schwartz et al., 2005; Schwartz & Martin, 2004). Some of the characteristics of adaptive expertise are the following:

- anticipation of challenges within ill-structured domains;
- flexibility in recognizing when to transfer knowledge across domains;
- recognizing and exposing the limits of one's own knowledge;
- view of the world as dynamic (seeing routines as insufficient);
- acknowledging to oneself and when one or others "doesn't know";
- responding with curiosity to (rather than ignoring) discrepancies in expectations or phenomena;
- allowing action to inspire new thinking, novel directions.

The path to routine expertise is paved with routine activity (like mathematical problem sets), and often leads to understandings that are limited in their robustness (Chi et al., 1988), or to applications of knowledge that result in high efficiency but low innovation (Schwartz et al., 2005). The path to adaptive expertise leads to knowledge and theories that are constructed in such a way that they help a practitioner to adapt prior knowledge to the specific task at hand (Barnett & Koslowski, 2002; Lin et al., 2005).

The growth of adaptive expertise is one way of explaining how design process can be so powerful for transforming teacher practice in ways that are context-adaptive. As an adaptive expert, one carries forward only those conceptions that do not inhibit the ongoing acquisition of new knowledge and which allow new, unexpected ideas to be received—even those that may require adjustment of prior ideas and schema (Crawford et al., 2005; Martin et al., 2005; Kulkarni et al., 2012). Teachers in this study are clearly working in this territory as they refine their understandings of how to be context-adaptive, through the use of design process in internal and external cycles of teaching.

Conclusion

This study points to some ways that teacher practice can benefit from employing design process as a strategy for context-adaptive teaching. Study participants were able to use design process to improve their designs for learning. Though design process was presented to study participants in a conventional way, these highly context-adaptive teachers applied it to improve their designs for learning in ways that were distinctive—and substantially different than how engineers and product designers might use design process (to improve a thing or experience).

In the current climate of rapid diversification and intense change in schools, teachers' ability to cultivate and skillfully use contextual knowledge is a highly valuable asset—design process may be a straightforward, strategic way to support context-adaptive teaching. The model proposed here for how these teachers used design process should be considered a topic for further exploration and elaboration through research—particularly as it relates to in-service teacher learning in schools and pre-service teacher education programs. As teacher education programs recalibrate their curriculum to value context-adaptive teaching outcomes, design process is a way to continue to reach out to today's teachers and administrators. Schools seeking to meet global standards as well as local community and cultural needs may find design process to be an effective tool for enhancing context-adaptive teacher practice.

Acknowledgments

I would like to express my sincerest gratitude to the Hawai'i participants in this study for their *aloha 'āina*, vision, persistence, and deep commitment to the well-being of current and future generations of *kānaka maoli*.

Notes

1 This "personal communication" came via email from the leadership of the American Educational Research Association's Division K to the entire body of Division K members in March 2011.

2 This definition is fundamentally different from the way that computer programmers use the term "context-adaptive," to refer to digital systems that adapt to the individual user within a platform's set parameters—for example, how an online testing program selects questions based on the accuracy of a user's previous answers.

References

Banathy, B.H. (1996). *Designing Social Systems in a Changing World*. New York, NY: Plenum Press.

Banerjee, B.H. (2008). Designer as agent of change: A vision for catalyzing rapid change. Proceedings from *Changing the Change*. Turin: Allemandi.

Barab, S.A., & Duffy, T. (2000). From practice fields to communities of practice. *Theoretical foundations of learning environments, 1*(1), 25–55.

Barnett, S.M., & Koslowski, B. (2002). Adaptive expertise: Effects of type of experience and the level of theoretical understanding it generates. *Thinking & Reasoning, 8*(4), 237–267.

Castagno, A., & Brayboy, B. (2008). Culturally responsive schooling for indigenous youth: A review of the literature. *Review of Educational Research, 78*(4), 941.

Chi, M.T.H., Glaser, R., & Farr, M.J. (Eds.). (1988). *The nature of expertise*. Hillsdale, NJ: Lawrence Erlbaum Associates.

Colby, S.L., & Ortman, J.M. (2015). Projections of the size and composition of the US population: 2014 to 2060. *US Census Bureau, Ed*, 25–1,143.

Collins, A., & Gentner, D. (1987). How people construct mental models. In D. Holland & N. Quinn (Eds.), *Cultural models in language and thought* (pp. 243–268). New York, NY: Cambridge University Press.

Crawford, V.M., Schlager, M., Riel, M., Toyama, Y., Vahey, P., & Stanford, T. (2005). *Developing expertise in teaching: The role of adaptiveness in learning through everyday practice*. Paper presented at the Annual Meeting of the American Educational Research Association Annual Conference, Montreal, Canada.

Darling-Hammond, L., Barron, B., Pearson, P.D., Schoenfeld, A.H., Stage, E.K., Zimmerman, T.D., Cervetti, G.N., & Tilson, J.L. (2015). *Powerful learning: What we know about teaching for understanding*. New York, NY: John Wiley & Sons.

Doherty, R.W., Hilberg, R.S., Pinal, A., & Tharp, R.G. (2003). Five standards and student achievement. *NABE Journal of Research and Practice, 1*(1), 1–24.

Dubberly, H. (2004). *How do you design? A compendium of models*. Retrieved from http://www.dubberly.com/articles/how-do-you-design.html.

Freire, P. (2000). *Pedagogy of the oppressed*. New York, NY: Continuum International.

Goodwin, A.L. (2010). Globalization and the preparation of quality teachers: Rethinking knowledge domains for teaching. *Teaching Education, 21*(1), 19–32.

Goodwin, A.L., Cheruvu, R., & Genishi, C. (2008). Responding to multiple diversities in early childhood education: How far have we come. In C. Genishi & A.L. Goodwin (Eds.), *Diversities in early childhood education: Rethinking and doing* (pp. 3–10). New York, NY: Routledge.

Goodwin, A.L., & Kosnik, C. (2013). Quality teacher educators = quality teachers? Conceptualizing essential domains of knowledge for those who teach teachers. *Teacher Development, 17*(3), 334–346.

Gruenewald, D.A. (2003). The best of both worlds: A critical pedagogy of place. *Educational Researcher, 32*(4), 3–12.

Gruenewald, D.A., & Smith, G.A. (Eds.). (2014). *Place-based education in the global age: Local diversity*. New York, NY: Routledge.

Johnson, Z. (2013). *"E Hoʻomau!" A study of Hawaiʻi teachers navigating change through generative praxis.* (Unpublished doctoral dissertation). Stanford University.

Jones, N., Ross, H., Lynam, T., Perez, P., & Leitch, A. (2011). Mental models: An interdisciplinary synthesis of theory and methods. *Ecology and Society, 16*(1), 46–58.

Kanaʻiaupuni, S.M., Ledward, B., & Jensen, U. (2010). *Culture-based education and its relationship to student outcomes.* Honolulu, HI: Kamehameha Schools, Research & Evaluation Division.

Kulkarni, C., Dow, S.P., & Klemmer, S.R. (2012). Early and repeated exposure to examples improves creative work. In H. Plattner, C. Meinel, & L. Leifer (Eds.), *Design thinking research: Building innovation eco-systems* (pp. 49–63). New York, NY: Springer.

Lampert, M. (2003). *Teaching problems and the problems of teaching.* New Haven, CT: Yale University Press.

Lin, X.D., Schwartz, D.L., & Hatano G. (2005). *Toward teachers' adaptive metacognition. Educational Psychologist, 40*(4), 245–255.

Martin, T., Rayne, K., Kemp, N.J., Hart, J., & Diller, K.R. (2005). Teaching for adaptive expertise in biomedical engineering ethics. *Science and Engineering Ethics, 11*(2), 257–276.

McCarty, T., & Lee, T. (2014). Critical culturally sustaining/revitalizing pedagogy and indigenous education sovereignty. *Harvard Educational Review, 84*(1), 101–124.

Nersessian, N.J. (2002). The cognitive basis of model-based reasoning in science. In P. Carruthers, S. Stich, & M. Siegal (Eds.). *The cognitive basis of science* (pp. 133–153). Cambridge, UK: Cambridge University Press.

Nussbaum, B. (2004, May 17). The power of design: IDEO redefined good design by creating experiences, not just products. *Bloomberg.* Retrieved from http://www.bloomberg.com/news/articles/2004-05-16/the-power-of-design.

Paris, D. (2012). Culturally sustaining pedagogy a needed change in stance, terminology, and practice. *Educational Researcher, 41*(3), 93–97.

Schwartz, D.L., & Martin, T. (2004). Inventing to prepare for future learning: The hidden efficiency of encouraging original student production in statistics instruction. *Cognition and Instruction, 22*(2), 129–184.

Schwartz, D.L., Bransford, J.D., & Sears, D. (2005). Efficiency and innovation in transfer. In J.P. Mestre (Ed.), *Transfer of learning from a modern multidisciplinary perspective* (pp. 1–52). Greenwich, CT: Information Age Publishing.

Smith, G.A. (2002). Place-based education. *Phi Delta Kappan, 83*(8), 584.

Smith, G.H. (1997). *Kaupapa Maori as transformative praxis.* (Unpublished doctoral dissertation). University of Auckland, New Zealand.

Trumbull, E., Sexton, U., Nelson-Barber, S., & Johnson, Z. (2015). Assessment practices in schools serving American Indian and Alaska Native students. *Journal of American Indian Education, 54*(3), 5–30.

Wiggins, G.P., & McTighe, J. (2005). *Understanding by design.* Alexandria, VA: ASCD.

11

TO SUCCEED, FAILURE MUST BE AN OPTION

David Kwek

As educators, we understand failure as an important part of the learning process. Do our students feel safe to fail or are they treading carefully to avoid failure? When wrong answers are penalized and corrections are perceived as punishments for making mistakes, students quickly learn the importance of getting the right answer at the first attempt. They learn that ideas are worthy of evaluation only when they have the perfect solution, or worse, when they are ready to put up a winning presentation. If we are serious about developing innovators who bravely persist in pushing frontiers, we must cultivate in students the right attitudes and mindsets to not see failures as final and to embrace every failure as a step towards success.

Encouraging Playful Experimentation and Meeting Real Needs

In my current role as a curriculum specialist, I work closely with schools to provide resource and professional development support to implement the Innovation Program that is organized by Singapore's Education Ministry, and which is open to Grade 5 and 8 students who have an interest in innovation and invention. In this eight-month program, students learn the skills for problem finding, generation of creative ideas, and testing of solutions. The creative problem-solving process, which emphasizes both divergent and convergent thinking, aims to stimulate the pupils' curiosity to understand the problem at hand and encourage them to embrace experimentation in generating and testing potential solutions. In a review of the program two years ago, we found that students had a tendency to quickly eliminate alternatives during the prototyping phase in order to converge on one specific solution. In particular, they were fixated on building polished mock-ups to impress others with aesthetics and sophistication.

This practice was problematic for two reasons. First, it went against the goal to stimulate students' curiosity about problems around them and for them to embrace experimentation while generating and testing potential solutions. As innovation expert Marc Rettig (1994) cautions, "high-fidelity" prototypes take too long to construct and involve too much emotional investment. Teachers lament the difficulty of convincing students with high-resolution prototypes to make changes because the amount of time and effort the students invest in building the "perfect" artifact set up their expectations for acceptance and success—not for failure. Second, in real-world problem-solving, the user is the expert, and would-be innovators need to let go of any ideas deemed not good enough. A polished model, however, discourages honest feedback because it gives the impression that the product is almost finished already. After all, it is very hard for people not to get defensive when they have spent a lot of time polishing something only for it to get changed significantly. The problem-solving process involves dealing with mistaken assumptions and making many, and sometimes radical, changes to original ideas. Treating an assumption or prototype as a fact can be very dangerous.

In a design thinking model, the value of an innovation lies with its intended user rather than with its creator. When students design an innovation and create a prototype that is polished and impermeable to feedback, this is counterproductive. To address this problem, our students needed to develop new mindsets so that they would look at ideas through the fresh eyes of a user and spend more time seeking through feedback the understanding they need for creating effective solutions. They needed to understand that the purpose of prototypes is not to impress users, but to learn from them. They needed to listen, rather than sell. In light of this, our Innovation Program team designed and piloted a series of prototyping lessons to facilitate a more iterative and user-centered innovation process. We also worked with a materials company to put together an innovation kit comprising a range of low-cost and versatile prototyping materials, which include base materials like Styrofoam, foam sheets, fabric swatches, and aluminium foil, and accessories like colored tape, wooden craft sticks, and abrasives. When the toolkit was first introduced to a group of Grade 5 students after the idea generation phase, students quickly immersed themselves in a do-it-yourself session. Initially, many of them were stuck as they struggled with constraints posed by their own ideas and the materials available. Yet because a time limit was imposed, they surprised themselves with accomplishments of becoming unstuck—their ideas and resilience were manifested as low-resolution but concrete artifacts that represented their points of view and were ready to be tested against user feedback.

When the students presented their innovation kit prototypes, we also observed that they were more open to feedback because they were less attached to their ideas. One student shared, "Our teachers gave us a lot of feedback on how to improve our prototype. We also expected to fail because it is only by failing that we know what to improve." This, in essence, describes why prototypes are built—as learning vehicles by which innovators "organically and evolutionally learn, discover, generate and refine designs" (Lim et al., 2008, p. 2). We could see embedded in the students' successive prototypes new thinking and experimentation that arose from feedback; and, more importantly, purposeful refinement to address the needs of their users. This process, which encourages the constant deconstruction and rebuilding of objects and ideas that most of us accept as static and fixed, fosters what Carol Dweck (2006) describes as the *growth mindset*. In fact, this iterative process often provides a crucial element of surprise as the student gains unexpected realizations that he or she could not have arrived at without producing a concrete representation of his or her ideas.

Principles for Designing Prototyping Lessons

Although exploration in the prototyping process is largely driven by the learner, it is informed by user feedback and inspired by the participation of adult facilitators. In designing our prototyping lessons, we used three key principles and saw how they were important in the process of learning:

- *Emphasize the value of immediate feedback.* A prototype simulates the experience of a proposed solution—one that a user can interact with. Because prototypes can be cheaply constructed, they can be shown to a lot of people and quickly updated based on feedback. Even before surveying the general public, students could test their prototypes among their classmates, teachers, and expert mentors to bring to the surface questions about the desirability, usability, and feasibility of their idea. This leads to early identification of problems and blind spots when it is still possible to fix them. It is rather obvious that an idea can be improved by removing its disadvantages; what is less obvious is that an idea can be improved by adding new advantages. If we teach our pupils to balance negative criticism with positive encouragement, our students will develop over time the confidence and competence to improve their ideas with honest feedback.
- *Emphasize process over product.* The teacher does not need to be an expert in prototyping, but he or she can help students clarify their ideas and intentions through reflective conversations. By limiting the prototyping time, students are encouraged to "fail fast" and learn by doing, rather than try to avoid failure by striving for initial perfection. In fact, teachers we have worked with realize that there is no need for much intervention once they confirm that the students are on a fruitful path. There will be times when students are stuck, but it is important to allow them to continue and find their own solutions. Jumping in too early takes ownership away from the students and may result in them giving up.

- *Encourage fluid experimentation.* The world is a construction kit with a diverse array of possibilities. Prototyping materials do not have to be cutting-edge and can be anything in the household—modelling clay, pipe cleaners, paper bags, tape, string, or anything you can bend, cut, or fold. We find innovation kits very useful because they provide the students with ready access to a wide range of materials for trying out innovative concepts and constructing early prototypes. The kits do not need to be all-encompassing, but the materials they contain should be chosen for inherent potential to encourage playful and low-fidelity prototyping and to stimulate thinking and ingenuity through their transformation into something totally new.

References

Dweck, C. (2006). *Mindset: The new psychology of success.* New York: Ballantine Books.

Lim, Y.K., Stolterman, E., & Tenenberg, J. (2008). The anatomy of prototypes: Prototypes as filters, prototypes as manifestations of design ideas. *ACM Transactions on Computer-Human Interaction (TOCHI), 15*(2), 1–27.

Rettig, M. (1994). Prototyping for tiny fingers. *Communications of the ACM, 37*(4), 21–27.

Treffinger, D.J., Isaksen, S.G., & Dorval, K.B. (2000). *Creative problem solving: An introduction.* (3rd Ed.). Waco, TX: Prufrock Press.

12

EMPATHY IN STEM EDUCATION

Kathy Liu Sun

Introduction

Many STEM-related issues, such as global health, technology development, and climate change, have significant impact on human society (Leach et al., 2005; Lubchenco, 1998; NGSS Lead States, 2013). Consequently, it is important that we extend our understanding of how STEM teachers can prepare students to develop the necessary skills and knowledge to better address and solve many of these issues that affect human populations, or what I will refer to as human-centered issues.

Reforms in science and engineering education have attempted to address the impact of science and technology on human populations and societal outcomes. One particular trend has been a focus on Science, Technology, and Society (STS) programs (NGSS Lead States, 2013; Yager, 1996). STS places an equal emphasis on (1) debating, criticizing, and evaluating particular scientific claims (Kolstoe, 2000) and (2) understanding how particular STEM-related issues affect particular populations (Mansour, 2009). This latter type of understanding may be gained through engaging in empathy. Thus, K-12 STEM education may significantly benefit from an emphasis on empathy to help students to better understand the changing ecology of STEM issues and to find science-based solutions that address the needs of particular populations.

This chapter reports on findings from a larger case study, which examined how K-12 teachers learned and implemented a human-centered approach to problem-solving *design thinking*. The term *design thinking* does not have a single authoritative definition (Buchanan, 1992; Kimbell, 2009). For the purposes of this study, I adopt Brown's (2008) definition of design thinking as a human-centered approach to problem-solving that focuses on identifying people's needs and embraces a philosophy of experimentation and collaboration. At the heart of design thinking's human-centered philosophy is empathy, which emphasizes the importance of engaging with other's experiences. This chapter examines the role of empathy in science and STEM-related education, specifically examining how science teachers conceptualize and integrate empathy in their classrooms. This chapter also examines the perceived benefits and challenges of engaging in empathy.

Theoretical Perspectives

Empathy

Empathy is often defined as the ability to "discern and identify others' affective states . . . or perspectives" (Eisenberg & Miller, 1987, p. 91). Ultimately, empathy furthers our understanding of the experiences of other human beings. The importance of empathy has been highlighted by mainstream media publications. *Fast Company* touted empathy as "the most powerful leadership tool" (Whitelaw, 2012). *Harvard Business Review* claimed that empathy was "The most valuable thing they teach at HBS" (Allworth, 2012).

In a review of empathy research, Eisenberg and Miller (1987) found that empathy was positively related with various pro-social behaviors and social competencies. For example, children who demonstrated higher levels of empathy were more likely to help other children and donate toys to peers. Additionally, research has also found empathy to be related to positive outcomes in specific academic domains. For example, there has been a considerable amount of research that has identified positive correlations between empathy and the study of history. Students who demonstrated higher levels of empathy were better able to engage in historical perspective taking and understand the rationale for particular historical decisions (see Davis et al., 2001). Other studies have identified empathy as an essential element in medical education, particularly around interacting with and interviewing patients (Bellet & Maloney, 1991).

Given the role of empathy in contributing to positive social outcomes and to greater success in particular academic domains, it is important that we extend our understanding of empathy and its potential influence in other academic domains. Empathy related to STEM education may be a particularly promising area of study because many STEM-related issues have significant impact on human populations. Thus, a deeper understanding of particular populations (gained through empathy) may lead to better solutions for various human-centered, STEM issues.

The Design Thinking Framework and K-12 Education

A human-centered approach to design recognizes that people are the inspiration for good designs or solutions to problems. Identifying and responding to people's needs allows for the creation of solutions that are meaningful, useful, innovative and necessary. According to Brown and Katz (2011), "the mission of design thinking is to translate observations into insights, and insights into the products and services that will improve lives" (p. 382).

Design thinking has gained popularity in various fields including engineering and business. Engineering schools have embedded design thinking related courses into their core curriculum (Dym et al., 2005) and various corporations and business schools are adopting design thinking strategies into their practices (Brown, 2008; Kimbell, 2009). However, design thinking is just beginning to find traction in the K-12 education sector. Few published studies have examined design thinking in a K-12 context. Carroll et al. (2010) conducted a qualitative study to examine the implementation of a design thinking curriculum in a middle school classroom at a public charter school. The study showed the promise of design thinking and its relevance to students' development of 21st-century skills, including their ability to work collaboratively, to solve problems iteratively, and to generate creative solutions. In another study, Carroll (2014) examined how mentors perceived the process of guiding middle school students through the design thinking process. Mentors identified the importance of sharing their experiences, building relationship with students, and making activities fun as essential for working with students through the design thinking process.

Design thinking has the potential to influence how teachers approach their lesson planning. A design thinking approach to instruction tends to be more student-centered, having students' active engagement and interests as central features of instruction. In addition to covering important disciplinary content, design thinking provides a space for students to identify problems and test their ideas.

Design thinking may also influence the types of activities that teachers design for their students. Teachers who learn about design thinking may also aim to teach design thinking to their students by providing hands-on challenges that focus on developing empathy and generating, testing, and refining ideas. Other iterative problem-solving processes that emphasize collaboration, such as problem-based learning, have been linked to improved student outcomes (Hmelo-Silver, 2004) and one might expect a similar impact when students engage in design thinking.

Teacher professional development shows promise for supporting teachers to learn new teaching and problem-solving strategies (Borko et al., 2010; Desimone, 2009), such as design thinking, that might engage students in empathy. However, when introduced to new teaching strategies or approaches, teachers often modify strategies to meet the needs of their particular students and contexts (e.g., Barab & Luehmann, 2003; Drake & Sherin, 2006). Consequently, how strategies are implemented will vary with teaching contexts. As teachers engage in new ways of teaching they may experience different challenges and affordances to particular teaching approaches (Cohen, 1990; Frykholm, 2004; Zielezinski, this volume). Understanding teachers' perceptions of these challenges and benefits may provide the necessary knowledge to help support teachers in continuing to implement new approaches to teaching.

This chapter examines the role of empathy in K-12 STEM education. The purpose is to understand how K-12 teachers who participated in a design thinking workshop perceived and implemented empathy in their classrooms. The chapter explores the following questions: How do K-12 STEM teachers conceptualize and implement empathy in their lesson planning and design of instructional activities? What are the benefits of empathy, as reported by STEM teachers? What challenges do STEM teachers face when trying to integrate empathy into their instruction?

The Setting and Analysis

This study builds on a three-day summer design thinking workshop for K-12 educators facilitated by the K-12 Lab at Stanford University's d.school. The workshop provided participants with first-hand experience of the design thinking process and opportunities to make explicit connections for how design thinking might be implemented in K-12 classrooms. Over the three days, participants were guided through the various stages of the design thinking framework while engaging in three different design challenges or problem-solving tasks.

The workshop leaders intentionally designed the first two design challenges to be unrelated to teacher practice, so that participants could become familiar with the design thinking process in a context in which they would have limited professional expertise. The goal was for participants to have the opportunity to see a problem from a fresh perspective. Only the third design challenge was a school-related task. Participants were given four hours to use design thinking to either solve a problem at their school site or to create a design thinking activity for staff and students at their respective school sites.

The participants worked in groups of three or four with an experienced coach. A total of 83 educators attended the workshop. These educators came from various institutions, including public and private K-12 schools, universities, and community organizations. The majority of participants were from the United States, but several came from other countries, including Senegal, Singapore, and the Netherlands. Due to the exploratory nature of this study, participants were not intended to be representative of educators at large. Rather, participants applied and were selected to participate in the workshop because they had expressed an interest in design thinking. The focus here is on the responses and experiences of K-12 STEM teacher participants of the workshop.

Data from post-workshop surveys and interviews, reflection group recordings, and content logs from recordings of the teacher planning session were analyzed to identify the role of empathy on teacher planning and instruction. In the analysis,

I initially focused on three middle school (grades 6–8) science teachers—Edith, Jessica, and Lance—who formed a group on the third day of the workshop.[1] This group of science teachers was interested in embedding design thinking into their science classes and sought to plan a design thinking lesson for their students. Edith, who was entering her second year of teaching, was a sixth-grade science teacher at a traditional metropolitan K-6 school. Lance was a first-year middle school teacher at a newly founded sixth- to twelfth-grade urban charter school. Jessica was a teacher with less than five years of teaching experience who taught middle school science at an urban school in its second year of operation.

Focusing on the groups' planning session allowed me to identify empathy episodes (instances where a participant talked about "understanding another's perspective" or explicitly mentioned the word "empathy"), which could be applied to analysis of all the data: transcripts of small group reflections, participants' short answer responses to post-workshop surveys, and transcripts of post-workshop interviews. I examined each of the empathy episodes and categorized them into four groups related to the research questions: (1) teacher engagement in empathy; (2) student engagement in empathy; (3) benefits of empathy; and (4) challenges of empathy (Table 12.1).

TABLE 12.1 Empathy categories

	Category of Empathy Episode	Description
How do K-12 STEM teachers conceptualize and implement empathy in their lesson planning and design of instructional activities?	Teacher engagement in empathy	Participant describes his/her own experiences engaging in empathy or attempting to empathize with students when planning a lesson. For example, teachers might discuss trying to understand a lesson from a student's perspective.
	Student engagement in empathy	Participant mentions how lessons were designed to provide opportunities for students to engage in empathy. For example, teachers might provide opportunities for students to interview other students to gain empathy.
What are the benefits of empathy on student learning, as reported by STEM teachers?	Benefits of empathy	Participant mentions a benefit of empathy for student learning or instruction.
What challenges do STEM teachers face when trying to integrate empathy into lessons?	Challenges of empathy	Participant mentions a challenge associated with trying to engage in empathy or having students engage in empathy.

Teacher Conceptualization and Integration of Empathy

In this section, I address the findings as they relate to the three research questions. I examine how STEM teachers conceptualized and integrated empathy into their classrooms, with a specific focus on lesson planning, classroom structures, and instructional activities. I also address the benefits and challenges to empathy, as reported and experienced by participating teachers.

Empathy as a Redistribution of Expertise in the Classroom

At the onset of their planning session, the three science teachers—Edith, Jessica, and Lance—initially began their lesson planning by generating a list of state-mandated science topics that they needed to cover. Several minutes into the brainstorm Jessica changed the direction of the conversation and stated, "maybe we can pick things that kids are straight out interested in." The group then shifted the brainstorm to identify things kids were interested in, such as "dissecting, building stuff, and interacting with the community."

In these initial moments of the science teachers' planning session, two different approaches to curriculum planning emerged: (1) beginning with a set of predetermined content standards and (2) starting with what students find interesting and then finding content that related to those interests. The latter approach was more reflective of the design thinking framework because it began with a human-centered focus that sought to identify users' interests, needs, or desires. The group of science teachers placed a particular lens on empathy that focused on the interests of their students, who would be the most immediate users of their lesson. After the second brainstorm, the teachers ultimately decided to design a lesson around a topic that was related to current events and one which they thought students would find interesting—addressing the devastation by natural disasters.

For the group of science teachers, an empathy-based approach to lesson planning translated to beginning with student interests. The emphasis was on making learning accessible, relevant, and enjoyable for students. At the end of the first hour of the science teachers' planning session, Lance realized this, as he stated, "our challenge was to design something that was engaging and interesting for our students."

This student-interest driven approach continued to be salient for teachers during the following school year, as Edith reported in her post-workshop interview:

> I really tried to make a change . . . and so I think through how to make it into a project, how to make it engaging from their perspective. Taking into consideration this fun aspect that they need to have I think is design thinking oriented. Just because you're trying to meet them where they are.

From Edith's perspective, taking a design thinking approach to lesson planning meant meeting students "where they are" and making activities that were "fun" and "engaging from their [students'] perspective."

Teachers also found opportunities to use empathy to address everyday problems encountered in their classroom or at their school sites that were not related to lesson planning. In Edith's case, she was able to take students' ideas and implement them into her classroom's structures. At the beginning of the year, Edith used empathy to work with her students to solve the challenge of homework. The transition from fifth grade to sixth grade was quite challenging for her students, especially with regards to the homework load, which Edith described as a "huge shock" for them. Edith had engaged in empathy work, recognizing that her students were "stressed out," and initiated a discussion with her students that resulted in a design thinking-style brainstorm to address the issue. She explained,

> We need to solve this. I'm here to help you, so I know I need to make some changes. But you also need to make some changes. So we had questions up all over the place. And then I basically said, "Ok, I assign [you] to different posters." You need to group these into like ideas because we need to iron this down because I need some action ideas, and you need some action ideas. So we made two lists: Ms. Z's actions and students' actions.

Edith created a brainstorm activity in which she and her students needed to engage in empathy. Edith had to listen to her students' needs and wants, and her students had to listen to her needs and wants before generating and testing ideas. Through this activity Edith demonstrated a user-centered approach to classroom design, as she sought student input and feedback for developing and modifying classroom procedures. She saw a student need and engaged with them to tackle the problem together, thereby integrating students' opinions and expertise in the creation operation of their classroom.

Edith's willingness to work with her students to address the homework challenge conveyed her value for students' expertise, experiences, and opinions. In this regard, there was a redistribution of expertise, as faculty relinquished some of their authority and gave students the opportunity to influence school and classroom procedures.

Empathy and STEM Content

In addition to using empathy to plan lessons and create classroom structures, teachers found opportunities for students to engage in empathy related to science content. Teachers created lessons based on science content that affected particular populations. For example, during the planning session on the last day of the workshop, the three focal school science teachers (Edith, Lance, and

Jessica) began planning a lesson based on a specific science-related topic that had an impact on human populations—the devastation from natural disasters. Ten months after the workshop, Lance created a design thinking activity for his students to address the earthquake that devastated Haiti in 2010. During this design thinking challenge students were to create a structure out of graham crackers and marshmallows that would withstand a simulated earthquake on a shake table. This particular design thinking challenge focused around a particular issue of impacting humans (the devastation in Haiti) and still managed to be both content rich (learning about earthquakes and engineering principles) and reflective of what students enjoy doing (e.g., building stuff[2]).

Although the design challenge addressed a current event issue related to science, Lance viewed it as an opportunity to engage his students in empathy. He described this design thinking challenge as "structural engineering with a personal understanding." In order for students to develop empathy for the people involved in the tragedy, Lance had his sister, who had worked in Haiti for five weeks after the earthquake, visit the class to share stories of what she had seen and done. The importance of empathy manifested in his post-workshop interview reflection about why he chose this particular design thinking challenge. Lance explained:

> I felt like that's a very good place to have students empathize and create service to understand how someone else on the other side of the world feels . . . I felt that was good way to build empathy . . . Where they get more empathy or understanding like why are we doing that? It's not just to learn about science. It's really that this is connected to people.

In the excerpt, we see how Lance wants his students to understand that the science content is connected to real people. By bringing in his sister, having students ask her questions, and watching videos related to earthquakes, Lance provided an opportunity for his students to gain a more "personal understanding" of the devastation of earthquakes.

Although projects with a human component gave students the opportunity to develop particular empathy skills, those skills were not necessarily easy to learn or to teach. Lance found it particularly challenging to get his students to ask focused questions and see the relevance of their interviews. Despite efforts to teach interview skills, he still felt his students were not mastering them. He often felt that his students were eager to build or create prototypes of their ideas before having a full understanding of the user needs. He explained, "I again really wanted to focus on empathy. And then they're like when are we going to build? I'm like, hold back. We haven't started really understanding, we're not going to build anything yet." Throughout his post-workshop interview, Lance expressed a similar desire to spend more time on empathy. Lance's comments revealed some of the challenges that may arise when introducing a user into a project—teachers will have the increased responsibility of teaching students how to develop empathy, and students may not fully engage in the empathy-building process, preferring to jump to solutions instead.

Edith had more success engaging her students with interviewing. After the workshop, Edith also looked for an opportunity to fit design thinking into existing projects. She had her sixth-grade students design a nutrition product for a fifth grader, using the project as an opportunity to teach the design thinking process to her students and to place emphasis on interacting with a user. Edith recounted:

> They had to come up with interview questions. And so they wrote those out, and then we talked about good interview skills, and then took notes when they interviewed their user. And then they had to synthesize it . . . because I wanted them to think about their users not just from their answers about nutrition but more of their life together.

Students needed to be explicitly taught how to interview and ask good questions, skills that are particularly relevant to the 21st-century skill of communication. Edith's students also needed to learn how to synthesize interviewee responses, not simply reporting facts but also seeking to understand how these facts played into their users' lives. The addition of a user fundamentally altered the nature of the end-of-unit project, requiring students to not only focus on content, but also on how the content related to a particular user. In this regard, the project gave the academic content (nutrition) a meaningful purpose (influencing a fifth grader's nutritional habits).

Broader Benefits of Empathy

The other workshop participants also felt that empathy was important. When asked to describe the most significant aspects of design thinking, the most common response, 11 out of 23 respondents, was empathy. Multiple respondents addressed the importance of understanding the user and the need for solutions that really address user needs. Several STEM teachers identified empathy as being a missing component in the science or engineering process. One teacher who was a former engineer identified empathy as a missing component of problem-solving. She wrote:

> Since I am an engineer by life job (only a teacher for 6 years) I have been using this approach for a long time with one difference—the Empathize mode. I think this is so important to have a user-centered design process. This is not a concept that is always embraced by engineers in problem-solving.

The former engineer, now science teacher, highlights the connection between empathy and user-centered design, and importance of embracing empathy in her engineering courses. The first two design thinking challenges at the workshop provided opportunities for participating teachers to engage in the design thinking process in an area in which they were not familiar. This experience challenged teachers not only to work beyond their disciplinary boundaries but also to understand another's perspective without making assumptions based on previous biases.

Teachers Gaining a New Perspective

In many ways the experiences and principles of design thinking, as they related to empathy and listening, were "not natural" for participants. During the workshops, teachers were placed in a variety of situations that fundamentally challenged their comfort levels, or as a workshop instructor stated, "challenged you as a person"—where they did not know everything, where they were not experts, where outcomes were uncertain, and where failure was guaranteed and encouraged.

During the first design challenge groups were tasked to find a solution related to university campus safety. Reflecting upon this challenge, one participant remarked to her group,

> We were given a challenge, and in our heads we automatically thought, "Oh, this is the issue, or this is what needs to be done." And actually speaking to someone, not only does it give you that point of view, but it also makes you step outside of your own point of view.

The participant realized the importance of stepping beyond her own point of view to learn from the expertise of perspective of another.

Another teacher participant, a public high school English teacher shared an important realization with her design challenge reflection group during the workshop relating to this issue of expertise. Although three of her four teammates had no previous affiliation with the university, they still thought they would be able to find a solution to the campus safety problems. They had assumed expertise in an area in which they clearly had little experience. She shared, "we may be experts in our content, but we're not experts in being a ninth-grade student sitting in a classroom learning." This participant made an important connection to teaching, recognizing the limited expertise and perspectives that teachers have on the experiences of their students.

The idea of assuming a lack of expertise raised particular discomfort around feelings of uncertainty for teachers. An elementary school participant's comments during her studio's reflection time illustrated this discomfort:

> My personality, I think [the] personality a lot of teachers have is that we like to know what our objective is and then we make this great plan to meet it. And it's very uncomfortable for me to have no idea what the end result is going to be . . . It's uncomfortable for me to just listen to the

situation and then build something, and it may turn out to be nothing of what I thought. I value it. I want to do more of it, but it's not natural for me.

Teachers also reported that they encountered challenges when using an empathy-based approach to design lesson plans. When trying to plan lessons that met students' needs and desires, teachers experienced tensions between the "old," standards-based approach to lesson planning and the "new," design thinking-based approach to lesson planning. This tension manifests in an exchange between Edith and Jessica:

> *Edith:* This is pushing me to not think about what they're learning, but just what they think is cool . . . and then try to relate it . . . Then I'm like, well, how am I going to teach about earthquakes?

> *Jessica:* This is what I went through last night when they were changing my way of thinking.

In the above exchange, Edith explicitly identified the tension between focusing on what students think is cool (students' interests) and focusing on what students will learn (content). Her use of the verb "push" suggested the presence of a tension, as it implied being challenged or forced to move in a particular direction. Jessica affirmed Edith's sentiments and described how she also wrestled with the new way of thinking. In stating, "They were changing my way of thinking," Jessica acknowledged that the design thinking approach to planning was different from her existing notions of planning. The shift in moving towards a more empathy based approach to lesson planning was not easy because such an approach did not perfectly align with existing approaches to teaching.

Conclusion

In examining how empathy impacted lesson planning and instructional activities two themes arose. First, teachers used empathy for lesson planning and activity design, as a gateway to better pedagogy and instruction. Second, teachers had their students engage in empathy, as a gateway to STEM content.

Findings from this study suggest that professional development focused on empathy-based problem-solving (design thinking) helped teachers to integrate empathy into their lesson planning and their STEM-related instruction. Teachers were given the opportunity to experience empathy from a learner's perspective, which gave them a new appreciation for their students' perspectives. This increased sense of empathy influenced teachers to shift their emphasis from content standards towards students' interests. Current trends in lesson planning focus on standards based instruction, where the primary focus of lesson planning centers on disciplinary content knowledge. Under this traditional model, teachers are often given a set of content standards that must be "covered" in their respective classes. However, design thinking provided a new lens through which the teachers could approach content. Because design thinking focuses on meeting a user's needs, teachers view their students as the users of their lesson plans. Such a perspective transformed their outlook on planning.

The findings illustrate how the implementation of empathy in designing lessons varied. In some ways teachers' perceptions attended to more superficial elements of empathizing with students and planned according to what they perceived to be students' interests. In other instances, teachers adopted a more genuine empathy stance and tried to create classroom structures that addressed students' observed and vocalized needs. For some teachers, empathy initially translated into doing activities students would consider "fun," "cool," or "engaging." Yet this interpretation of empathy was a somewhat superficial understanding of empathizing with students because empathy with students can be much more than identifying topics simply because students are interested in it or because they think it is "cool." Empathy might include these things, but it is more about understanding students and their deeper needs as learners. Engaging in empathy to design lessons at a deeper level might mean finding ways to make lessons accessible to students with particular needs, such as those having language barriers or lacking particular skills. Engaging in empathy to design lessons might also mean working with students to address scientific problems and needs that students observe in the world. Or it might also mean engaging with students about their stresses and needs to design better learning environments to address their perceived issues.

Teachers were focused on listening to student needs and shifting plans accordingly—an approach drastically different from the traditional model of teaching where the teacher is supposed to be completely in charge and in control of the direction of the lesson. Such challenges highlight the fact that learning to engage in empathy is a process for both the teachers and the students (Sun, 2013). Teaching with empathy must be mastered like other kinds of teaching.

Findings from this study contribute to our understanding of how we might support teachers to adopt a more empathy-based approach to their instruction. Teachers who attempt to engage in an empathy-based approach must first make the mental shift from being one who "controls" instruction to one who designs instruction based on student input. Teachers may need additional support for how to engage students in empathy. If students are having trouble with asking follow up questions, teachers can design activities related to analyzing interview questions and identifying good probing questions. Teachers can also support students in their documentation and recording of their empathy experiences. For example, teachers might work with students to take notes or summarize interview findings, as Edith did with her students. Additionally, if students are more interested in building, as Lance mentioned, then perhaps teachers could develop ways to integrate empathy into building activities by incorporating, for example, empathy interviews and analysis around student prototypes.

From a research perspective it is important that we extend our understanding of how teachers can make empathy a more integral component in their STEM lessons. Future work might examine (1) classroom implementation of STEM curriculum that has an empathy component and (2) the impact of integrating empathy into STEM education on various student outcomes (i.e., academic achievement, dispositions towards science, etc.). Ultimately, such research and work with teachers may be particularly important for better preparing K-12 students to effectively tackle many of the complex, human-centered, and STEM-related issues of the 21st century.

Notes

1 All names are pseudonyms.
2 "Building stuff" was generated by the science teachers as one thing students are interested in.

References

Allworth, J. (2012, May 15). Empathy: The most valuable thing they teach at HBS. *Harvard Business Review.* Retrieved from https://hbr.org/2012/05/empathy-the-most-valuable-thing-they-t.

Barab, S.A., & Luehmann, A.L. (2003). Building sustainable science curriculum: Acknowledging and accommodating local adaptation. *Science Education, 87*(4), 454–467.

Bellet, P.S., & Maloney, M.J. (1991). The importance of empathy as an interviewing skill in medicine. *Jama The Journal of the American Medical Association, 266*(13), 1831–1832.

Borko, H., Jacobs, J., & Koellner, K. (2010). Contemporary approaches to teacher professional development. *International Encyclopedia of Education, 7*(2), 548–556.

Brown, T. (2008). Design thinking. *Harvard Business Review, 86*(6), 84–92.

Brown, T., & Katz, B. (2011). Change by design. *Journal of Product Innovation Management, 28*(1), 381–383.

Buchanan, R. (1992). Wicked problems in design thinking. *Design Issues, 8*(2), 5–21.

Carroll, M., Goldman, S., Britos, L., Koh, J., Royalty, A., & Hornstein, M. (2010). Destination, imagination and the fires within: Design thinking in a middle school classroom. *Journal of Arts and Design Education, 29*(1), 37–53.

Carroll, M.P. (2014). Shoot for the moon! The mentors and the middle schoolers explore the intersection of design thinking and STEM. *Journal of Pre-College Engineering Education Resarch (J-PEER), 4*(1), 14–30.

Cohen, D.K. (1990). A revolution in one classroom: The case of Mrs. Oublier. *Educational Evaluation and Policy Analysis, 12*(3), 311–329.

Davis, O.L., Yeager, E.A., & Foster, S.J. (Eds.). (2001). *Historical empathy and perspective taking in social studies.* Lanham, MD: Rowman & Littlefield.

Desimone, L. (2009). Improving impact studies of teachers' professional development: Toward better conceptualizations and measures. *Educational Researcher, 38*(3), 181–199.

Drake, C., & Sherin, M.G. (2006). Practicing change: Curriculum adaptation and teacher narrative in the context of mathematics education reform. *Curriculum Inquiry, 36*(2), 153–187.

Dym, C.L., Agogino, A.M., Eris, O., Frey, D.D., & Leifer, L.J. (2005). Engineering design thinking, teaching, and learning. *Journal of Engineering Education, 94*(1), 103–119.

Eisenberg, N., & Miller, P.A. (1987). The relation of empathy to prosocial and related behaviors. *Psychological Bulletin, 101*(1), 91–119.

Frykholm, J. (2004). Teachers' tolerance for discomfort: Implications for curricular reform in mathematics. *Journal of Curriculum and Supervision, 19*(2), 125–149.

Hmelo-Silver, C.E. (2004). Problem-based learning: What and how do students learn? *Educational Psychology, 16*(3), 235–266.

Kimbell, L. (2009). Design practices in design thinking. Paper presented at European Academy of Management.

Kolstoe, S.D. (2000). Consensus projects: teaching science for citizenship. *International Journal of Science Education, 22*(6), 645–664.

Leach, M., Scoones, I., & Wynne, B. (Eds.). (2005). *Science and citizens: globalization and the challenge of engagement.* London and New York, NY: Zed Books.

Lubchenco, J. (1998). Entering the century of the environment: A new social contract for science. *Science, 279*(5,350), 491–497.

Mansour, N. (2009). Science-technology-society (STS): A new paradigm in science education. *Bulletin of Science, Technology & Society, 29*(4), 287–297.

NGSS Lead States. (2013). *Next generation science standards: For states, by states.* Washington, DC: The National Academies Press.

Sun, K. (2013) *Teacher learning in a professional development context: An analysis of tensions.* Paper presented at American Educational Research Association Annual Meeting, San Francisco, CA.

Whitelaw, G. (2012, April 30). Empathy is the most powerful leadership tool. *Fast Company.* Retrieved from http://www.fastcompany.com/1835574/empathy-most-powerful-leadership-tool.

Yager, R.E. (Ed.). (1996). *Science/Technology/Society as reform in science education.* Albany, NY: State University of New York Press, Albany.

PART IV

Inspiring Teaching: Design Thinking in the Classroom

13

PROFESSIONAL DEVELOPMENT THAT BRIDGES THE GAP BETWEEN WORKSHOP AND CLASSROOM THROUGH DISCIPLINED IMPROVISATION

Jennifer Knudsen and Nicole Shechtman

The Bridging Professional Development project (which we refer to as Bridging PD) helps middle school mathematics teachers learn to *teach for argumentation*. Mathematical argumentation is a fundamental practice of mathematicians. We treat it as a social process in which students make conjectures and justify mathematical statements in classroom discussion. The purpose of an argument is to find out as a group whether a mathematical statement is true or not. The Common Core Standards for Mathematics (Common Core State Standards Initiative, 2010) have given new urgency to the need for argumentation to be taught in every classroom. To "construct viable arguments and critique the reasoning of others" is one of eight practice standards in the Common Core, along with others such as problem-solving and reasoning abstractly. The practice standards are relatively new to many teachers and are an important lever for engaging students in conceptually rich mathematical discourse.

Bridging PD, funded by the National Science Foundation to bring mathematical argumentation to a diversity of urban settings, addresses multiple facets of teacher knowledge and pedagogical practice, including teachers' own understanding of mathematical argumentation and the teaching moves they can use in the classroom to facilitate argumentative discourse. The PD is designed to bridge the gap between what teachers learn in a workshop and what they then apply in their classrooms. We have offered Bridging PD in three different in-service professional development formats, including summer institutes and Saturday workshops. Bridging PD belongs to a genre of research-oriented projects on professional development to support mathematics teachers in mathematical discourse. Among these are the JAGUAR project on algebraic justification and argumentation (Staples et al., 2012), the Mathematics Discourse in Secondary Classroom Project on the development of six specific teaching moves for supporting rich mathematical discourse in the classroom (Herbel-Eisenmann et al., 2013), and the Accountable Talk approach addressing norms and practices for discourse that has accountability to the learning community and the disciplines (Michaels et al., 2012).

Although we did not originally conceptualize Bridging PD in terms of design thinking, our work is very much in line with the design thinking approaches in this volume. At the heart of our project, we are supporting teachers to be design thinkers in the classroom and with their own practice. To begin to teach for argumentation, many teachers need to make some fundamental shifts in how they approach teaching. Fostering mathematical argumentation requires moving beyond traditional classroom discourse, which can be characterized as the initiation-response-evaluation approach where the predominant pattern is that the teacher initiates questions, students answer, and the teacher tells them whether they are correct or incorrect (Mehan, 1979). Teaching for argumentation requires a more facilitative approach that allows classroom discourse to be a collaborative activity in which students take on more of the mathematical authority and responsibility for constructing their own conceptual understanding. Like design work, collaboratively constructing mathematical arguments is not formulaic; the path is unforeseen and must be invented by the participants through creative discussion. This kind of process is called "collaborative emergence" (Sawyer, 2004). Indeed, doing design work and facilitating mathematical argumentation have much in common. Both are structured, collaborative activities with definable stages that are useful guidelines for this activity. Both are "serious fun" that results in products—a designed object, a proven mathematical statement— that are important, and in which participants experience the joy of creating. Furthermore, to become skillful at this kind of discourse, the teachers themselves must design their own practice that they can use flexibly and improvisationally in the classroom.

To support the facilitation of collaborative argumentation in the classroom, Bridging PD draws on a growing body of research that conceptualizes teaching as *disciplined improvisation* (e.g., Borko & Livingston, 1989; Burnard, 2011; DeZutter, 2011; Sawyer, 2004, 2011). Researchers in this milieu connect the professional practices of teaching with methods used in improvisational arts such as music and theater, in which experienced performers produce their work creatively as an ensemble in the moment without a script (Johnstone, 1979; King, 2001; Sawyer, 2011). They recognize the power of improvisational approaches to help teachers develop classroom learning environments that support the productive collaboration and intellectual risk-taking (Lobman, 2011) that are essential to making "bold conjectures" (Shechtman & Knudsen, 2011). *Discipline* is a critical component. Improvisation does not mean anything goes; it requires training, practice, and expertise in the underlying structures of the art form (Sawyer, 2011). Improvisers must be disciplined in their mastery of a shared tool kit that can be used creatively. Furthermore, we use improvisational activities to promote teachers' design thinking as they construct new practices for themselves. Improv activities give teachers opportunities to rapidly prototype new practices with each other in a safe workshop environment, receive constructive and supportive feedback, and iterate on what they are learning before they take it to the classroom.

Bridging PD addresses educational equity and preparing students for the 21st-century workplace, as can design thinking in educational settings (Goldman & Zielezinski, 2016). We believe that, on principle, students should have access to argumentation because it is a high-level disciplinary practice. It is a way to balance the primarily skills-based curriculum that many low-achieving districts have adopted. Mathematical argumentation is highly related to 21st-century workplace skills, as is design thinking. For example, making logical connections among abstract ideas and interacting with others to clarify their ideas are 21st-century skills necessary for an increasing number of good jobs (Partnership for 21st Century Skills, 2011). Additionally, collaboration and connected thinking are central to both mathematical argumentation and design.

In the rest of this chapter, we examine the key elements of the Bridging PD approach and discuss the research to date on what teachers learn in Bridging PD and what happens in their classrooms.

Facilitating Mathematical Argumentation: An Illustration

To make this all more concrete, here is a specific fictionalized example of a mathematical argument among three students addressing a common middle school topic, facilitated by their teacher. The conjecture they are discussing is whether all squares are rectangles. There are several key points to note. The first is the co-construction among each of the actors of the conjecture and justification. This includes both construction of ideas and constructive critiques of others' ideas. The second is the *teaching moves* that the teacher uses to facilitate this collaborative mathematical argumentation process. Moves are simple behaviors that are aimed at a specific purpose or purposes. Here, we see the teacher uses such moves as prompting for clarification, revoicing, making sure that multiple voices are heard, facilitating agreement, and strategically adding mathematical content to the discussion.

Discourse Moves		How the Moves Further the Argument
Jeri:	All squares are rectangles, you know.	Jeri makes a *conjecture*.
Kim:	No, that can't be. Squares don't have unequal sides, and every rectangle I have ever seen has unequal sides.	Kim provides a *justification* that the conjecture is false by offering a definition of rectangle based on her experiences with them.
Teacher:	What do you think, Malak?	The teacher brings in a third view.
Malak:	Unequal sides? That's not a rectangle. It's . . . it's a warp-angle.	Malak *critiques* Kim's argument.
Teacher:	Kim, you mean rectangle, not warp-angle (whatever that is), right?	The teacher asks students for clarification to address Malak's issue.
Kim:	Yeah.	
Teacher:	Well, what more do you need to say to make your statement into one about rectangles, not just warp-angles, which are really just plain old quadrilaterals with four unequal sides?	The teacher asks Kim to *refine her definition* of rectangle and clarifies what Malak meant by warp-angle using standard mathematical language.
Kim:	They have to line up. I mean two opposite sides are equal and the other two are equal, too.	Kim *refines* her definition.
Malak:	Yes, you have to put that "opposite" in there or it doesn't work to tell you what rectangles are.	Malak *agrees*.
Jeri:	See—that's the rule for a rectangle. But it doesn't say they can't all be equal. The square has opposite sides equal, no matter which way you look at it, so it has one opposite pair and another opposite pair—each equal but they are all equal.	Jeri uses Kim's definition to *justify* the conjecture that squares are included as rectangles.
Teacher:	Here's what I think you are saying: All rectangles have opposite sides equal. Don't forget, they have to have 90 degree angle corners, too. So take any square . . .	The teacher *revoices* the beginning of the argument, inviting students to complete it.

Malak:	It has opposite sides equal and 90 degree angle corners, too. So any square is also a rectangle. That's what I said, right?	Malak *refines* the definition of rectangle and agrees with Jeri's conjecture.
Teacher:	Right!	The teacher voices shared agreement.
Kim:	This is different than when I learned shapes back in kindergarten.	Kim contrasts this new view of rectangles with her old one.
Teacher:	Well, you are way past kindergarten, Kim. This is the real thing—real math.	

These students work together to define a rectangle and understand the relationship between squares and rectangles—addressing a commonly held misconception. They move through stages of conjecturing, justifying, and concluding, with refining and critiquing as important activities along the way.

Using New Norms for Constructing Arguments Together

Both classroom mathematical argumentation and design thinking in school require new norms for how students are to work together. Such norms should include expectations that are in alignment with the rights and responsibilities of individuals engaged in creative collaborative work. Figure 13.1 shows a list of some key rules, or norms, as used in theatrical improvisation that inspired the norms we use in our Bridging PD workshops. The norm to say "Yes, and" is perhaps the most fundamental: it captures the right of every participant to have his or her ideas heard and the reciprocal responsibility to hear everyone else's ideas. The "Yes, and" norm promotes awareness that rather than simply negating what a classmate is saying, the task in argumentation is to thoroughly understand what the other person is saying so as to consider the possibility that it is true. This is similarly pertinent to the empathizing stage of design thinking. Further, both collaborating designers and arguers must say yes to each other's ideas by accepting them even while critiquing and refining them.

An important part of disciplined improv is the use of improv games to establish the norms. These games have simple rules to follow. The rules vary to help participants develop expertise in different aspects of improv—and their analogs in argumentation. The participants may vary the characters, setting, and central problem to solve so that a wide variety of scenes are played out. The improv games are useful for setting norms in both classrooms and professional development workshops.

Rules of Improv

1. Say "YES, and..."

2. Don't negate

3. Give and accept offers

4. Make mistakes

5. Make the ensemble look good

FIGURE 13.1   Rules of Improv used in Bridging PD workshops (for examples, see Johnstone, 1979; Lobman, 2011)

Gift giving is an improv game that helps develop the norm "Yes, and." In the game, a giver acts out offering a wrapped package to a receiver, such as by hoisting an imaginary heavy package. The receiver identifies the gift and thanks the giver, for example, "A Frida Kahlo painting! Just what I wanted!" The giver then explains why that gift was chosen for the receiver, for example, "I knew you like her work." It's important that the giver responds in the moment to whatever the receiver names as the gift; it's not OK to say, "No, that's not what I gave you." This game helps both arguers and designers establish norms for their playful work. As one of our Bridging PD teachers said, "A conjecture is a gift," referring to its role in the emerging argument and the way it should be received by arguers. So it is with designers' contributions during ideation and prototyping. Even if a conjecture is ultimately found false or a prototype discarded, the argument or the design is furthered.

Another fundamental rule, "Make mistakes," encourages arguers to concentrate on producing ideas and communicating them. This is not a typical norm in a traditional mathematics classroom, yet it is critical to learning, to making good arguments, and to making good designs. It is often the case that more mathematics concepts are uncovered in exploring what is ultimately found to be a false conjecture. Likewise, while no idea is wrong in brainstorming during ideation, the design thinking that leads to abandoning an idea can ultimately be more important than if a straight path from ideation to product were taken. Hence, productive failure (Kapur, 2008) is a theme in argumentation as well as in design thinking. In our example argument, Kim made a definition of rectangles that was subsequently found inadequate—she had simply defined irregular quadrilaterals. But Kim's offering led to the insight that opposite sides of a rectangle must be equal and that this didn't preclude the case where the two pairs are equal and

Conjecturing

- Look for math patterns that make sense to you.
- Think about more than just one case.
- Be creative.
- Don't judge other people's conjectures.

Justifying

- Look for reasons why a conjecture is true or false.
- Consider examples and counterexamples.
- Build off of other people's ideas.
- Generalize.
- Try to convince others of your ideas, but keep in mind that you could be wrong. . .which is OK.

Concluding

- End an argument when your class is convinced that the conjecture is true (or false).

FIGURE 13.2   How to do math argumentation

ultimately to the conclusion that a square is a rectangle, too. The failure led to the productive resolution of the truth of a conjecture.

Another important set of norms that we emphasize in Bridging PD are the sociomathematical norms associated with the structure of an argument, the phases of conjecturing, justifying, and concluding. To support these norms and help scaffold discussions, we provide teachers with a poster to use in the classroom (see Figure 13.2). There are notable parallels between design thinking and argumentation. Imagine replacing "conjecture" with "design" and "truth" with "usefulness," "practicality," or "elegance." For example, "Look for reasons why a conjecture is true or false," becomes, "Look for reasons why a design is useful, practical, or elegant." Then the norms for argumentation and design do not seem very far apart. The conjecturing phase of argumentation is an analog of the ideation stage of design thinking, and justifying has similarities with prototyping and testing the design.

Designing New Teaching Moves to Facilitate Argumentation

Even in the somewhat tidy argumentation scenario presented earlier, it's easy to see that the teacher had to be on her toes. The argument may not flow so easily.

Problems of equal participation could have arisen: What if Malak had been reluctant to raise his objection? At one point, the teacher decided to summarize what the students had said. When is the right time to summarize? Additionally, could the teacher have taken a less directive role in the argument? The information that right angles are necessary to a rectangle could have come from the students, for example. Did Kim's comment that it's different from kindergarten mean she understood or was left in a muddle? The answers affect how the teacher would have concluded this argumentation session. Responding to these complexities is challenging. Of course, teaching in general can be challenging, but teaching for argumentation is different from giving a traditional lesson, with definitions first, examples second, and practice problems third (Yackel & Cobb, 1996). Teaching for argumentation requires a lot of improvisation.

As part of Bridging PD, we also use several pedagogies inspired by improv and other theatrical methods to help teachers design new teaching moves to deal with these types of challenges. For example, early in the workshop, to get teachers thinking about teaching moves, we have them read through scripts of classroom discourse and discuss their reactions. Like actors in their first time through a script together, teachers sit at a table and read their assigned parts. The simple experience of reading aloud what a teacher might say often provides insights. In one Bridging PD workshop, a teacher told us that in her classroom, she provided plenty of opportunities for students to explain their reasoning. But then, when taking part in a read-through, she recognized that the teacher in the script asked questions, but most of them were questions with short answers that did not require much explanation at all. "That is me," she said, with some surprise. The perspective acquired through the script reading affords teachers the opportunity to see differences between what they do and what they say. These differences are contributors to the gap we are trying to bridge—between what happens in the workshop and what teachers later do in the classroom—and the next activities are designed to bridge that gap.

Teaching games—inspired by improv games—bridge the gap by helping teachers develop and practice new teaching moves. For example, one game called *Open and Closed* contrasts two types of teaching moves by having teachers in small groups take on the roles of teacher and students and play out a scene with two different sets of rules. Teachers might be assigned, from the dialogue presented earlier, the characters of students Jeri, Kim, and Malak and their teacher, with the setting being just the first two lines of the dialogue where Jeri and Kim disagree. The problem is to bring the class to agreement on whether or not squares are rectangles. The same scene is played in two rounds. In the first round of the game, the teacher can ask only open-ended questions of the "students." For example, she can ask, "What do you think?" In the second round, the reverse is true. She can ask only closed-ended questions or give instructions or information. She could ask, "What is the definition of a rectangle?" or even provide a definition of a rectangle. After playing out the two rounds, the teachers uncover possible purposes for open- and closed-ended questioning and thus prepare to use them both in their classrooms. To be clear, we are not saying that one type of question is better than the other in teaching for argumentation but that both can and should be used, purposefully.

The norms of collaboration are important foundations for playing teaching games. Playing out teaching scenes with other teachers can be stressful; teachers can feel judged or inadequate if things don't go perfectly. Improv games like *Gift Giving* help set norms that ameliorate these feelings and help teachers work together productively to uncover information about teaching through the games. For example, in classroom scenes teachers can be tempted to play the most difficult students—the ones who disrupt class and refuse to participate. The "Make the ensemble look good" rule creates an atmosphere of support where those playing students don't have to behave like model students, but they do have to help build opportunities to try out pedagogical moves (other than classroom management) within the game.

We also give teachers an opportunity to try out their new teaching moves in rehearsals of lessons they plan to deliver in the classroom. In theater, a rehearsal is the final step between preparation and performance, so the Bridging PD workshop ends with rehearsal time for each teacher. Each teacher gets 20 minutes in which to marshal her peers to help her act out some possibly problematic aspect of teaching for argumentation. A teacher may be concerned about how to conclude an argument. She can set up a scene that comes toward the end of a lesson, assign specific student roles to other teachers, and play it out. She can try out new teaching moves learned in the workshop and deal with dilemmas that might arise. For example, can summarizing what students have said so far help everyone understand what has been said, or might it close down thinking? Is it possible to know that the whole class understands? These are important and not easily answered questions. They are represented dramatically in the rehearsal. The rehearsal is close enough to classroom practice to give it veracity, but it is not the actual high-stakes performance with students. It provides teachers with insights that they can take back to the classroom and provides another opportunity to try out new teaching moves. Rehearsal is an idea that is used in pre-service teacher preparation, too, with the goal of providing close approximations of practice (Grossman et al., 2009) for novice teachers (Lampert et al., 2013).

In preparation for rehearsal, teachers do what we call visualizing a lesson, enabling them to consider rapid prototypes of their teaching moves. Working in pairs, one teacher describes aloud what she would do for a particular lesson, down to the level of what she would write on the board and where. The other teacher creates a written outline based on this visualization. After both teachers have had a chance to take each role, they create detailed lesson plans from which they can improvise in rehearsals as well as in class. The lesson plans do not constrain teachers' improvisation but instead provide a map from which to chart the improvisational route of teaching.

We can consider teachers as design thinkers as they go through all these activities: they are designing a new way to teach. As teachers take on the role of students, they must *empathize* with them, understanding, for example, what a student new to argumentation may bring to the activity as they play out what such a student might do. Even reading scripts offers the opportunity to empathize with the students and teachers being represented. When setting up a teaching game, teachers must *define* teaching problems, similar to defining a design challenge, such as how to bring students to agreement on a particular conjecture. They need to *prototype* new teaching moves, trying them out in the game in rapid succession to see which have utility and how. Then, through rehearsals, they *test* their newly designed teaching moves, to see how they might work in practice. The ultimate test, however, is how the moves function once teachers have embarked on teaching argumentation with their students back in their classrooms.

Research

Integral to the design and development of the Bridging PD model was research on teacher knowledge, teachers' practice and students' opportunities for doing mathematical argumentation, and student learning. For each of three configurations of the program, we conducted or are conducting studies that examine the discourse occurring in teachers' classrooms.

Bridging PD I

Design and Methods

We designed our first Bridging PD study to answer the question, *Through participating in the Bridging PD program, do teachers grow in their specialized* mathematics knowledge for teaching *(MKT)* (Hill et al., 2005) *and do they increase argumentative talk in their classrooms?* The program was implemented in a two-year small-scale randomized impact study. With a particular focus on teachers of underserved student populations, we recruited middle school math teachers from high-poverty urban districts in the San Francisco Bay Area. Each year was a stand-alone program—year 1 addressed argumentation with the content of similarity, and year 2 addressed argumentation with the content of coordinate geometry. Most teachers attended for either year 1 or year 2, although a few attended for both years.

All teachers were randomly assigned to the treatment group or the control group. Teachers in the treatment group had the full two-week Bridging PD—MKT in the first week and pedagogy in the second (teaching moves to facilitate argumentation). Teachers in the control group had the MKT workshop in the first week but in the second week attended a different PD session of equal value to them but targeting different pedagogical knowledge (vertical coordination across grade levels). This experimental manipulation enabled us to examine the impacts of the first week's MKT PD alone versus the MKT PD *coupled with* the PD on teaching moves and bridges to classroom practice.

There were two main outcome measures for all teachers in both groups. The first was a pre-workshop and post-workshop MKT assessment aligned with the content of the MKT in the workshops. Each assessment asked teachers questions about similarity or coordinate geometry, whichever was the topic of that year's curriculum unit. Some questions were pure math questions and others were set in the context of student work.

Here is an example of the type of item we used:

> Jamal missed yesterday's lesson on graphing equations. Ms. Jones is working with him individually to help him catch up.
>
> She draws the following graph and states, "The line is a graphical representation of the equation y = x + 3."
>
> Jamal asks, "What does that mean?"
>
> In the space below, give a mathematically correct explanation that is appropriate for seventh graders.

The second main outcome measure was observations of argumentative talk in the teachers' classrooms. We observed and videotaped teachers in both treatment and control groups for two days in their classrooms teaching with materials covered in the first week (MKT). We used the videotapes to make transcripts

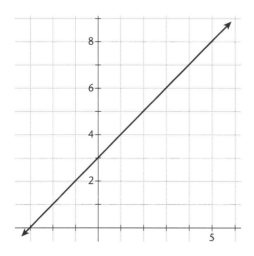

of all the whole-class discourse. We developed a coding scheme for counting the number, duration, and type of arguments occurred. The protocol comprises two passes through a classroom transcript. In the first, coders identify all segments of argumentative talk, coming to agreement on where statements' mathematical justifications begin and end. In the second pass, within these segments of argumentative talk, coders counted the number of student statements and the occurrences of various types of teaching moves, such as open-ended and closed-ended questions, orchestration of participation, and complexity of the intellectual work demanded of the students.

Findings

We found several positive results. The changes in teachers' scores on the MKT assessment between the beginning and end of each workshop indicated that teachers in both the treatment and control groups grew in their understanding of the mathematics. In year 1, the focus was on argumentation about similarity, and there was a moderate effect size of .5 [$t(23) = 4.2, p < .001$]; in year 2, the focus was on argumentation about coordinate geometry, and there was a moderate effect size of .3 [$t(20) = 4.5, p < .0001$]. The number of student statements made in argumentative discourse in treatment classrooms was approximately double that in control classrooms in both years 1 and 2 (Figure 13.3). In year 1, this difference was statistically significant with a large effect size of 1.4 [$t(13) = 2.6, p < .05$], whereas in year 2, this difference was a marginally significant trend with a moderate effect size of .7 [$t(14) = 1.4, p = .18$]. Similarly, in the treatment group we observed a greater number of teaching moves facilitating student argumentative talk. In year 1, teachers used more closed-ended questions [$t(11.5) = 2.2, p < .05$], open-ended questions [$t(12.0) = 2.8, p < .05$], and moves to facilitate and encourage participation by multiple students [$t(11.8) = 2.4, p < .05$].[1] In year 2, there were nonsignificant trends, indicating that treatment teachers did more of each of the examined teaching moves. More detail on these findings as well as case studies will be in a forthcoming article by the authors.

Although these main effects were substantial, significant variation also existed between teachers in how much argumentation occurred in each classroom. As designers, we wanted to know whether there were any patterns that might indicate consistent reasons why teachers might underperform and whether we might be able to design additional supports for the teachers. Therefore, we examined potential mediating variables that might contribute to more or less classroom argumentation. The most important mediator was teachers' prior MKT. In both years, middle school math teachers came to our PD with a wide range of prior knowledge—on both years' pretests, teachers' scores spanned the full range, from less than 15 percent correct to 85 per cent and higher. This had important

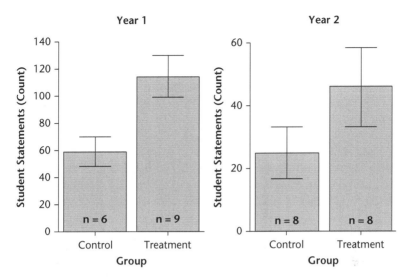

FIGURE 13.3   Argumentative talk: mean counts ($\pm$ standard error) of student
statements

Note: The number of statements is not comparable across years because the curriculum materials
were different.

consequences in the classroom. Whereas treatment teachers overall had more
argumentative talk in their classrooms, the average length of the arguments was
highly related to their content knowledge.

Our qualitative investigations in the PD and classrooms also revealed that the
interpersonal practices of mathematical argumentation were novel for many teachers
and that teaching for argumentation was challenging regardless of prior specialized
content knowledge for teaching. In the PD, teachers expressed uncertainty and
skepticism about using what they perceived to be more open-ended practices in
their classrooms. It became apparent in PD discussions they needed more support in
setting up their classroom culture so that argumentation was a possibility.

Bridging PD II

Design and Methods

In our second Bridging PD project, a design research study addressed core
research question was, *How can we extend and expand the Bridging PD model to
enhance students' opportunity to engage in argumentation and learn mathematical content?* We extended the program in four ways:

1. developed a two-week replacement unit, *Argumentation with Triangles* (on
    geometry content), with more explicit supports for teachers with weak MKT;

2. added a set of tools that teachers could use to establish classroom norms and structure interpersonal practices for argumentation;
3. provided richer opportunities for students to engage in argumentation through group work, written argumentation, and using dynamic representational software (The Geometer's Sketchpad);
4. examined students' understanding of content and competency in argumentation through assessments and interviews.

We examined four teachers' implementation of the unit and what their students learned. The teachers taught the triangles unit at the beginning of the school year so it could be used to establish classroom social and sociomathematical norms. We asked each teacher to select a target class that we would observe most days of the unit. Across teachers, we observed a range of classes, from an advanced geometry class to regular seventh-grade math to a class that supported the needs of students with learning disabilities. An assessment was administered to the students in the target class before and after the unit. We used the pre-test and post-test to identify students with a range of ability in written mathematical argumentation and conducted follow-up interviews to examine their ability to make spoken arguments. To analyze classroom discourse, we reviewed the videos and observation notes to examine how argumentation was or was not supported by the teaching moves focused on in the PD. We did not use predetermined codes but used a more open-ended analytic technique to relate student and teacher moves.

Findings

In all the target classrooms, students demonstrated substantial learning gains, with an effect size of 1.45 [$t(96) = 9.94$, $p < .0001$], on average gaining 10.31 points out of 36 from pretest to post-test (Figure 13.4).

Through this design study, we continued to identify challenges for practice and opportunities for improvement. Not surprisingly, interview findings indicated that after two weeks of instruction, students were successful in basic argumentation, yet there was still room for growth in argumentation skills. This pointed to the need for a longer, more comprehensively integrated PD program. Additionally, in a focus group, project teachers discussed challenges they faced with struggling students, providing important insights into the learning needs of a variety of students. Case studies from our analysis of classroom discourse are forthcoming and address teaching moves as scaffolds for content or argumentation or both.

Bridging PD III

In current work, we are collaborating with a large urban district to offer a two-year program of professional development for mathematics teachers. Our research questions address how teaching practice and students' participation in

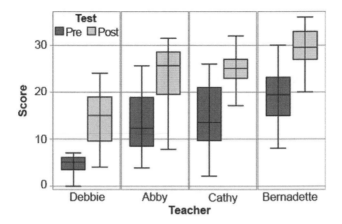

FIGURE 13.4 Student learning results for the Bridging PD triangle unit

argumentation can change over the course of much longer professional development than we have previously been able to offer—and how teachers can include all students in argumentation. Using a quasi-experimental design, we are collecting data before, during, and after the two-year PD and will also be able to track what was learned in the workshop into the classroom in a set of case studies. During a first year of co-design with district teachers and staff, we adapted the materials developed in Bridging I and II and created online tools that would be useful in learning and planning to teach for argumentation: an argument database that houses scores of arguments students might make, searchable by standard or by key words, and a "conjecture cloud" where teachers can visually arrange conjectures to determine how to integrate all students' contributions into a class discussion. We used the design thinking process that Goldman and her colleagues use (Carroll et al., 2010 regarding middle school kids; Goldman & Bullock, 2016 regarding teachers) with our co-designer teachers. The research and practitioner teams learned from each other and built new knowledge as well as products, improvisationally.

Conclusion

Bridging PD is very much in line with other design thinking approaches to education. Mathematical argumentation requires the same kind of spontaneous, cooperative action as improv theater while maintaining the rigor of a search for true mathematical statements. That same spirit of improvisation connects argumentation with design thinking as well—in embracing the ideas of others and taking risks that can lead to failure, with the insight that failure leads to productive discourse and design solutions. As design thinkers in the classroom and with their own practice, teachers work to make fundamental shifts in how they approach classroom mathematical discussions. Teaching for argumentation means facilitating and orchestrating complex mathematical discussions in which mathematical truths emerge collaboratively. This requires a lot from teachers. They need not only an understanding of the mathematics, but also a pedagogical repertoire that they can use flexibly and improvisationally in the moment as discussions unfold. As part of Bridging PD's multipronged approach, methods adapted from theatrical improv provide teachers with norms and practical tools that they can use to set expectations that support productive struggle and collaboration and scaffold generative conversations in the classroom. In PD, improv methods can also help teachers rapidly prototype, try out, and get feedback on their own new practices in a safe environment before taking them back to the classroom. While our research examined the Bridging PD intervention as a whole rather than the effects of the improv specifically, our findings and new work in three studies suggest that this approach can have tangible impacts on teachers' practice and their students' access to the critical high-level disciplinary practice of argumentation. Both doing design work and facilitating mathematical argumentation can be serious fun that supports equity and the development of important skills for the 21st century.

Note

1 Note that t statistics were adjusted to accommodate unequal variances.

References

Borko, H., & Livingston, C. (1989). Cognition and improvisation: Differences in mathematics instruction by expert and novice teachers. *American Educational Research Journal, 26*(4), 473–498.

Burnard, P. (2011). Creativity, pedagogic partnerships, and the improvisatory space of teaching. In R.K. Sawyer (Ed.), *Structure and improvisation in creative teaching* (pp. 51–72). Cambridge: Cambridge University Press.

Carroll, M., Goldman, S., Britos, L., Koh, J., Royalty, A., & Hornstein, M. (2010). Destination, imagination and the fires within: Design thinking in a middle school classroom. *International Journal of Art & Design Education, 29*(1), 37–53.

Common Core State Standards Initiative. (2010). *Mathematics standards*. Retrieved from http://www.corestandards.org/Math/.

DeZutter, S. (2011). Professional improvisation and teacher education: Opening the conversation. In R.K. Sawyer (Ed.), *Structure and improvisation in creative teaching* (pp. 27–50). Cambridge: Cambridge University Press.

Goldman, S., & Zielezinski, M. (2016). Teaching with design thinking: Developing new vision and approaches to 21st century learning. In L.A. Annetta & J. Minogue (Eds.), *Connecting science and engineering education practices in meaningful ways: Building bridges* (pp. 237–262). Switzerland: Springer International Publishing.

Grossman, P., Compton, C., Igra, D., Ronfeldt, M., Shahan, E., & Williamson, P. (2009). Teaching practice: A cross-professional perspective. *The Teachers College Record, 111*(9), 2055–2100.

Herbel-Eisenmann, B.A., Steele, M.D., & Cirillo, M. (2013). (Developing) teacher discourse moves: A framework for professional development. *Mathematics Teacher Educator, 1*(2), 181–196.

Hill, H.C., Rowan, B., & Ball, D.L. (2005). Effects of teachers' mathematical knowledge for teaching on student achievement. *American Educational Research Journal, 42*(2), 371–406.

Johnstone, K. (1979). *Impro: Improvisation and the theatre.* London: Faber & Faber.

Kapur, M. (2008). Productive failure. *Cognition and Instruction, 26*(3), 379–424.

King, K.D. (2001). Conceptually-oriented mathematics teacher development: Improvisation as a metaphor. *For the Learning of Mathematics, 21*(3), 9–15.

Lampert, M., Franke, M.L., Kazemi, E., Ghousseini, H., Turrou, A.C., Beasley, H., & Crowe, K. (2013). Keeping it complex using rehearsals to support novice teacher learning of ambitious teaching. *Journal of Teacher Education, 64*(3), 226–243.

Lobman, C. (2011). Improvising within the system: Creating new teacher performances in inner-city schools. In R.K. Sawyer (Ed.), *Structure and improvisation in creative teaching* (pp. 73–93). New York, NY: Cambridge University Press.

Mehan, H. (1979). "What time is it, Denise?": Asking known information questions in classroom discourse. *Theory into Practice, 18*(4), 285–294.

Michaels, S., O'Connor, M.C., & Hall, M.W. (with Resnick, L.B.). (2012). *Accountable Talk® sourcebook: For classroom conversation that works.* Pennsylvania, PA: University of Pittsburgh Institute for Learning.

Partnership for 21st Century Skills. (2011). *Framework for 21st century learning.* Retrieved from http://www.p21.org/our-work/p21-framework.

Sawyer, R.K. (2004). Creative teaching: Collaborative discussion as disciplined improvisation. *Educational Researcher, 33*(2), 2–12.

Sawyer, R.K. (2011). What makes good teachers great: The artful balance of structure and improvisation. In R.K. Sawyer (Ed.), *Structure and improvisation in creative teaching* (pp. 1–24). New York, NY: Cambridge University Press.

Shechtman, N., & Knudsen, J. (2011). *Bringing out the playful side of mathematics: Using methods for improvisational theater in professional development for urban middle school math teachers.* Lanham, MD: University Press of America.

Staples, M.E., Bartlo, J., & Thanheiser, E. (2012). Justification as a teaching and learning practice: Its (potential) multifaceted role in middle grades mathematics classrooms. *Journal of Mathematical Behavior, 31*, 447–462.

Yackel, E., & Cobb, P. (1996). Sociomathematical norms, argumentation, and autonomy in mathematics. *Journal for Research in Mathematics Education, 27*(4), 458–477.

14

THE MATERIALITY OF DESIGN IN E-TEXTILES

Verily Tan, Anna Keune, and Kylie Peppler

> *The red, white, and blue star-shaped buttons caught Peter's eye on the first day of the electronic-textile workshop—they connected with Peter's patriotic sentiments. He decided to combine these buttons with a shirt with the same colour scheme that he had designed prior to the workshop. The upcoming 4th of July holiday gave him inspiration to create a 'display of fireworks' on his t-shirt using LEDs on top of the star-shaped buttons, and he added sound effects through low alternating notes from a buzzer.*

Peter was one of the teachers who attended an electronic-textile, or e-textile, workshop as part of a summer professional development program in a mid-Atlantic town. In this vignette, what do we perceive as bringing about Peter's design decisions? Most conventional views of design would see Peter acting on and transforming the materials: Peter created the fireworks display with LEDs and the sound effects using a buzzer. On closer examination, the materials also appear to have agency, priming Peter's design choices. For example, the color of the materials seemed to prompt Peter's patriotic emotions, to work on his imagination, and to influence his actions toward a coherent design of a patriotic fireworks display. Imagine if these materials were not available and instead were replaced by glittering neon buttons or other materials not conducive to a patriotic theme. How then would Peter's artifact have been conditioned, and what form would the artifact have taken?

Traditionally, design has been perceived as a humanist endeavor, where the designer is the agent of the activity, concretizing an abstract theoretical concept into an artifact (Nelson & Stolterman, 2012; Cross, 1982). The designer brings about the "courses of action aimed at changing existing situations into preferred ones" (Simon, 1982, p. 129), and makes decisions about the materials, proportion, and tools to achieve a desired outcome (Nelson & Stolterman, 2012). The designer is acting in an effort to provide a service (Löwgren & Stolterman, 2004). Design has also been defined as "a reflective conversation with the materials of the design situation" (Schön, 1983, p. 76). Here the designers' capabilities to listen and respond to the cultured and contextualized material are foregrounded. The designer makes decisions that bring about a desirable result amidst contextualized interactions in the discovering, designing, and reflecting (Schön & Wiggins, 1992). In these views, we often forget that the materiality of design conditions much of the direction of design. Like Peter in the summary of his design process above, it is hard to untangle just how much the person acts on the material to transform it, or *in what ways the materials condition the particular design artifacts that are nursed into being.*

We have been increasingly interested in looking at design through a materialist, post-structuralist, and post-humanist view that takes a "material turn" (Braidotti, 2013). In this view, agency is no longer owned and produced by human agents or designers alone, but is dispersed and distributed to different materialities or their assemblages and emerges as a consequence of their intra-actions (Barad, 2007). As opposed to "interactions," intra-actions do not presume independent entities and relations. Through agential intra-actions, boundaries and properties of the "components" of design become determinate, which in turn make particular embodied concepts meaningful. Hence, we focus not only on the actions of the designer, but also on the transformative agency of the materials. How is intention and agency shared between the designer and (perhaps preconditioned by) the materials themselves in the design process? A skilled designer selects appropriate starting materials to envision the project (knowing that other materials will take the project in an unwanted direction). Design materials become active agents that extend their reach from being and acting in the world, and designers become entangled with the being and acting of things (Barad, 2007; Rogers, 2009).

A "Material Turn" in Design

In his seminal work, Schön (1983) eloquently discussed the reflective interactions between the materials of the design and the designer, suggesting that these three entities (material, designer, and design artifact) are engaging in an interactive back-and-forth. It is this interaction between the material of design and the designer's craftsmanship that Nelson and Stolterman (2012) highlight as requiring our attention if we want to theorize and understand how design comes about. Their definition of materials in the design process goes beyond the physical material, encompassing also the ideas and cultural contexts within which design takes place. Thinking and doing are intertwined as the designer engages in dialogue with the materials. While the materials are attributed with a "voice" with which they "talk back" to the designer, informing them about what can or cannot be done, it is the designer who selects which materials to bring to the design situation, which material voices are invited and heard, and how they are interpreted. Here, the material acts through the designer, facilitating the human intentions and expressing the desired design artifact. This suggests that the human designer acts with agency over the material to bring a design into becoming.

The becoming of a design continues after design time, once a design artifact is placed in use with those people for whom it was intended (e.g., Fischer, 2013). Specifically focusing on the act of tailoring digital design artifacts, Henderson and Kyng (1992) suggest that supporting design in use is desired as it increases agency of how artifacts can be shaped to better fit their particular situations of use. This notion of tailorability is tightly connected with human agency: at design time, a person made it possible for the design artifact to be tailored in the future, and, in this way, agency is intentionally transposed across time to another person who may tailor.

Design can be a process of mutual learning (e.g., Blomberg & Karasti, 2012). This process of reaching intersubjectivity is facilitated through materials of design that help "discuss current situations and envision future ones" through design-by-doing (Löwgren & Stolterman, 2004). Flexible and loosely structured materials are provided to participants of design, including paper prototypes or cardboard mock-ups to co-create dialogue about potential designs through the materials selected as communicative tools. These materials communicate unfinished and not-yet-thought-through designs and are intended to conjure up playful ways into design, in which participants communicate implicit understandings through visual and tactile means rather than words alone (Brandt et al., 2012). These are well-intended material ways for providing participants with expressive means and a voice to shape the process and product of design.

In the new materialist perspective of design, the role of physical materials is not subordinate to the agency of the designer. This may mean that objective, normative, or subjective messages that are embedded in the materials at creation and through extended use are foregrounded through the way materials are intra-acting with the human agents. The ways of doing that the materials communicate can be explored and they can teach us things that may be transferred to other materials (Cabral & Justice, 2013). They respond to the designer as well as make bids for action that can favor certain responses of the humans above others, evoking patterns of actions that can stretch across time and space. This highlights the importance of questioning which materials to invite to the design situation in order to expand the voice of the participants, and begs the question: what are the patterns that drive the material agent into the design, and how can we use this productively to invite design that is not preconditioning the results?

New domains are particularly advantageous for exploring this dynamic between material and designer because nearly everyone has something new to learn in the design process in terms of properties of materials and their functionality. We illustrate these aspects through focal cases of participants designing with e-textiles—fabric-based artifacts embedded with electronics and small, wearable computers connected with conductive thread. The process of crafting with e-textiles allows participants to customize both the form and function of their artifacts (Buechley et al., 2013). E-textiles offer unique opportunities to explore the materiality of design, which pertains to the emergence of designs through an empirical process of material making and discovery (Orth, 2013). Furthermore, the computational aspects of e-textile designs, their "programming materiality," can emerge through similar cycles of experimentation and surprise (Berzowska, 2005).

Prior research on e-textiles focused on the designer in looking at aesthetics, remixing, and repurposing of designs (Fields et al., 2012; Kafai et al., 2011, 2012). Additionally, in the science, technology, engineering, and mathematics (STEM) domains, e-textiles effectively introduced circuitry concepts to youth (e.g., Peppler & Glosson, 2013). With regards to materiality, we looked at how e-textiles can potentially rupture traditional gendered scripts around electronics through the purposeful nexus of traditionally "masculine" and "feminine" tools and practices, which implicitly give girls hands-on access and leadership roles in the design process that are consequential for both learning and participation in STEM (Buchholz et al., 2014). This chapter extends this earlier work by exploring the agency of the design materials in conditioning the outcomes of design. We present the analysis of four focal cases of novice designers working on e-textiles to illustrate this phenomenon.

Workshop Description

Setting, Objectives, and Participants

Four focal cases were selected from among ten participants in a two-day (14-hour) e-textile workshop involving K-12 teachers in a mid-Atlantic town. Teachers signed up for the workshop as part of their Science, Technology, Engineering, Arts, and Mathematics (STEAM) professional development, which was a new priority of the school district. The district, seeking to integrate engineering and computer science into all subject areas and grade levels, commissioned the e-textiles workshop as one of several STEAM-related professional development activities. The goal of the workshop was to invite educators to explore e-textiles through personal projects as active participants and future facilitators of similar activities. Exploring the e-textile materials through design projects was intended for educators to explore connections between the materials and the STEAM fields they taught or planned to teach in their classrooms. On the first day of the workshop, participants were introduced to simple e-textiles circuitry, after which they sewed a practice project. They were then introduced to the LilyPad Simple development board (a wearable computer), learning to program it with the visual programming software Modkit (http://www.modkit. com/micro). On the second day, participants worked on design projects. They were invited to bring a personal item to combine with a variety of materials provided by the workshop, such as buttons, sequins, ribbons, and a variety of fabrics.

Data Sources and Analytical Techniques

The design processes of all participants were captured through (1) pictures of participants working on their projects to capture the development of the artifacts over time; (2) participants' planning documents to reference initial starting points; (3) close-up pictures and videos of the final artifacts to compare design projects across participants; (4) daily observation notes to document the researchers' impressions; and (5) audio-recorded, semi-structured interviews (15–20 min) conducted at the end of the workshop to capture the participants' own reflections on their design artifact and process. Interview questions included: "What do you like most about your design?" and "Describe the process of making your e-textile. If there were something you could change about your e-textile design, what would it be?" Through the informal interviews, we hoped to unearth the tension between the designers' intentions and the affordances of the materials used. The metadata of the documents—each data point had a time-stamp—allowed us to re-construct a temporal narrative of the design processes. The combination of this data helped paint a broad picture of the design process, with the interview data providing a first-person perspective on the thoughts behind the designs. In this way, we sought to better understand the intra-actions between humans and materials in the workshop through augmented qualitative observations.

Focal Cases

To select focal cases, we searched the data for participants who actively sought to realize a specific design idea through their project, as opposed to those participants who took a more exploratory, tinkering approach to design. Of these two categories, the former more clearly demonstrates what we would traditionally describe as human agency in the design process, leveraging the materials on hand to execute an idea. By focusing on these cases, we sought to understand how material played a role in what could readily be seen as a human-centered design process. Of the five projects fulfilling this description, we further narrowed our selection by looking for cases with detailed documentation resulting in rich datasets for analysis. This produced three focal cases. For comparison, we chose a fourth focal case that did not meet the criteria. Participants of the first three focal cases brought additional materials from home for the personal project, whereas the participant in the fourth case only made use of what was available at the workshop.

To visualize the design processes, pictures and observation notes for each selected participant were placed on a timeline using Popplet (http://popplet.com/), an iOS and web-based visual mapping tool for capturing and organizing ideas. Audio interviews were transcribed so that important observation excerpts and periodic images of the design could be placed along a design timeline. Design moves were identified, including the initial ideation stage, and attempts were made to list the moves chronologically. From there, intra-actions of designer and material (i.e., how the materials were physically handled in the design process) were documented in relation to time.

We took a new materialist view of the participant's design process, placing emphasis on the material patterning of activity. The intra-action among the material is not limited to its impact on the designer using those materials, but rather the collection of designers and materials in the room leading to memetic intra-actions. One material can have a subconscious impact on the activity and material selection of other localized designs. For example, the introduction of motors can encourage a subconscious inclusion of spinning into even non-technical designs (e.g., spinning materials on fingers, the drawing of spirals, etc.) that was absent prior to the introduction of the motors. We see this as an emerging patterning of intra-action, where one material can create a motif that is explored in other designs and by other designers in unforeseen ways.

The materialist approach made visible how material agency was manifest and how it acted in the design processes of individual participants as well as how it stretched to encompass the overall workshop and the memetic intra-actions across participants and project specific materials. In the following section, we bring together four focal cases for further discussion that range in their intentionality and purposeful selection of materials in the design process. Through these cases, we look at the intersection of how we might see the material impacting the design process and the implications for design more generally.

Materials Evoking Artistic Expression

Peter, the designer in our first vignette, created a design that leveraged red, white, and blue star-shaped buttons—all materials that were provided in the workshop. He was an experienced art teacher with strong patriotic sentiments and likely gravitated towards these materials given his interests. On day 1 of the workshop, after seeing the buttons, Peter remarked, "I think we live in the greatest nation . . . I am always doing things with red, white, and blue." In fact, Peter had designed a t-shirt with the same colors and patriotic theme (see Figure 14.1) prior to the e-textiles workshop, and he decided to bring it the following day to incorporate it into his project. The upcoming 4 of July holiday and the programmable LED lights seemed to lead Peter toward a fireworks-inspired e-textile design. He programmed two pins of the LilyPad to create coordinating blinking lights with the LEDs. He then attempted to design for the

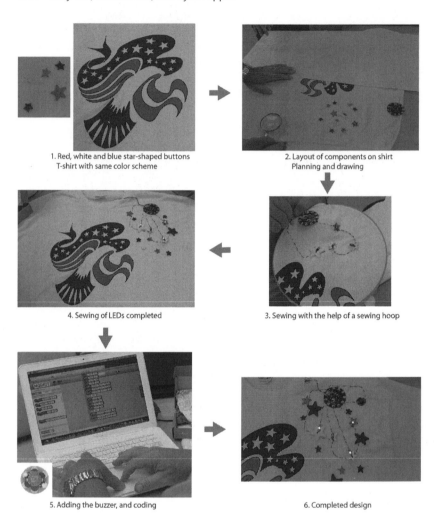

1. Red, white and blue star-shaped buttons
T-shirt with same color scheme

2. Layout of components on shirt
Planning and drawing

4. Sewing of LEDs completed

3. Sewing with the help of a sewing hoop

5. Adding the buzzer, and coding

6. Completed design

FIGURE 14.1 Photograph of Peter's e-textile design employing patriotic theme

following effect: "explosion of fireworks off in the distant sky, and the fact that the buttons are large, medium, and small, it's that feeling of foreground, middleground, background." Peter worked to create this by outlining the LilyPad on paper, laying the other components in place, and drawing the sewing lines. This drawing communicated constraints, especially the complexities in sewing. Having struggled with sewing on Day 1 of the workshop, Peter chose four LEDs instead of the originally planned six LEDs to avoid the crossing of sewing lines or short circuits. His plan was to join two LEDs to each pin. Compared to other participants, he sewed especially meticulously, making use of tools like a fabric pencil to draw sewing lines on his shirt, a sewing hoop, and magnifying glasses. To evoke the loud popping of exploding fireworks, Peter added a buzzer to his design and programmed it to produce low alternating notes. Peter explained his choice of notes, "I am no musician . . ." but explained that he was searching for a fireworks-like sound effect. The other participants were also incorporating musical tunes in their designs.

Materials Demanding Preservationist Techniques

Mary, a technology integration teacher in her first year of teaching, had a personal interest in fine arts. To the e-textiles workshop, she brought a square-shaped fabric reproduction of Van Gogh's painting, *The Starry Night*, as the foundation for her e-textiles project (see Figure 14.2). The reproduction, while skewed on the color palette, aptly represented the short brushstrokes that, through swirling arrangements, give the post-impressionist painting idealized motion. Mary's design objective was to augment the stars of the print using LED lights that she would program to blink. She decided to use six LEDs, underscoring the vibrancy of the painted stars through illumination, which she would sew on top of the stars. Furthermore, Mary aspired to include a programmable buzzer into her design that would play a fragment of Don McLean's song, "Vincent (Starry Starry Night)," an homage to Van Gogh and his work. The fabric reproduction of the painting intra-acted with the designer and the other materials of the project (i.e., LEDs, song, circuitry). Here, it is precisely the alignment between the material and the intentions of the designer that brought Mary's project together. In Mary's words: "I really like how it came together in the end . . . I liked thinking about how you could make it, like, integrate it into an already-created idea." Starting with the painting offered Mary material constraints within which to locate and fixate her design. Here we see a technological complexity unfold, which is tightly coupled with the complexity of the material and aesthetic representation. This is analogous to the observations of our prior e-textiles workshops, where e-textile projects that leveraged a blank canvas (e.g., unicolored canvas bags or t-shirts) led to less complex designs, both in terms of circuitry and the designer's meaningful expression.

The choice of the painting and its aesthetic began to intra-act with the crafting techniques employed in the project. Mary laid out the LilyPad, LEDs, and buzzer on the fabric, and sketched the circuitry on paper. The sense of the picture being an art piece appeared to invoke conscientiousness on Mary's part to maintain its aesthetics; she was unwilling to let her stitches be seen on the front of the picture: "My design was on top of my stitching, because I already had a picture that I wanted, just to light up from behind. . . . I don't necessarily like how sewing looks if it's not done on a machine. It needs to be perfect." Mary's concern over marring Van Gogh's painting with stitching produced a preservationist response to the material. Mary was compelled to preserve the look and feel of the original painting, seeking out an alternative to a visible running stitch

FIGURE 14.2 Photograph of Mary's design inspired by Van Gogh's *The Starry Night*

for the conductive thread. With the help of a facilitator, Mary found a solution that consisted of adhering translucent glue to the conductive thread at the backside of the fabric, which allowed energy to flow between the LEDs and the LilyPad invisibly to beholders without shorting the circuit. Struck by the hidden properties of the glue, Mary reflected on what her learning might mean for her teaching: "So I used the glue instead. I thought it was really interesting, thinking how it is an insulator. Because I was just thinking of it as a craft supply. But it would be a whole other lesson for students to talk about what is conductive and what is an insulator."

In sum, there were many aspects of the material that conditioned Mary's decision-making. Primarily, the painting evoked a preservationist mentality, which Mary used to augment but not disrupt the sanctity of the painting in her design. The painting acted as a conduit, attracting design choices that would shape the meaning of the rest of the material.

Materials Driving Memetic Spread

Steve, a technology literacy (and previously music) teacher, brought to the workshop a shirt that belonged to his four-year-old daughter. The shirt featured a heart-shaped outline that was colored with a sparkling print rendering the American flag (see Figure 14.3). He chose the shirt as a continuation of the illumination of the LEDs he planned to sew into the shirt: "This [shirt] seemed to stand out, because it already had sparkles on it, stars on it, or adding the twinkle to them kind of seems to fit right in." Steve, like Mary, wanted to augment the theme of the e-textile through the use of the melodic buzzer. Due to his musical training, Steve invested time into programming the LilyPad buzzer to play a fragment of the national anthem, continuing the America motif of the shirt's print. "I wanted to find pieces of music that were patriotic, since it is a patriotic shirt." Steve, also like Mary, expressed a desire to hide the e-textile stitching within the t-shirt so that the circuitry would not disturb the visual aesthetic of the illustration on the shirt.

In assemblage, Steve and the design surfaced a connected challenge to the visually concealed stitching and LilyPad components. Steve's design was for his four-year-old daughter, and he was concerned that the LilyPad or the other components could scratch against her skin: "I wanted [the electronic components] to be hidden a little bit. But the problem with hiding something is that you have this device up against your skin, which could scrape, or cut, or irritate." He circumvented these nuisances by sewing the LilyPad onto a fabric square and tucking the fabric square to the back side of the shirt to form a protective barrier between the wearer's skin and the electronics.

During the workshop, the capabilities of a temperature sensor intrigued Steve as he considered the special needs of his daughter: "I have a daughter who has epilepsy, and it is actually triggered by her body temperature being so high. Then [the design] would be able to see, set, or maybe the shirt will start lighting up, I know her temperature is getting high while she is playing outside. Then I could quickly get a cooling rag . . . to put on her, so her temperature could come back down." Specifically in this statement, we see the intra-actions between Steve the designer, the temperature sensor, and his daughter's needs. Steve conceptualized the idea of using the temperature sensor and the LilyPad

FIGURE 14.3 Photograph of Steve's heart-shaped rendition of the US flag

on the shirt as a "fever detector" for his daughter. He articulated his plan to program the LEDs to light when her temperature goes up, as an alert signal.

Steve's case is indicative of the intra-action between the materials and the designer in determining an emergent agency for the design. Steve's design process presents the conditioning of the available materials on ideation, as opposed to solely the idea formation conditioning the selection of materials: it was the introduction of the new materials that prompted the new ideas. Such a perspective underscores the material basis of human behavior and decision making. Across the vignettes, we see an intra-action among Steve's, Mary's, and Peter's projects: Steve's shirt continued the patriotic motif of Peter's design, Steve applied preservationist techniques similar to those Mary had employed (and maybe conditioned by the introduction of the nearby re-print of the Van Gogh painting). Both motifs, the patriotic ornamentation and the preservationist technique, were exceptional outliers to the hundreds of workshops we conducted. We hypothesize that the introduction of the Van Gogh painting and the red, white, and blue buttons guided the designs in those directions. From a new materialist point of view, we can see memetic spread among the designs.

Materials Facilitating Learning

Sophie was a fourth-grade teacher who started her teaching career after working as a risk analyst. Unlike the other highlighted participants, Sophie did not bring any of her own materials to the workshop. Instead, she used an undecorated canvas bag that was contributed by another participant as the basis for her e-textiles work. As one of the teachers who would be using e-textiles to teach circuitry, Sophie focused on learning the technicalities, such as polarity, making tight connections, and diverse debugging practices. Her first priority was for the computation and circuitry to work on her project, and to be sure she knew enough to guide her own students. Throughout her interview, Sophie returned to her students: "I honestly enjoyed it from start to finish because the beginning part, designing [the circuit], that works your brain, that is tough. It is a good challenge for your brain, and if it is a challenge for my brain, I can only imagine how it is going to challenge the students." Her design featured four LEDs programmed for a "strobe light" effect, with the circuitry visible on top of the canvas bag (see Figure 14.4). The on-off effect of the strobe light subtly communicated a modal morph of the thematic motif underlying the visual stitches. The stitches created a binary pattern of above and below the fabric surface, and the strobe light mimicked that. Sophie intended to use her project as a sample that she could show to her students. While the patriotic motif also made it around to Sophie, who connected the idea of "fireworks" to her design in her retrospective reflection, the materials conditioned her work in subtler, less consequential ways. For example, the decorations provided in the workshop caught her attention after she completed the circuitry design. As an afterthought, she hot-glued buttons of

FIGURE 14.4 Photograph of Sophie's strobe light circuitry for a canvas bag

flower shapes and of various sizes in layers on top of the circuitry and canvas bag. Sophie explained her enjoyment of decoration and added: "Oh, just the creativity, how you could design anything you want." With this, she expressed hope that the instructional piece she produced would communicate the possibilities of e-textiles as educational materials beyond straightforward circuitry learning: "I want to keep it so I can show it as an example."

Discussion

The cases presented here each speak to the ways that materials initiate ideas that can take off and spread across participants and projects. In Mary's case, the *Starry Night* picture influenced the choice of sparking LEDs, tune, and techniques of sewing to maintain aesthetics. Peter's t-shirt drew inspiration from the red, white, and blue buttons seen on Day 1 of the workshop, intra-acting with the spatial position of the buttons, LEDs, and buzzer tone. In Steve's project, the potentially scratchy surface of the LilyPad inspired the alternative circuitry design that employed similar preservationist techniques of other designs in the workshop. Sophie's case illustrates a subtler effect of materials, where a generic canvas bag did not initiate specific ideas or themes, and decorative materials were not considered in the ideation stage.

As with many design endeavors, the materials chosen early in the process ended up conditioning future design decisions and selection of subsequent materials. While experienced designers understand the affordances of particular materials for an idea and will seek out the appropriate materials for those design decisions, at times the full consequences of those choices in the design process are not fully known from the beginning. They stay in the background or unravel through design, becoming clear only after design-time.

Our research is pointing to the agency unfolding as people and things intra-act in the design process, resulting in an intra-action between material and instinctual choice. Each of the vignettes provided here reveal the designers making choices based on the originally selected materials, revealing the importance of the designers' material selection can be—understanding that they need to work *with*, and not *against*, their materials. This back-and-forth between the designer and their materials speaks to the often under-theorized weight that materials play in the design process.

The implications for how we think about the preparation of future designers cannot be missed. Cross (2006) describes how designers are "immersed in material" and how they draw upon these materials in their thinking. Importantly, good designers need to have the "ability to both 'read' and 'write' in this culture: they understand what messages objects communicate, and they can create new [objects] . . . which embody new messages" (p. 9). Material knowing (i.e., knowing what things are, how things work, and what meanings they represent) is very important to the process. Purposefully introducing a wide range of material early in development—a shared goal of early childhood educators, but less emphasized in K-12 education—encourages this type of material knowing. For example, early childhood classrooms often include free play where children can explore the forms, parts, and uses of diverse materials, such as geometrically complex seashells, simplistic wooden blocks, and printing patterns with found objects like Osage oranges. An implicit understanding of the affordances and constraints, as well as an appreciation and knowing about composition and social meanings of materials, are practiced. By contrast, in schools, less diverse materials are part of everyday learning situations. Students miss out on continued unraveling and surfacing of more complex ideas that are embedded within the materials of early childhood. An equal emphasis on the cultural, historical, and social meaning of the material is crucial. Materials come to us with a set of designed agendas, and sedimented with historic, cultural, and social identities that must be reckoned with in the design process. As we design our everyday learning environments, we need to consciously engage these material histories as we select materials (digital and physical) to be used in the design process as well as when we design physical learning spaces.

This material perspective of design conditions us to rethink the design of our learning environments, particularly those in which we provide materials to engage participants in design. Besides exposing participants to different types of materials to help them touch, feel, imagine, and connect to their ideas and imagination, the physical environment should also support the discovery of new properties of materials, new techniques, and the incubation of new ideas. In K–12 contexts this could involve active engagement with materials and discussions of what the materials mean to youth during brainstorming sessions. This discussion could create an openness or receptivity (attention) to the materials, connecting to youth's inner thoughts and ideas (Chamorro-Premuzic, 2009), leading to creative design processes.

Conclusion

Through four focal cases, we attempt to shift focus from the designer as the only active agent in design to understanding more about the materiality of design. Agency during design can emerge from the intra-action of the designer and materials. Even the more subtle ways in which material agency presents itself through design, as in the case of Sophie's e-textile, could be explored through closer examination of exploratory, tinkering approaches to design in which the designer did not enter the design spaces with concrete ideas. Makerspaces that provide a variety of tools and materials can empower designers to react and respond to the different materials that in assemblage spread a wide array of messages, patterns, and motives across making projects. These learning environments can enable designers to uncover the physical and sociocultural meanings of materials and become spaces for capturing geo-historic records of new material ways. In an effort to shift agency over to the designer, we need to focus on both the educational environments and the building of records.

References

Barad, K. (2007). *Meeting the universe halfway: Quantum physics and the entanglements of matter and meaning*. Durham, NC: Duke University Press.

Berzowska, J. (2005). Electronic textiles: Wearable computers, reactive fashion, and soft computation. *Textile, 3*(1), 58–75.

Blomberg, J. & Karasti, H. (2012). Positioning ethnography within Participatory Design. In J. Simonsen & Toni Robertson (Eds.), *Routledge international handbook of participatory design* (p. 86). New York, NY: Routledge.

Braidotti, R. (2013). *The posthuman*. Cambridge, MA: Polity Press.

Brandt, E., Binder, T., & Sanders, E.B.N. (2012). Ways to engage telling, making and enacting. In J. Simonsen & Toni Robertson (Eds.), *Routledge international handbook of participatory design* (pp. 145–181). New York, NY: Routledge.

Buchholz, B., Shively, K., Peppler, K., & Wohlwend, K. (2014). Hands on, hands off: Gendered access in crafting and electronics practices. *Mind, Culture, and Activity, 21*(4), 278–297.

Buechley, L., Peppler, K.A., Eisenberg, M., & Kafai, Y.B. (Eds.). (2013). *Textile messages: Dispatches from the world of e-textiles and education.* New York, NY: Peter Lang International Academic Publishers.

Cabral, M. & Justice, S. (2013). Material learning: Digital 3D with young children. Proceedings from *FabLearn 13: Conference in Digital Fabrication in Education,* Stanford University, October 2013, Palo Alto, CA.

Chamorro-Premuzic, T. (2009). Creative design process. In B. Kerr (Ed.), *Encyclopedia of creativity, vol. 1* (pp. 191–194). Berkeley, CA: Sage.

Cross, N. (1982). Designerly ways of knowing. *Design Studies, 3*(4), 221–227.

Cross, N. (2006). *Designerly ways of knowing.* London: Springer-Verlag.

Fields, D., Kafai, Y., & Searle, K. (2012). Functional aesthetics for learning: Creative tensions in youth e-textile designs. In *The future of learning: Proceedings of the 10th international conference of the learning sciences* (ICLS 2012) (Vol. 1, pp. 196–203). Sydney, Australia. Retrieved from http://www.scribd.com/doc/109869021/ICLS2012-Proceedings-Vol-1-2012.

Fischer, G. (2013). Meta-design: Empowering all stakeholder as codesigners. In *Handbook on design in educational computing* (pp. 135–145). Routledge: London.

Henderson, A. & Kyng, M. (1992, January). There's no place like home: Continuing design in use. In *Design at work* (pp. 219–240). Hillsdale, NJ: Erlbaum Associates.

Kafai, Y., Fields, D., & Searle, K. (2011). Everyday creativity in novice e-textile designs: Remixing as interpretive flexibility. Proceedings from *ACM Creativity & Cognition* (pp. 353–354). Atlanta, GA.

Kafai, Y., Fields D., & Searle, K. (2012). Making learning visible: Connecting crafts, circuitry and coding in e-textile designs. In *The future of learning: Proceedings of the 10th international conference of the learning sciences (ICLS 2012)* (Vol. 1, pp. 188–195). Sydney, Australia. Retrieved from http://www.scribd.com/doc/109869021/ICLS2012-Proceedings-Vol-1-2012.

Löwgren, J. & Stolterman, E. (2004). *Thoughtful interaction design: A design perspective on information technology.* Cambridge, MA: MIT Press.

Nelson, H. G. & Stolterman, E. (2012). *The design way: Intentional change in an unpredictable world.* Englewood Cliffs, NJ: Educational Technology Publications.

Orth, M. (2013). Adventures in electronic-textiles. In L. Buechley, K. Peppler, M. Eisenberg, & Y. Kafai (Eds.), *Textile messages: Dispatches from the world of e-textiles and education* (pp. 197–214). New York: Peter Lang International Academic Publishers.

Peppler, K. & Glosson, D. (2013). Stitching circuits: Learning about circuitry through e-textile materials. *Journal of Science Education and Technology, 22*(5), 751–763.

Rogers, Y. (2009). The changing face of human-computer interaction in the age of ubiquitous computing. In A. Holzinger & K. Miesenberger (Eds.), *Usability for e-inclusion, Lecture notes in computer science* (pp. 1–19). Berlin Heidelberg: Springer.

Schön, D. (1983). *The reflective practitioner: How professionals think in action.* London: Basic Books.

Schön, D.A. & Wiggins, G. (1992). Kinds of seeing and their functions in designing. *Design studies, 13*(2), 135–156.

Simon, H. (1982). *The sciences of the artificial* (2nd ed.). Cambridge, MA: MIT Press.

15

FINDING YOUR FIT

Empathy, Authenticity, and Ambiguity in the Design Thinking Classroom

Molly B. Zielezinski

When undertaken in the classroom, design thinking teaches youth to confidently solve complex problems and lays the foundation for them to become the innovators and creative thinkers we need to tackle the problems of the 21st century (Carroll et al., 2010). While the application of this approach in the classroom is gaining more traction and popularity, the best practices for implementation are sometimes less clear. When bringing design thinking to schools, there is no magic formula or baseline curriculum because the context for implementation varies so widely. The subject matter, grade level, classroom norms, curricular objectives, and a whole host of other variables can either support or constrain a teacher's effort to begin this new practice in her classroom. Although these contextual features shape the effectiveness of design thinking for student learning, my work with students and teachers has helped me identify several key ideas in this approach that are relevant regardless of context. Following is a brief discussion of my journey to design thinking, after which I present each of these fundamental understandings and discuss their relevance for those interested in leveraging design thinking as a pedagogical tool.

I attended my first design thinking workshop in 2008, as a teacher introduced to the process through a Stanford d.school boot camp. My experience was similar to that of others learning the process for the first time. It ignited a spark within my fellow teachers and me, casting a wide light of possibility and promise. We walked away from this introductory workshop alive with the frenetic buzz, excited by the multitude of ways to apply the process and tools in our classrooms. I was instantly hooked and in the years that followed, I became both a practitioner of design thinking in my own middle school classroom, a student of design thinking in my doctoral program at Stanford, and a teacher of design thinking to hundreds of educators from around the country. Through these three lenses, I have had the opportunity to witness the common pitfalls for those getting started with design thinking. Overcoming these obstacles in my own classroom and then guiding teachers from a wide variety of contexts around the very same stumbling blocks led me to reflect on the nature of design thinking. What is most important about this tool? How might teachers capture the essence of the process without falling prey to the most common pitfalls encountered when getting started on this path? The following insights seek to answer these questions for those who wish to begin to use design thinking in the classroom.

No. 1 Design Thinking Tools and Mindsets Are Not Just for Design Challenges, They Can Also Be Used as Standalone Activities

Back in 2008, my boot camp ended on a Saturday evening. Stoked by the fires of innovation, I spent all day Sunday at my desk eager to plan new design-laden lessons. This is when I encountered my first hurdle. Poring over the state standards in science and math, I struggled both to find a place where design thinking would fit as a pedagogical tool and to ensure that each student would adequately engage with a given state standard in the time available to teach that content. In that moment, I wish someone had told me that I did not need to develop a streamlined design challenge in order to start incorporating design thinking into my classroom. Committing to a complete challenge felt risky and overwhelming given how new I was to the process, and because I had limited time allotted for covering specific content that would be wasted if my challenge proved ineffective. Later, I learned that design thinking does not have to be a step-by-step process where teams progress neatly through each stage of the process. Instead it can be operationalized with individual stages, tools, and mindsets that can be applied as stand alone activities within a lesson.

The individual tools can be inserted anywhere within a lesson, with or without the shell of a start-to-finish design challenge, and still invigorate engagement. This looks different in every classroom but can include such tasks interviewing fictional characters using the book as a data source, brainstorming classroom processes (such as how all the students can visit the new class pet in an orderly fashion or 10 different approaches to solving a story problem in math), using an empathy map to unpack the meaning of a historical speech, and so on. The list goes on and on but the point is that, even when used à la carte, these tools are effective for developing the habits of mind and problem-solving skills that are typically associated with a complete design thinking challenge. Furthermore, students gain confidence and fluency with each opportunity to practice an individual tool or technique and the teacher builds her knowledge of how each can be leveraged to support specific educational objectives. As such, applying parts instead of the whole process lowers the barrier to entry for teachers looking to experiment with design thinking in their classrooms immediately while also providing them with the experiences they need for effectively designing complete challenges later on.

No. 2 Choose Your First Challenge Wisely

When the time arrives to facilitate your first challenge with students, never start with a topic for which your students already have strong feelings. A neutral entry point will allow the learner to utilize their complete cognitive load for engaging in the design process without being distracted by emotional hot buttons or personal expertise. For example, do not ask students to redesign homework policies or teachers to set out to improve technology use in their own classrooms. These are fine challenges for those with some experience but for a newcomer to design thinking controversial topics are ill advised, especially those with solutions that may personally impact the person who is designing. This is because when you are learning the process and tools associated with design thinking, your brain must work to master a new set of skills. If the focus of a design challenge is something you feel quite strongly about, your ego and self-interest in the outcome will hinder your ability to focus clearly on the process. Design thinking is messy and at times it is uncomfortable because you are being asked to spend time defining problems, avoid jumping directly to solutions, and doing so through an empathic lens. When a newcomer is a relative expert on a certain topic (as students are on homework and teachers are on their own classrooms), they feel immediately qualified to provide solutions and they feel a certain level of investment in these solutions. To give learners the time and space to become acquainted with the process, it is imperative to choose challenges that have a neutral entry point.

No. 3 Empathy is Not Just the First Step;
It Is an Essential Perspective That Frames All Design
Thinking Tools and Techniques

Empathy is the major feature of design thinking that sets it apart from most methods of engineering design and problem-solving. In the classroom, it provides a meaningful answer to the age-old question "Why are we doing this?" As learners are exercising empathy, it becomes clear that the motivation underlying the design thinking task is to meet the needs of a specific other.

Figure 15.1 depicts the five basic steps in the Stanford d.school design thinking process (Plattner, 2010). You see here that you begin a design challenge by empathizing, but it is important to remember that you don't put empathy aside once this step is completed. The entirety of the design process is conducted through an empathic lens. In the first stage, a specific individual or "user" is identified and each stage from that point forward is conducted with intense

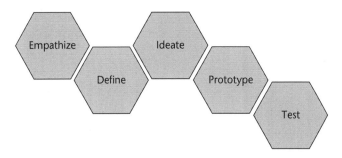

FIGURE 15.1 Design thinking process (Plattner, 2010)

regards for your user. As such, empathy is inherent in the educational objective of a complete design challenge.

For example, in a typical fifth-grade math lesson we might see the following objective: *Students will be able to find the area of irregular shapes.* If the same skill were exercised using design thinking as a pedagogical tool, we would see a similar objective situated within an empathic frame. *Students will be able to identify key statements from interviews with the Head Counselor and campers at the YMCA. They will make decisions about the allocation of camp activities to different available learning environments taking into account information from the interviews as well as the area of each learning environment.* These hypothetical lesson objectives illustrate a shift in perspective from decontextualized acquisition of knowledge and skills to an empathy-driven approach to teaching and learning that is responsive to human needs. This type of shift supports student engagement by providing context and purpose within their lessons. Yet reframing alone is not sufficient for introducing design thinking; for a new pedagogical tool to be effective it must also be well-scaffolded. It is not enough to ask students to consider the perspectives of a relevant other; the way to do this must be clearly modeled in a variety of forms and subsequently coached by the teacher as students practice.

If you think of empathy like a muscle, you see that empathy skills can be toned, defined, and strengthened by working out. The tools and processes within design thinking are the fitness regime for the empathy muscle, and with practice and repetition students become more comfortable flexing their empathy muscle. Some à la carte empathy activities include conducting open-ended interviews,[1] creating empathy maps,[2] writing point of view statements,[3] video observation,[4] and what/why/how observations.[5] Activities such as these can be integrated as scaffolds to support empathy and should be first introduced through teacher modeling and then student practice in teams that are guided by the teacher. Ongoing coaching and frequent check-ins are important for keeping novice design groups focused on the user throughout the process.

No. 4 Be Mindful of Modifications, a Choice to Preserve Authenticity in the Face of Time Constraints

When leading newcomers through a complete design challenge, there is one place that empathy is often omitted due to time constraints and it is one illustration of how real time modifications can have big implications for learning. Design challenges inevitably take more time than planned and when the time finally comes that all design teams have a prototype in hand it is tempting to move from here to sharing out and calling an end to the challenge. This sequence, which I have done myself at times, fails to take advantage of a meaningful opportunity to engage the empathy muscle. In the sequence of your design challenge, testing usually comes after the development of a prototype. In the testing stage, you present your original user with your prototype and get their feedback on what you have created. This is important because the design team has been away from the user for considerable time and may have unintentionally begun to emphasize their own preferences and ways of thinking or just plainly made incorrect inferences about the user's thoughts and feelings. The process of getting user feedback is an important reality check, a formative assessment that tells the novice designer what they have done correctly and where they could improve.

It is also sometimes logistically challenging to get the original design challenge users back to your classroom a second time, another reason this part is tempting to skip. When you can get users back, it is a powerful experience for them, as they have the opportunity to engage with a design intentionally and authentically crafted to meet their needs. They feel listened to, and when this happens, their response to the prototype serves as validation for the intellectual work done by students to this point. The testing stage also opens a space for dialogue, so the students can hear genuine feedback on improving their designs. This is a much more authentic form of feedback than teacher comments on an essay or red x's on a math quiz. It is purposeful, contextualized, and individualized. Once this feedback is given, it is important to then give design teams time to iterate on their prototypes based on feedback. This helps novice designers begin to embody the mindset "fail forward," teaching them that risk taking is rewarded by the opportunity to improve on their design and make use of the authentic feedback. It also instills a culture of purposeful iteration and revision that can be transferred to other academic endeavors such as writing. As such, we must be mindful of all that is lost when, as is often the case, testing or iteration are left out because time is short instead of privileged as hands-on activities that are crucial for learning.

In a complete design challenge, modifications and real time experiments are both inevitable and encouraged, and can have big impacts, both positive and negative. When making changes on the fly, take a moment to weigh what you specifically aim to improve against what the original activity offers that would be lost and, to the extent that it is possible, avoid compromising authenticity in favor of efficiency. The example above arises when you are coming to the end of the time allotted for a design challenge and it seems impossible to fit testing, iteration, and a final share out of what each team has made (this last part, while not a formal part of the process, is always irresistible as each team has been creative and innovative, developing ideas worth sharing). To preserve authenticity in this situation, engage in testing and iteration rapidly instead of cutting out either completely. Although not ideal, in a pinch, testing can be done in ten minutes and iteration in five minutes (or these can also be stretched across hours or days, depending on your overall scope and sequence of the challenge). It feels fast but the choice to include them means the value of a complete design cycle has not been lost.

Authenticity arises in real, valid, and genuine opportunities for learning and takes many forms in a design challenge, including genuine interactions with group members and users, inference-making grounded in observations and evidence, opportunities to grapple deeply with the perspective of another, negotiating your vision in conjunction with group members as you build prototypes, obtaining feedback from your user, and so on. These are not learning for learning's sake, but activities situated in a valid context and driven by the purpose of solving a unique problem for a real person. Having facilitated numerous design challenges and participated in many others, I have developed a sense of when you can push through rapidly and when to slow down and engage deeply over the course of a challenge in a way that will preserve the opportunities for authentic learning. Based on this, some suggestions related to the pacing of a complete challenge include:

- Be lavish with time during the empathy and define stages of your challenge. This is the time for students to make authentic connections and uncover deep insights. This type of work is often unfamiliar and can sometimes feel uncomfortable as students are asked to make inferences about their user without confirmation that these inferences are completely correct. Allow them to linger in the ambiguity of not knowing instead of hurrying through a moment of discomfort.
- In brainstorming, absolutely emphasize quantity of ideas over quality. This seems counter intuitive but it is important to keep any evaluation of ideas out of this phase. It is imperative that students do not judge themselves or others when brainstorming. No suggestion is rejected and all ideas are worth sharing. It often helps to include a quick demonstration or activity to demonstrate what bad brainstorming looks like. A judgment-free brainstorming space allows for many ideas to be generated quickly, including mundane ideas, solutions that already exist, and also the hidden gems. The actual group brainstorming itself can be done in as little as 10 to 15 minutes if time is tight. Once brainstorming is done, students can then rank their best or favorite ideas.

- Don't let students linger too long on selecting which idea they would like to prototype. Give them tools to scaffold group decision making and if a group is truly divided, let them prototype more than one idea. Tools for scaffolding decision making might include idea clustering (grouping those solutions that are similar or able to be combined), ranking the ideas, or structured voting, where each student gets a certain number of votes or certain types of votes. Also encourage students to make selections considering the perspective of their user and vote according to what idea best meets the needs of this person.

- Decide in advance whether you want prototypes to be low resolution, quick, detailed working models or something that will move to a next stage of production. Use your learning objectives as a filter to help you decide, communicate your decision clearly to your students, and plan your time to reflect this decision.

- Finally, always add some flex time into the pacing plan for a design challenge; that way if and when you go over time, you have accommodated for this in advance. This will help prevent you from having to make hard decisions when groups are engaged deeply in a certain activity but the time allotted has run out.

None of these suggestions are hard and fast rules but each are worth considering when time is tight. When managing a challenge from start to finish, a teacher must make many micro-decisions along the way. Prioritizing authenticity, through within-group interactions, engagement with a user, empathy work, and gathering feedback, can be a useful lens for guiding choices to maximize learning in the face of time constraints.

No. 5 Lean Into the Ambiguity, Reject Efficiency to Make Room for Innovation!

The previous suggestion makes the case that pacing can be very important, not only for testing and iteration but also throughout any design thinking activity. United States culture, particularly in schools, is characterized by a drive for efficiency—better, faster, more, now! We move same-age students through a series of subjects, using bells to signal their next dose of learning. The world outside of schools is a much messier place that is often characterized by unwieldy problems with blurry boundaries across many disciplines and ways of thinking. As such, our efficiency model of schooling is no longer aligned nor practical for the 21st-century learner. Design thinking is also at odds with this efficiency model. To truly solve problems takes time and rather than rushing to solutions, good designers lean into the ambiguity that characterizes the early stages of a design challenge, they linger with the uneasiness of the unresolved problem before them, and embrace the pace needed to define these problems, posit user-centered solutions, and develop prototypes. While time is a premium resource in any classroom, rushing through any design activity undermines the utility of design thinking in establishing a learning culture of inclusiveness, risk-taking, and thoughtful problem-solving and innovation.

Conclusion

When bringing design thinking to schools, there is no perfect path. Yet my experience has helped me to identify a few key points that may smooth some rough spots on the journey. First, teachers interested in design thinking have options! Design challenges can be done by implementing all the tools, the entire process, or through exercising one tool or process step in an à la carte way. There is no need to wait for a perfectly manicured design challenge to get started. Next, when facilitating that first complete challenge with newcomers select design challenges outside their realm of expertise so that they can focus on engaging in the process without being distracted by prior knowledge, ego, or desired outcomes. Also, remember the importance of empathy throughout the design thinking process, both at the onset of a challenge and throughout the process, as well as in individual tools, specifically user testing and iteration of prototypes as a way for novice designers to evaluate their progress and begin to embody important design mindsets such as "fail forward" and "improve through iteration." Finally, arriving at effective solutions to complex problems takes time. Whenever possible step away from the efficiency model of education and embrace the pace and mindsets needed for authentic problem-solving and innovation. In my experience, when an educator dives in to design thinking with these guidelines in mind, the students' increased engagement, motivation, and grit is palpable and the transformation in the learning environment is rapid and powerful. Design thinking is a pedagogical approach that balances form and flexibility. The tools and techniques of design thinking, when used as a whole or deployed as stand alone activities, support active engagement and empathy driven problem-solving and empower students to become innovators and creative thinkers equipped for the challenges of the 21st century.

Notes

1 https://dschool.stanford.edu/wp-content/themes/dschool/method-cards/interview-for-empathy.pdf.
2 https://dschool.stanford.edu/wp-content/themes/dschool/method-cards/empathy-map.pdf.
3 https://dschool.stanford.edu/wp-content/themes/dschool/method-cards/point-of-view-madlib.pdf.
4 https://dschool.stanford.edu/groups/k12/wiki/fe13b/Video_Observation.html.
5 https://dschool.stanford.edu/wp-content/themes/dschool/method-cards/what-why-how.pdf.

References

Carroll, M., Goldman, S., Britos, L., Koh, J., Royalty, A., & Hornstein, M. (2010). Destination, imagination and the fires within: Design thinking in a middle school classroom. *International Journal of Art & Design Education, 29*(1), 37–53.

Plattner, H. (2010). *Bootcamp Bootleg*. Palo Alto: Design School Stanford. Retrieved from https://dschool.stanford.edu/wp-content/uploads/2011/03/BootcampBootleg 2010v2SLIM.pdf.

16

ANALYZING MATERIALS IN ORDER TO FIND DESIGN OPPORTUNITIES FOR THE CLASSROOM

Charles Cox, Xornam Apedoe, Eli Silk, and Christian Schunn

Design and Its Introduction to Both Teachers and Students

For K-12 science and math teachers, technology and engineering have always been relevant topics, albeit typically of a tacit or peripheral nature. Often teachers either purchased technology or constructed an apparatus from the technologies at hand and then employed it to demonstrate an application of a scientific principle, perhaps describing the behavior of the apparatus mathematically. For example, firing a projectile at a falling object in order to demonstrate that both are accelerating downward at the same rate (in the case of the projectile, neatly along the path of a parabolic arc). The focus was on the science and mathematics aspects of STEM, rather than on the properties of the technology or how to construct it.

One reason for this emphasis on the science and mathematics over the design could be that scientific theory testing and mathematical generalizability are regarded with more respect in an academic context. In schools, design might be viewed as having the lower status of "empirical application." In the example of the projectile and falling object, a demonstration of the principle that makes the surprising but accurate prediction of falling and projectile objects colliding might seem more fundamental than having students consider how to aim the projectile initially for a consistently successful collision of the two (i.e., an application of the principle). The demonstrator tinkers beforehand until the demonstration performs consistently, but does not really discuss the significance of that coordination effort with the students. The most basic aspects of design are not discussed because these can be complex, messy distractions that students will find hard to understand.

Another possible reason for this emphasis on the abstract and general over the application of the design might be that the analytical aspects of science and mathematics (which are often considered challenging) might actually be more accessible than concepts or processes of design. Analyzing idealized scientific principles might seem easier than instructing students on the messiness of how to create the equipment used to generate the data that is needed for the analysis.

Whether the reason for privileging analysis over design is one of ease or one of relative importance, K–12 teachers are now facing a challenge of making design more visible and central to their students. Interestingly, this situation is similar to what occurred in engineering higher education in the recent past. Analysis had supplanted design for years, and during the 1960s to 1990s undergraduate engineering curricula had become predominantly theory driven (Nicolai, 1998; Seely, 1993) to the detriment of learning about design and application. Because an undergraduate engineering degree is a professional degree that should produce individuals who can enter the engineering workforce, representatives of the engineering professions protested this state of affairs. These protests led the National Science Foundation (NSF) to fund multiple research projects about what design is and how experts use it. Later, the Accreditation Board for Engineering and Technology (ABET) revised their standards toward including design in undergraduate curricula. The result is that design, especially when done collaboratively in teams, has indeed become a staple of engineering higher education (Lattuca et al., 2006).

The engineering professions demanded that higher education provide experience with design, and so administrators designated a place for design in their curricula and instructors made the necessary changes to include design activities in their courses. Those events reveal two reasons design is important enough to address with K–12 students as well. First, engineers are expected to perform design as a significant portion of their professional careers, and K–12 students should be exposed to the authentic nature of engineering in order to make informed decisions about their undergraduate study and career choices. Second, now that engineering undergraduates are expected to engage in the practices of engineering via the curriculum, K–12 students with little prior exposure to design activities will struggle more than peers who might have already developed basic design skills.

Interestingly, the performance expectations for design in K–12 classrooms have many similarities to those in higher education. However, there are some significant differences between K–12 and university engineering programs that need to be addressed. Teacher experience with design as an explicit focus of instruction is at the head of the list. At the most basic level, experience in engineering design cannot be expected from K–12 teachers who never had to learn it or teach it. While it is reasonable to expect that lack of preparation will change in the near future through various pre-service and in-service professional development opportunities for new and existing teachers, we propose to accelerate the process with our guidelines for evaluating and revising design-related materials for K-12 classroom use.

Before we present the guidelines, we begin with making a case for why they are worth considering. First, we describe some basic competencies associated with design at a nitty-gritty level that may be more understandable and concrete than the more vague standards statements that currently exist. Then we walk the reader through how we analyze a design task to assess whether it aligns with a subset of these competencies. We selected a design task that we anticipated would help students learn and demonstrate these competencies. On closer inspection, we identified limitations in the implementation of the design task that likely impeded students' abilities to attend to these competencies. We do not go into all the details regarding the design task and its administration because it is not the goal for this chapter to have teachers implement this particular design task with their students. Instead the point is for K-12 teachers to have an example of how to structure a design task in ways that foreground design concepts and processes.

Finally, with this concrete example in hand, we present a tabulated set of guidelines for K-12 teachers inexperienced with design instruction. Use of these guidelines might support initial evaluation of materials in terms of selecting ones that already have useful properties for teaching design as well as determining where materials could be further improved.

The Range of Design Competencies

Due to the expanded mathematics goals in the Common Core State Standards Initiative (2011), and the expansion in the Next Generation Science Standards (2012) to include engineering design competencies, K-12 teachers need to find, create, or adapt classroom activities related to those competencies. By design competencies, we refer to the following, described in terms that highlight the social (internal) and societal (broader) aspects of design practices:

- recognizing ill-structured and ill-defined conditions that are found unsatisfactory by some specified population (concept of problem finding);
- conjecturing about the limitations and resources that problem solvers have at their disposal (concept of problem scoping);
- analyzing the preferred conditions of the various stakeholders in that population (concept of problem defining);
- deriving the range of problems that could be addressed once different stakeholders see different problems (concept of problem refining);
- synthesizing paths to bridge from existing to preferred conditions (process of exploring solutions);

- evaluating the consequences of these paths in terms of effects on different stakeholders (process of evaluating solutions);
- iterating possible versions of a path in order to refine or otherwise improve it (process of improving solutions);
- throughout the design process, working collaboratively in order to exploit multiple sources of expertise, such as critique provided by experts (processes involving collaborative skills);
- communicating one's conceptualizations of problems and possible solutions in order to elicit feedback (processes involving communication skills).

We include this list (derived from Appendix I – Engineering Design in the Next Generation Science Standards, 2012) to identify potential areas on which to focus when considering how to analyze and improve design-related materials. The list is not exhaustive and excludes various other design concepts and processes or "Learning and Innovation Skills" such as critical thinking, communication, collaboration, and creativity (Partnership for 21st Century Skills, 2011). Indeed, because of the expansive nature of design, many teachers will need to revise their beliefs about the range of content that could be considered engineering and design.

The next consideration should be to identify when and in what ways to incorporate design productively in learning and instruction. Design is often resorted to when *resolving* ill-structured and ill-defined problems. Note that there is a clear distinction between solving and resolving, in that ill-structured and ill-defined problems are not really solvable to the extent that there is a unique solution and that such a solution can be reached in a prescriptive linear manner (Rittel & Webber, 1973). By way of contrast, $x + 3 = 8$ has a clear single solution, and an experienced problem solver in algebra knows exactly how to start solving such a problem. Instead, design typically requires multiple iterations in order to educe and refine its possible directions (Günther & Ehrlenspiel, 1999; Kolodner et al., 2003; Louridas, 1999; Schön, 1992).

The ill-structured and ill-defined nature of design permeates all of the design competencies that we have identified, from problem finding through to communicating solutions. Even an experienced designer does not know how to start applying a design process in order to make sense of a wicked problem except by taking a stab based on "theoretical interests, the special problem under investigation, his conjectures and anticipations, and the theories which he accepts as a kind of background: his frame of reference, his 'horizon of expectations'" (Popper, 1957, p. 172), nor how to end except by satisficing (Simon, 1957). As a result, problem framing, exploring alternative solutions, and getting feedback on ideas are all critical aspects of effective design.

As a consequence for teaching, the complexity and messiness of design means that design processes do not lend themselves either to being modeled in simple analytic terms (i.e., always follow these simple steps; Lesh et al., 2000) or to being parsed as traditional learning objectives. Our goal is to show how it may be possible for teachers to embrace the ill-structured and ill-defined nature of design in how they understand and implement design activities in their classrooms.

Preparing to Teach Design: A Way of Teaching, Not Just a Thing to Teach

After a few years of teaching, K-12 teachers have knowledge of how to teach, they have knowledge about content with which they are familiar, and they have knowledge about how to teach the content with which they are familiar (pedagogical knowledge, content knowledge, and pedagogical content knowledge, respectively; see Davis & Krajcik, 2005). All this knowledge was hard won through gaining experience and tapping expert advice, as is the case for any profession. Since most K-12 teachers have little or no expert guidance to/on design, the aggregation of knowledge of design concepts and processes and how to teach them might be daunting. In short, if K-12 teachers have not previously thought about teaching design, how do they even know where to begin seeking advice?

We propose that resolving the challenge of introducing design activities requires development of teachers' awareness about using design as a reactive pedagogy, a kind of augmentation of their pedagogical content knowledge. By reactive design pedagogy, we mean an iterative give and take between teacher and student as a conversation that explicitly examines the nature of the problem being addressed, the process being used to address it, and the concepts being developed through that process. It is a questioning of the expertise that the students are bringing to bear. For example, a reaction to a student's presentation of a problem description or possible solutions might include suggestions for avenues that have not yet been considered. The student presents an interpretation of the situation at hand, and the teacher reacts, providing material for the student's further reflection about resolving the situation or problem. A reactive pedagogy is critical in design instruction because the nature of design cannot be reduced to a series of linear steps that when applied work progressively toward a well-defined goal. Instead, rich experiences in design learning are more likely to result when there is explicit support for students to consider multiple, alternative possible ideas, to utilize both forward and backward reasoning, and to refine their understandings and solutions iteratively.

Reactive design pedagogy requires teachers to maintain conversations with their students about content, process, and result. That does not mean the target design competencies are treated in a haphazard manner, but rather that the sequence of encountering and mastering solution paths and competencies will probably vary from class to class or student group to student group. Teachers have to be prepared to react to those differences, whether by steering the conversation (e.g., getting back to the target design concept or design practice) or allowing it to take its direction and then analyzing the unexpected results in order to determine why they occurred. As such, teaching using design places responsibility on both students and teachers, who will need to master dealing with both ambiguous situations and the unexpected consequences that arise from their interventions. With that in mind, we next describe a design task to illustrate the limitations of a task as given. We examine how the task might be altered using reactive design pedagogy in ways that explicitly foreground and support development of design competencies.

A Simple Example Design Task: The Block Tower Task

In the analysis done for this section, we do not present all details of the design task itself or exactly how to fix all aspects; instead we focus on the opportunities for reactive design pedagogy that the task could provide. We also call attention to an aspect of the task that we had not anticipated—the production of a fundamental design discourse that we were not prepared to react to or exploit. The example is followed by guidelines we delineate for how a teacher deliberating about the use of this task could have analyzed it and refined it before deploying it.

The *block tower task* involved stacking wooden blocks in order to make a tower. Middle and high school students participated in the task in teams of three or four, either during a science fair or as part of a summer enrichment program. Each team of students was given approximately 50 blocks (1.5 cm x 2.5 cm x 7.5 cm each) and the student teams were to stack the blocks on a platform (12 in x 12 in) that would shake when activated. A trial was defined as successful if no blocks were vertically displaced during 20 seconds of shaking. Students could make as many trials as they wished within a 20-minute time limit, and the team that made the tallest tower that withstood shaking was declared the winner.

As background resources, every team was also provided with a set of short documents that emphasized five features block towers might have. Each of the features had two distinct levels: *internal density* (hollow or solid), such that hollow towers had fewer internal members than solid ones did; *shape* (pyramidal or rectangular), such that pyramidal towers were wider at the base than at the top, while rectangular towers were the same width at both top and bottom; *symmetry*; location on the shaking platform; and stacking patterns of block layers. Figure 16.1 shows a block tower with hollow and rectangular features.

We explored the use of two different guidelines given to student teams to test their effects on how successful student designs were and what they would learn from the design process. Teams in the *individual features* group were encouraged to focus on the effect of one feature of a tower, the implication being to conjecture

FIGURE 16.1 Example of block tower before shaking

how the feature contributed resistance to shaking (although the feature being considered was allowed to vary from trial to trial), and how to take advantage of the feature over a series of trials in order to make a taller tower (VOTAT or varying one thing at a time, per Tschirgi, 1980). We thought this strategy would improve student learning of factors that influence the success of a tower.

For the other treatment, the *systems of features* group, teams were encouraged to examine how combinations of a tower's features affected shaking resistance in each trial (the combination was allowed to vary from trial to trial). This process is a variation on HPTC, or "holding particular things constant" (Apedoe & Schunn, 2009) in that the teams in this group were encouraged to consider interactions among block features rather than establishing one on which to focus. We thought this strategy would improve the efficiency of finding a very successful solution.

The design task was one that professional engineers would classify as non-trivial: side-to-side shaking is a dynamic lateral loading for which computer-aided analyses would likely be employed. It is also important to note that both VOTAT and HPTC can be of great value to professional engineers modeling structural systems, with each approach having a particular advantage depending on the situation. It turned out that neither approach on its own was sufficient to support students' engagement in sophisticated design concepts and processes in this design task implementation. One issue was that the affordances of the materials and the setup made it difficult for students to make intuitive conceptual connections between the features that were identified in the support materials and the performance of their designs. After all, how should students have approached the task without the experience or computational resources of professional engineers?

The students first had to find a structure that would resist the applied stresses before they could use strategies to modify that structure for comparison. The students used what they had previously understood about structures, and several teams attempted to apply the easily recognizable premise of leaning blocks against one another to make triangles and tetragons, assemblies that they knew would normally resist deformation. Teams spent a lot of their 20-minute time limit arguing about how to make sense out of the task constraints: lateral loading that does not act like gravity. The blocks, the structural technology they had been given, were fundamentally ineffective at resisting the loading. In short, instead of facilitating observation of how students adopt and modify analysis strategies such as VOTAT and HPTC, we presented a phenomenologically baffling situation for students to deal with in a very short period of time.

What the Block Tower Task Almost Did: Reveal Student Design Practices in Discourse

A reactive design pedagogy would call for modifying the task in ways that would provide more support to the students to engage in authentic aspects of design. In particular, the task could have been structured such that students engaged in a discourse that eventually would have enabled them to deal with the problem through increasingly sophisticated processes and concepts.

To promote rich design practices, a design task should involve a *wicked* problem (Rittel & Webber, 1973)—no fully specified statement of the problem, no single best solution, no well-defined stopping rules or set of permissible operations, no straightforward guidelines on solution directions. The block tower task required students to exhaust the assemblies of braced frames with which they were familiar (triangles and tetragons), and to start ideating and iterating after failures—in other words, to resort to design as a way of dealing with the unknown. The task was not, however, an entirely wicked problem because the mission of building the tallest tower that withstood shaking was a definitive problem formulation and there was a clear criterion for a winner.

The winning team constructed their tallest tower with a hollow interior that allowed for slight lateral displacement of individual blocks as part of a non-rigid unbraced frame (similar to that in Figure 16.1). Post-interviews with the students revealed that their tower frame's lateral load resisting attributes were unintentional, and that the students had no vocabulary to describe why their tower worked. This lack of relevant language was fundamentally limiting to what students could learn and how teachers could guide them. But the students did have an artifact as a starting point from which to develop intent and then communicate it. Getting started by making something to be the object of critique is in and of itself a non-trivial design event and a crucial component of design thinking.

Design thinking values communication of a concept as an elicitation of others' expertise in a discussion—a design conversation—demonstrating effectively reactive design pedagogy.

While students did not initially have a vocabulary for describing design concepts, they were beginning to develop one (primarily of shapes and secondarily of words) around this task. Gubrium and Holstein (2000) make an important distinction between discursive practice (the real-time structuring of a reference to a concept or object under scrutiny) from discourse-in-practice (recognition of the boundaries within which that structure's components may be drawn and assembled). The creation and modification of towers engaged students in a *discursive practice* related to designing, pushing them to come to terms with a *discourse-in-practice*. In the situation of the block tower, discursive boundaries were not yet apparent to students at the beginning, but become accessible to them as a consequence of initiating the discursive practice for which the creation of an artifact (or, more correctly, a succession of artifacts) is necessary (Engeström, 1987; Hewitt & Scardamalia, 1998; Krippendorff, 1989). By developing a discourse for describing their design, the students were learning how to design: confronting a wicked problem, choosing a way to make sense of it, and framing approaches to dealing with it.

Strategies That Could Improve the Discourse During Design

To reinforce reactive pedagogy, the design task could encourage students to reflect on their processes by explaining them to someone else in the form of a decision tree. Students can also benefit from analyzing the audience's reaction to the presentation of the decision tree. Recall that "decision-based design cannot account for or suggest a process for how concepts and alternatives are generated—and this is often regarded as the most creative and hard-to-model aspect of design thinking" (Dym et al., 2005, p. 107). A decision tree cannot sufficiently describe all aspects of design process but rather following a trail of decisions in a structured way leads to conversations about why and how students made those decisions and what the consequences are from, say, not following alternative paths.

Sara and Parnell (2004) describe a critique process, which can be thought of as another kind of design conversation that challenges and hones students' development of productive discourse about design. This process involves the use of outside critics (e.g., a practicing engineer) who are invited by the teacher to the class:

> Students present their work visually and/or verbally to a panel that might include tutors, visiting critics and fellow students, in order to receive feedback. Through this dialogue, a useful learning opportunity is created for the whole group, and in particular, students are expected to learn valuable lessons that can be taken through to their future work. In this way,

reviews provide the opportunity for reflection on the project; the processes that the student used and the finished product.

(p. 57)

With regard to possible critique strategies, Kolodner and colleagues (2003) outline a number of effective options ranging from in-class pin-up sessions to public presentations that are used in their middle school curricular units.

It should be noted here that critiques do require some preparation in order for students to get the most benefit from them. Students need to understand the function of their artifacts as vehicles for eliciting expertise and to treat the critique process as a way of garnering others' expertise in order to expand and augment their own catalogs. Even though the critical reaction from either a teacher or an outside expert is crucial to teaching design, it is not as common a feature of other pedagogies, and can require some getting used to by everyone involved, in order to promote a productive dialog.

Interpreting Design Opportunities: How the Guidelines We Present Here Can Benefit Teachers

We return to the main question: How do K-12 teachers find new ways (or modify existing search strategies) to incorporate engineering or other design activities in the classroom? We reviewed what happened with our block tower task with teachers in mind. We thought about how we would have better facilitated useful design discursive practice in students. The design task did allow the creation and manipulation of an artifact. This is a core element for encouraging student-generated design activities and concepts as a means to reach a relatively sophisticated engineering discourse-in-practice that could serve as the basis for reactive design pedagogy. The guidelines below present more suggestions for aligning classroom materials with the range of competencies that were discussed earlier in this chapter.

The guidelines refer to the block tower task but can be applied to most examples of design tasks. We have divided the guidelines into two tables: the first table (Table 16.1) deals with design concepts and the second table (Table 16.2) with design processes. Design concepts can be applied *to things to make* and design processes can be applied *to ways to make them*, with an understanding that not all things to be made are necessarily physical artifacts (e.g., sometimes processes or services can be designed).

Example Modifications of Materials to Support Particular Design *Concepts*

The materials for a design task can be sequenced in a classroom in order to progressively produce three kinds of concepts: design models, user models, and system images that act as interpretive vehicles between the models. Norman connects the designer's problem-solving and user considerations in terms of the differing models or representations:

> The *design model* is the designer's conceptual model. The *user's model* is the mental model developed through interaction with the system. The *system image* results from the physical structure that has been built (including documentation, instructions, and labels). The designer expects the user's model to be identical to the design model. But the designer doesn't talk directly with the user—all communication takes place through the system image. If the system image does not make the design model clear and consistent, then the user will end up with the wrong mental model. (emphasis in original) (1990, p.16)

Visualization is a recurring challenge in design that involves many underlying concepts for students to identify and tackle. There is a frustration that presenters often face during a critique when backgrounds for presenter and reviewer do not align sufficiently for optimal communication. There is also the consideration for third party users of a design concept who will not have the designer on hand to explain the concept.

Rosson and Carroll (2009) describe another set of concepts that teachers might employ to engage students with the users of the design and other stakeholders in wicked problems in order to facilitate this communication challenge. Students can be helped to recognize people just like them or resemblances among folks in families or communities doing things similar to what the students might do. Other variations can also work: even the exact opposite strategy can work as long as students are asked to make an explicit comparison of how others are different from them. In all of these approaches, the ability to communicate design thinking in ways that push the design forward is what the teachers are helping students to develop.

TABLE 16.1 Suggestions for modifying the block tower task for design concept emphasis

Concept Addressed	How This Relates to the Current Block Tower Task	How the Block Tower Task Could Be Made a Stronger Example of the Concept
Systems consideration by zooming in and out at various scales and scopes in order to address: systems, subsystems that	Currently missing: context adjacent to blocks is not considered	• Provide additional structures that could be affected by block failures and award points for maintaining block failures within building footprint, even if members shift vertically

are components of systems, super-systems of which the systems are a part, system boundaries, and contextual extra-systems outside a given system's boundaries	Currently missing: whose need is being addressed by this investigation is unknown	• Search for whose need is being met by a new built form • Analyze needs, resources, and constraints (any or all of which may be revised later) • Distinguish needs from measurable requirements and solutions
	Currently missing: physics intuitions are not leveraged—novice participants do not have previous experience with lateral forces and are not allowed to modify blocks to attempt resisting lateral stress	• Allow modification of blocks • Provide tools to perform modification
	Currently missing: no supporting tools for reflection on design idea performance—although function is known and structure is by default limited to compressive stacking, behavior of the built form is indeterminate and indeterminable beyond the affordances of a massing model (crude sketch model intended to show how the shape and proportions of the overall building result from its larger and smaller volumes in relation to one another)	• Storyboarding with regard to smaller scales of detail and intermediate scales of human interaction (not to be finalized, but rather discussed in passing with the intent of establishing relationships across scales and then returning for another pass later on)
Alternatives to familiar phenomena	Currently missing: making sure novel elements are salient—clues about unfamiliar phenomena (such as lateral forces) that are being introduced, and how to deal with them, because you can't index and retrieve strategies that you don't already have	• Distinguish lateral stress from gravity • Lead students to consider that they must consider an unfamiliar stress in addition to gravity

Example Modifications of Materials to Support Particular Design *Processes*

The term *design* can refer either to the concept being formulated (design as a noun) or to the formulation itself (design as a verb), but there is an important deep connection between the two during learning. In particular, we think more attention to the rules given in the design task and allowing some breaking of rules can be powerful for allowing better design content and better design process.

When implementing the block tower task, we often imposed constraints on the participants with respect to: individual features and systems of features, how to classify each of those, how much time the platform shook, and when the time for the task had expired. Additionally, there are other critical design procedures associated with the block tower task that we have not yet discussed: the ones students themselves individually impose upon the problem, and the ones generated by having to work with one another.

Dealing with those in turn, we start with constraints that students themselves imposed on the task. Never did we tell the participating students that they could not scratch up the block surfaces to increase friction between layers, or whittle notches in the blocks, or otherwise modify them in order to transfer forces throughout a block frame by making connections between block members. If a teacher's aim is to support the development of students' independent critical thought and reflection, contributing to discourse generation and increasing the range of possible solutions, then material that allows the constraints of the

TABLE 16.2 Suggestions for modifying the block tower task for design process emphasis

Practice Addressed	How This Relates to the Current Block Tower Task	How the Block Tower Task Could Be Made a Stronger Example of the Practice
Iteration, both as refinement of a single approach and as development of multiple concurrent approaches to the problem	Currently missing: expert and peer social drivers of refinement—there are no experienced designers as participants, such as those from outside the classroom	• Include a participant whose zone of proximal growth is only a little more advanced than those of the other participants in order to derive some advantage from reciprocal teaching • What to create for a critique and how to steer it toward critic expertise you want to tap • How to recognize unanticipated critique value

		• How to sift what students receive from critics in order to separate what is to be kept as useful
	Works as an example: experiential drivers of refinement—generating ideas, recording them (although not for participant use), and iteratively testing them	• Making video available in real time for analysis • Providing external memory storage/retrieval for consultation
	Currently missing: material selection as presented to students is overly constrained	• If a variety of materials were allowed, they could be chosen for an iteration, fixed for that iteration, and then revised for the next iteration
	Works as an example: materials can be stacked in a variety of ways	• Allowing opportune intervention by supplementing blocks with everyday objects
	Currently missing: opportunities for addition of material are prohibited	
	Works as an example: attempting to initiate reflection after each trial	• Structure and administer reflection to probe for evidence of either single feature consideration or system of features consideration and how that was manifested in the assembly
	Currently missing: reflection curtailed by time constraints	
Primary processes of design and processes associated with higher order thinking: analysis of problems, synthesis of resolutions, and evaluation of alternatives	Works as an example: uses interactive/iterative design methodology, explores alternatives, explores scope of constraints (individual features and systems of features), examines existing designs, encourages reflection on process	• Functional decomposition might involve separating the problem of height from that of resistance to periodic lateral stress, and then combining solutions (or portions of solutions) in order to satisfice both criteria
	Currently missing: exploration of alternatives to problem representation as given—using functional decomposition, exploring graphic representation, redefining constraints, exploring user perspectives	• Exploring user perspective involves the manufacture of personas and their relationships with the tower's construction

problem to be manipulated might be preferred (Mehalik & Schunn, 2006). In that case, any problem statement accompanying the material is not consumed whole, but instead deconstructed by the teacher in order to determine how definitions, such as user needs, were arrived at (Faste, 1987), and any initial constraints become susceptible to revision if there is a way to arrange benefits to otherwise under-represented stakeholders. In other words, the teacher can ask students to consider which initial constraints in the design problem should be reconsidered.

Summary

Again, while we use engineering design as a reference throughout, it must be explicitly understood that our analysis and suggestions are neither comprehensive in a general sense nor exhaustive in any particulars. We expect the teacher to modify or augment the suggestions as needed for the situation and materials at hand.

To retrace our steps, we presented a list of design competencies that are now to be found on teachers' plates, and we conjectured that teachers, especially those without experience in teaching design, would be looking over materials to be used in their classrooms. We then followed with an analysis of a design task (the block tower task) that we ran with students in middle school and high school. That task, as a representative of materials which teachers might encounter when looking for ways to teach design, led us to two main points. The first point is that the teacher should be wary of tasks, such as the block tower task, without prior analysis. This point arose from our recognition that the task did not result in the learning that was expected, although it did lead to some unintended but beneficial outcomes.

The second and main point is: guidelines for searching materials might be helpful, especially for teachers who are inexperienced in teaching design. We crafted guidelines based on the block tower task and our ideas about how we might have changed it. Our intent is for the guidelines to serve as a starting point for informing teacher choices and modifications. As teachers become more sophisticated in their practice of reactive design pedagogy, further inspection of existing materials in consultation with these guidelines will yield not only many more directions in the implementation of those materials, but also a much wider range of competency related novel materials.

In conclusion, we anticipate two ways to use the guidelines: assessment of material for suitability and likelihood of expansion beyond the original intent of the material. When assessing material for usefulness in design instruction, teachers might consider which concepts or processes are to be emphasized and then review whether or not those can be expected from an implementation of the material. A purposeful application of the guidelines we have provided could lead to the discovery of possible expansion of existing materials and the addition of more affordances that the materials provide.

References

Apedoe, X., & Schunn, C. (2009, April). *Understanding how students solve novel design challenges.* Poster session presented at the National Association for Research in Science Teaching (NARST) Annual International Conference, Garden Grove, CA.

Common Core State Standards Initiative. (2011). Retrieved from http://www.core standards.org.

Davis, E., & Krajcik, J. (2005). Designing educative curriculum materials to promote teacher learning. *Educational Researcher, 34*(3), 3–14.

Dym, C., Agogino, A., Eris, O., Frey, D., & Leifer, L. (2005). Engineering design thinking, teaching, and learning. *Journal of Engineering Education, 94*(1), 103–120.

Engeström, Y. (1987). *Learning by expanding: An activity-theoretical approach to developmental research.* Helsinki: Orienta-Konsultit.

Faste, R. (1987). *Perceiving needs* (Society of Automotive Engineers Technical Report 871534). Warrendale, PA:SAE International. Retrieved from http://www.fastefoun dation.org/publications/perceiving_needs.pdf.

Gubrium, J., & Holstein, J. (2000). Analyzing interpretive practice. In N. Denzin & Y. Lincoln (Eds.), *Handbook of qualitative research* (2nd ed.) (pp. 487–508). Thousand Oaks, CA: Sage.

Günther, J., & Ehrlenspiel, K. (1999). Comparing designers from practice and designers with systematic design education. *Design Studies, 20*(5), 439–451.

Hewitt, J., & Scardamalia, M. (1998). Design principles for distributed knowledge building processes. *Educational Psychology Review, 10*(1), 75–96.

Kolodner, J., Camp, P., Crismond, D., Fasse, B., Gray, J., Holbrook, J., Puntambekar, S., & Ryan, M. (2003). Problem-based learning meets case-based reasoning in the middle school science classroom: Putting Learning by Design™ into practice. *Journal of the Learning Sciences, 12*(4), 495–547.

Krippendorff, K. (1989). On the essential contexts of artifacts or on the proposition that "design is making sense (of things)." *Design Issues, 5*(2), 9–39.

Lattuca, L., Terenzini, P., & Volkwein, J. (2006). *Engineering change: A study of the impact of EC2000.* Baltimore: ABET.

Lesh, R., Hoover, M., Hole, B., Kelly, A., & Post, T. (2000). Principles for developing thought-revealing activities for students and teachers. In A. Kelly & R. Lesh (Eds.), *Research design in mathematics and science education* (pp. 591–646). Mahwah, NJ: Erlbaum.

Louridas, P. (1999). Design as bricolage: Anthropology meets design thinking. *Design Studies, 20*(6), 517–535.

Mehalik, M., & Schunn, C. (2006). What constitutes good design? A review of empirical studies of design processes. *International Journal of Engineering Education, 22*(3), 519–532.

Next Generation Science Standards. (2012). Retrieved from http://www.nextgen science.org

Nicolai, L. (1998). Viewpoint: An industry view of engineering design education. *International Journal of Engineering Education, 14*(1), 7–13.

Norman, D. (1990). The design of everyday things. New York: Doubleday/Currency. Retrieved from http://www.scribd.com/doc/23317082/Design-of-Everyday-Things-by-Donald-Norman.

Partnership for 21st Century Skills. (2011). *Learning and Innovation Skills.* Retrieved from http://www.p21.org/overview/skills-framework/60.

Popper, K. (1957). Philosophy of science: A personal report. In C. Mace (Ed.), *British philosophy in mid-century* (pp. 155–189). London: Allen & Unwin.

Rittel, H., & Webber, M. (1973). Dilemmas in a general theory of planning. *Policy Sciences, 4*(2), 155–169.

Rosson, M., & Carroll, J. (2009). Scenario-based design. In A. Sears & J. Jacko (Eds.), *Human computer interaction: Development process* (pp. 145–164). Boca Raton, FL: CRC Press.

Sara, R., & Parnell, R. (2004). The review process. *CEBE Transactions, 1*(2), 56–69.

Schön, D. (1992). Designing as reflective conversation with the materials of a design situation. *Knowledge-Based Systems, 5*(1), 253–264.

Seely, B. (1993). Research, engineering, and science in American engineering colleges: 1900–1960. *Technology and Culture, 34*(2), 344–386.

Simon, H. (1957). *Models of man: Social and rational.* New York, NY: Wiley.

Tschirgi, J. (1980). Sensible reasoning: A hypothesis about hypotheses. *Child Development, 51*(1), 1–10.

17

DEVELOPING POWERFUL, PORTABLE DESIGN THINKING

The Innovators' Compass

Ela Ben-Ur

Why Create a Design Thinking Compass?

I am fixated on this question: Might design thinking (DT), in connection with other practices, have the potential to empower everyone, regardless of age or role, whether alone or together, to creatively move and grow through any challenge?

This question emerged over my years as a practitioner, leader, learner, teacher, and coach in places of world-class design education and practice, and as a parent. I've seen that our big challenges—whether succeeding in second grade, creating new technologies, or finding happiness—require us to individually and collaboratively navigate many diverse challenges: technical and human, personal and professional. Different people and processes (including DT) find new possibilities within these problems in common ways. What if we could learn to recognize these, adapt them in all big *and* little things we do, and build on our discoveries?

I've explored this question in K-12 education with many wonderful educators in different geographies, kinds of schools, and grades. We've glimpsed the empowering potential of DT as we've challenged ourselves to invoke it in new ways. Here's a simple example. The most enthusiastic student in a weekly fifth-grade design elective missed a field trip because of incomplete homework. Her teacher and I asked about this, gesturing to a large "Innovators' Compass" (to be described shortly) in the classroom and jotting down her replies:

> *Ela Ben-Ur (EB):*   What's going on—what are your observations?
>
> *Student:*   We're adopting my [5-year-old] cousin because her mom had a breakdown. She wants to play with me all the time.

Teacher:	How do you feel about that?
Student:	I want her to like me. I want to make her happy because everyone's not happy when she's unhappy.
Teacher:	What do you think the core challenge might be? What matters?
Student:	Adjust to my cousin wanting to play all day. I feel like a 34-year-old. How do I make her happy?
EB:	What are some ideas?
Student:	I could play with her for 15 minutes and then do homework.
Teacher (trying a "thought" experiment):	Do you think you'd stop?
Student:	Hmm, no.
Teacher:	Any more ideas?
Student:	I could let Nana say it's time to do homework. Or do homework with [my cousin]?
EB:	Which will you try first as an experiment?
Student:	Ask Nana, "In 40 minutes, can you tell us it's time to do homework?"
EB:	How was this for you?
Student:	Good. I haven't thought about it so much before. [The Compass is] an organizer to help me get through life. It goes through certain steps to get your challenge done.

The next week, we wondered if she'd even remember her idea:

EB:	Did you try something with your homework?
Student:	It worked! I asked Nana to tell us after 35 minutes. We did that all week.

Such real-life situations are a crucible demanding the most powerful and portable form of DT. I've stretched DT in new kinds of situations, helped by complementary methods. I've strived to embody DT in a form people quickly get, *feel*, use, adapt, and share. I used increasingly simple slides, worksheets, or posters; these still felt like too much stuff, and too little that stuck in real situations (including my own!). All along, I've updated my visualization of DT. In March 2012 I took the first departure from an IDEO model. I added axes to *show* the directions DT stretches us, and how different DT phases iteratively pursue those. I added short descriptions to *summarize* (not only symbolize) the phases. However, not until preparing to coach multiple educators (unfamiliar with DT and working on separate initiatives) at once in an August 2014 workshop did I think to use this as the primary *tool* for discussion and action. I realized that the axes formed a tangible workspace and evoked a compass to navigate it. The educators I worked with were able to use those first Compasses to start digging deep into their own challenges—identifying empowering observations, ideas, and experiments. Since then, I've evolved this approach daily in every challenge I face, coach, teach, lead, and parent.

A compass is a concrete, portable, powerful *tool* that fits in our pocket or phone. It's *top-of-mind* whenever we're getting started . . . or getting stuck. It instantly *orients* us in fundamental directions (here, essential *practices* of DT). It bridges to, and between, our fledgling inner compass (DT *mindsets*) and more specific or sophisticated tools (DT and other *processes*). It *empowers* our independent navigation through any settings, conditions, or situations that test even practiced mindsets. It *invites* us to decide where we'll use it or put it away, stay or wander, and speed up or slow down.

Unpacking the Compass

The Compass (see Figure 17.1) strives to capture the *what*, *why*, and *how* of powerful DT in a workspace that *works* for anyone at all times.

The *cardinal directions and center* align our orientation around *how* and *why* DT is powerful. In our greatest moments we're able to see the past and present in new ways so we can see the future in new ways, from details to big picture. DT and

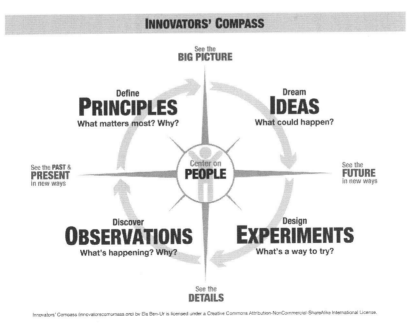

FIGURE 17.1   The current Innovators' Compass

its complementary practices help us recognize and move in these cardinal directions. The potential we discover is often found in people (including ourselves) and things around us. DT (re)centers us on all people involved, drawing on "human-centered" empathy at all times.

We reference these directions and center as we move around the four *quadrants*, on paper or in our minds, to help feel how each quadrant is powerful in its own way—related to, yet distinct from, the others. Clockwise from lower left, these are: noticing details of the past and present in new ways (discovering new *observations*); zooming out for new perspective on how everything connects to see what matters most about the past, present, and future (defining guiding *principles* that can serve as our "North Star"); exploring broad future options (dreaming new *ideas*); and zooming in to the most essential details of an idea to try (designing *experiments*).

Each quadrant offers us new possibilities by exploring the fundamental *landmarks*— observations, principles, ideas, experiments—of *what* we use to navigate in DT and everyday life. Each landmark has a simple description to help us recognize it (e.g. *observations* are "What's happening? Why?"). The inquiries in the student "homework" dialog earlier leveraged these landmarks and descriptions. We can get to each landmark in different ways, much like we can "ascend" or "hike" to the peak of a mountain. Whether we "brainstorm," "ideate," or "dream" in the upper right, we seek *ideas* that reflect the big picture of what might be possible and who/what might be of help. I like the mnemonic "discover, define, dream, design" for memorability, but I have used others.

The grey arrows offer the natural journey of DT processes (exploring clockwise from observations) when we don't have a clue where to start. However, the full space is open, helping us own it. We use each landmark to find the others. If we suddenly have an idea, we can capture it, then return to explore the observations and principles behind it, or move forward with a simple experiment. As we work directly in it, the Compass helps us see and feel where we have explored, as well as where to go next. Different people and different innovation "processes"—from "Lean" cycles of rapid evolution, to deliberate design processes, to tinkerers' individual "flow"—explore the quadrants with different emphases, patterns, and paces (Figure 17.2). The Compass helps us visually embrace and support how these work together.

The processes shown in Figure 17.2 use visual, verbal, and/or physical methods to explore a quadrant. We can multiply our creativity just by exploring the quadrants in any visual, verbal, and physical ways we can think of. Look, listen, and experience; use pictures/diagrams, physical movements and making, in addition to words.

With a Compass up in the staff/classroom and one in everyone's notebook (or phone!) there's always a reference if needed. This helps liberate us to adapt the language and "size" to the setting and scale of the challenge, people involved, and available materials—including none! Later we can always capture or enlarge it

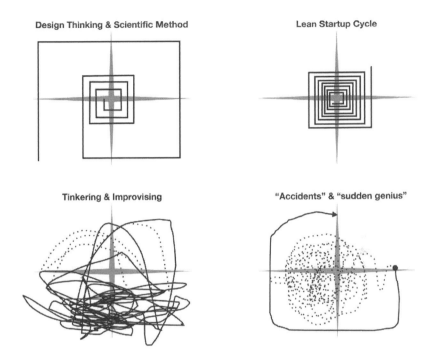

FIGURE 17.2 Connecting different conscious (solid) and subconscious (dotted) "processes" with the Innovators' Compass

(in the middle of a larger piece of paper, extending the axes). Drawing and adapting the Compass helps us internalize it and develop our own internal compass over time.

The Compass is not a map. Instead, it helps us make our own maps. We capture our discoveries meaningfully for ourselves and others with a visual orientation that's recognizable even without labels. A movable format (digital or stickies) lets us organize and synthesize each quadrant. Alternatively we can just look at what's there to gain inspiration for our next steps. After a while, we start working on "new" problems and realize we or others already have a relevant "map." We see patterns across observations, principles, ideas, and successful experiments—and develop a growing global awareness that can guide us.

Let's make your first map now.

Experiencing the Compass

Find a piece of paper. Draw the two main lines with a circle (or heart) at the center. Copy any labels you like, or leave more space to write and draw your own thoughts. Now let's take a journey through the Compass. Your mind may naturally wander to a different area of the Compass than you're "working on"; jot your thoughts down there and return.

(Center) PEOPLE. Take a few deep breaths. Tune in to a question, challenge, or opportunity that you and perhaps others are experiencing right now. It can be anything you're starting, or feeling stuck about—for an example, as immediate as getting yourself to try this Compass! If it's clear, put it at the top. If not, don't worry. Put any people who might be involved, or invited, in the center. If you can't be with those people now, make sure to note your assumptions or questions for them in the following parts. In the example of "Getting myself to try the Compass," you'd represent yourself and anyone you'd thought to "Compass" with.

(Lower left) OBSERVATIONS. What's happening? Ask "Why?" again and again. Notice new things without judging or analyzing. What do people (including you!) do, say, think, and feel? What's happening in your environment? What's happened in the past that might be relevant? In our example: "I don't have a piece of paper. I'm thinking 'I should try it' because I know we learn by doing. I've seen DT work. I'm kind of curious. I'm afraid I'll do it wrong. I see the other person is busy. *I assume* they'll think this is silly."

(Upper left) PRINCIPLES. "What matters most, now and in whatever happens next? Why do those things matter? Are "problems" coming to mind? Turn them into principles. Principles might seem to compete with one another. This is reality; the next part of the Compass explores creative ways to fulfill them all. Again in our example: "Get as much *learning* in this time as I can. Work on our *relationship*, because it's more lasting than these issues. Help this feel *safe* for us both." The statements, words, and/or images you end up with will inspire your ideas and actions.

(Upper right) IDEAS. To fulfill those principles "What could happen?" Explore as many approaches as you can. From whom/where could those come? Look for potential in everyone and everything around you. If it's easier you can start with subsets of principles (e.g., by creating "How might we …?" questions) to start generating ideas, and build on those toward finding ideas that fulfill all principles. If you find yourself judging an idea, ask: "Do I have a principle behind that concern? If not, is there a new one to capture? Either way, does that *really* matter?" In any case, move on to the next idea! Don't invest time designing details of an idea yet; first look to see what kinds of ideas are out there. For example, "Do a first round solo. Schedule a time with that person, giving them time to prepare themselves. Draw in the cover of this book [*Wait, I shouldn't! Is that a principle? No—it doesn't matter if I do!*]." And so on.

(Lower right, and onward) EXPERIMENTS. What idea (or smallest workable set of ideas) seems like a promising step to fulfill your principles? Capture any questions/doubts about it. Ask "What's a way to try?", seeking the least (time/money/risk) needed to answer your questions/doubts. For example, for those concerns about how to write or meet, "See how a first mark in pencil feels." Or "See if they'll arrange a meeting." Then DO it! Openly share your questions as you do.

Do this before reading further. Spend five minutes on it. Observe what happens; what people (including you!) do, say, think, and especially feel as a result. Expect to be surprised! If you're not "there" yet, ask "Why?" and go around again! Capture new observations, principles, ideas, and experiments to move forward—you can separate iterations with a line or another color. If related challenges arise, start a Compass for them!

Reflect, using another simple Compass. Observe your Compass experience: what did you (and others) do, say, think, or feel differently? Any principles, ideas, or experiments about using the Compass in the future?

The Compass in School

The Compass offers a tangible workspace for exploring possibilities in any situation. It works over months or in just seconds—on a whiteboard, digital document, scrap of paper, in conversation, or in our minds. The formats can blend together as we tune into opportunities to use the Compass any time we or others are starting something or feeling stuck.

Use of the Compass in conversation gives young children language for their natural observation, imagination, and experimentation. Even before age four my daughter knew she could get away with *anything* when trying an "experiment" and that if it wasn't working we'd "look at it" for observations and new "ideas"; she knew our four house "principles" (Care; Communicate; Conserve; get Curious, Creative, and even Crazy—just be Careful and Clean up); and she knew to offer *me* observations and ideas when *I* was frustrated! We can document Compass experiences for young children. Later they can do so themselves with pictures, then also words. A second grader worked on his experiences of exclusion and found new confidence in class. A third grader "unblocked" his writing by *writing into* a Compass.

Compasses serve well to introduce, scaffold, and reflect on major cycles of school projects. Students can "speed date" several potential projects with quick Compasses before choosing one. My co-experimenters (K-12 and college educators) and I similarly encourage students to design presentations and papers with a Compass: balancing observations about what they're excited to share and what their audience hopes to experience, creating a few guiding principles, and playing with several approaches before committing to one. Along the way, we help students "center and re-enter" frequently to proactively sense technical, interpersonal, or personal challenges and quickly use a verbal or visual Compass to help. And when students ask for college or career advice we'll leverage observations of their most/least fulfilling/frustrating/etc. moments, to find principles, ideas, and experiments for them to explore.

We try to walk this talk because creative grown-ups enable creative students! In meetings, the Compass helps fuel generative communication and collaboration around new issues and ideas. We'll create a Compass in a digital document

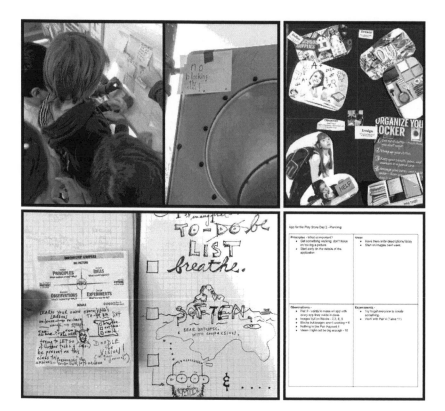

FIGURE 17.3 Diverse Compasses used by students to address their recess challenges together (top left, with experimental prototype) and find an individual project to "Make their mark" (top right); and by teachers to responsively design their lives (bottom left, with experimental prototype) and classes (bottom right)

for student-centered teaching plans; after class we'll capture reflections in this planning Compass for next year, and start a Compass for the next class. I put a big Compass in the classroom for us all to offer ongoing observations, principles, ideas, and experiments for the class, soliciting these especially at the semester's midpoint and end. I informally "Compass" before and during class to check in with myself and my students, revisit important principles, and sense tweaks to try in light of those (even just a deep breath!).

What's Next?

Our aspiration for this work is the development of a common, flexible practice that builds the inner Compass of both individuals and collectives in order to navigate the world's ever-growing complexity. That eventual practice nurtures the "4Cs" of 21st-century learning (Communication, Collaboration, Critical Thinking, and Creativity) and more. It centers us on compassion, connecting us to ourselves and others. This supports our curiosity, creativity, and courage as we all (re)explore what we know, think, dream, and do. It builds our critical thinking as we learn to sense when to begin or end, where to go next, and what to take with us between its quadrants. It inspires us to be both comprehensive systems thinkers and concrete doers. As a simple visual tool, it inherently invites collaboration and communication among members of our school and societal ecosystems. Most importantly, it enables a choice for finding new possibilities to fulfill our collective principles, rather giving up or just getting by.

Inspired experimenters fuel this work so please experiment with us! How might we:

- further share and measure impact—both individual and cultural?
- use the Compass to support "experimentation" in science, writing, art, etc?
- leverage the common verbal and visual orientation to nurture connections between compass users in different geographies, in K-12, and beyond?
- exchange observations, principles, ideas, and experiments with a growing community, and continue to evolve this work?

I continue to be inspired by hearing things like "It's deeply orienting me right now," or "We bumped into each other and used a Compass to . . .," or children invoking pieces of it here and there. If we can in fact "empower everyone, regardless of age or role, whether alone or together, to creatively move and grow through any challenge," it's a destination worth the journey.

Acknowledgements

A few "lead user" experimenters: (K-12) Artemis Akchoti, Michael Dawson, Kevin Day, Garrett Mason, Caroline Meeks, Audrey O'Clair, Kaleb Rashad, Faith Blake, Dan Ryder; (College and beyond) Dan Coleman, Sara Hendren, Caitrin Lynch, Linda Gerard, Meli Glenn. Thought and program partners: Maya Bernstein, Hassan Hassan, Ben Linder, Otto Scharmer. Communication design collaborators: Jennifer Audette, Amy Leventhal, Kelly Sherman.

My family.

INDEX

Taylor & Francis eBooks

Helping you to choose the right eBooks for your Library

Add Routledge titles to your library's digital collection today. Taylor and Francis ebooks contains over 50,000 titles in the Humanities, Social Sciences, Behavioural Sciences, Built Environment and Law.

Choose from a range of subject packages or create your own!

Benefits for you

» Free MARC records
» COUNTER-compliant usage statistics
» Flexible purchase and pricing options
» All titles DRM-free.

REQUEST YOUR FREE INSTITUTIONAL TRIAL TODAY

Free Trials Available
We offer free trials to qualifying academic, corporate and government customers.

Benefits for your user

» Off-site, anytime access via Athens or referring URL
» Print or copy pages or chapters
» Full content search
» Bookmark, highlight and annotate text
» Access to thousands of pages of quality research at the click of a button.

eCollections – Choose from over 30 subject eCollections, including:

Archaeology	Language Learning
Architecture	Law
Asian Studies	Literature
Business & Management	Media & Communication
Classical Studies	Middle East Studies
Construction	Music
Creative & Media Arts	Philosophy
Criminology & Criminal Justice	Planning
Economics	Politics
Education	Psychology & Mental Health
Energy	Religion
Engineering	Security
English Language & Linguistics	Social Work
Environment & Sustainability	Sociology
Geography	Sport
Health Studies	Theatre & Performance
History	Tourism, Hospitality & Events

For more information, pricing enquiries or to order a free trial, please contact your local sales team:
www.tandfebooks.com/page/sales

 Routledge
Taylor & Francis Group

The home of
Routledge books

www.tandfebooks.com